W9-AAR-634

Oddly Normal Volume 1

WRITTEN & ILLUSTRATED BY
OTIS FRAMPTON

WITHDRAWN

Published by Viper Comics
9400 N. MacArthur Blvd., Suite 124-215
Irving, TX 75063
USA

First edition: May 2006
ISBN: 0-9777883-0-X

This volume collects issues 1-4
of the series Oddly Normal.

Jessie Garza president & publisher
Jim Resnowski editor-in-chief & creative director
P.J. Kryfko assistant editor
Jason M. Burns assistant publisher

VIPER COMICS | **WWW.VIPERCOMICS.COM** | **EST. 2001**

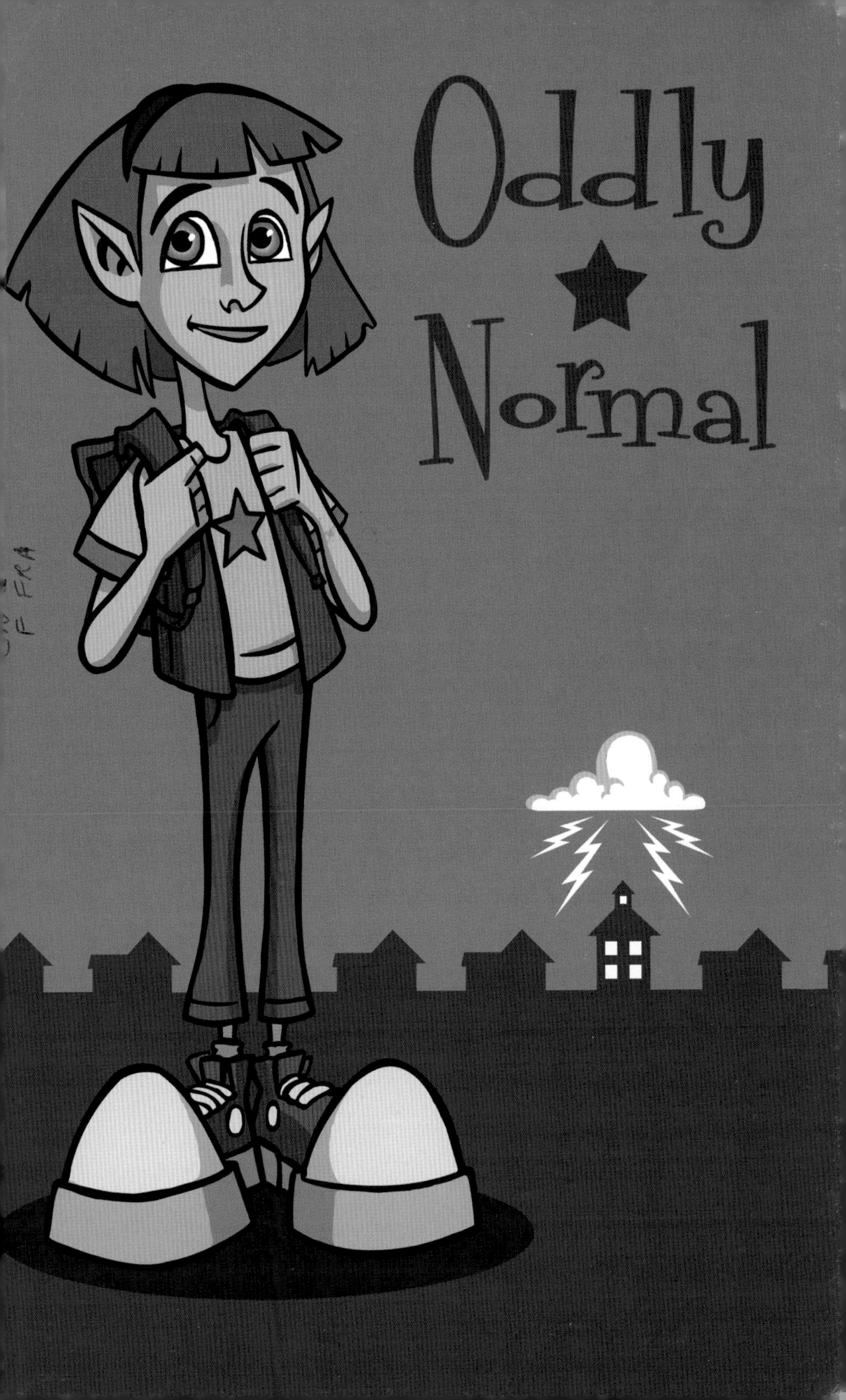
Oddly
Normal

Chapter 1

Be Careful What You Wish For

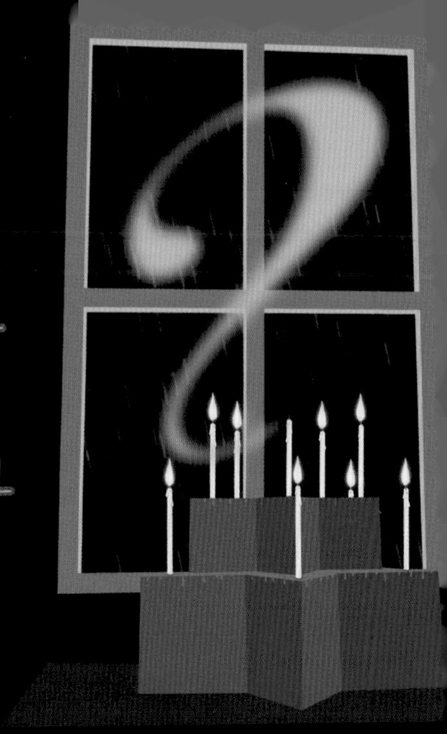

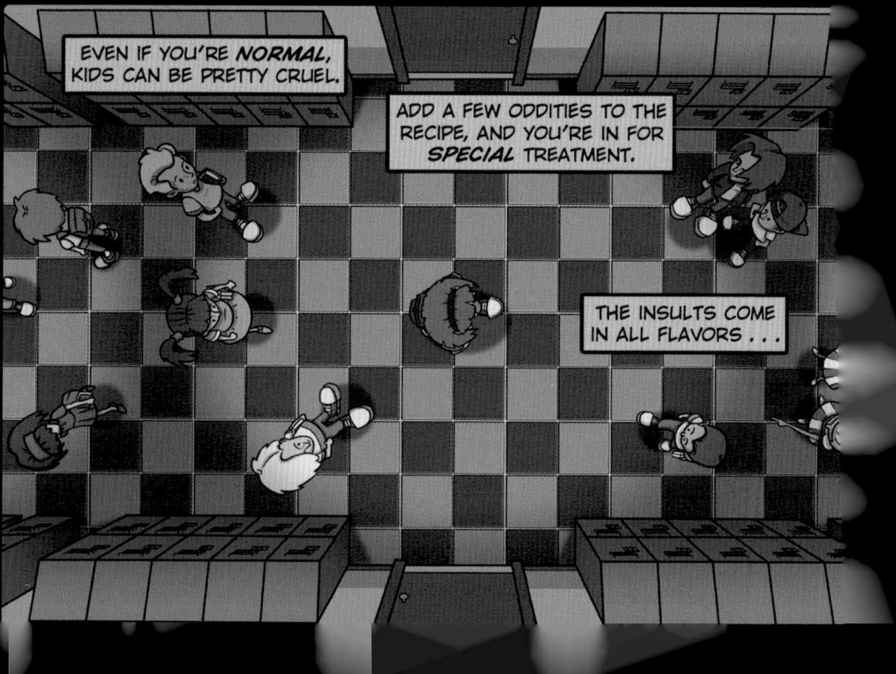
EVEN IF YOU'RE NORMAL, KIDS CAN BE PRETTY CRUEL.
ADD A FEW ODDITIES TO THE RECIPE, AND YOU'RE IN FOR SPECIAL TREATMENT.
THE INSULTS COME IN ALL FLAVORS . . .

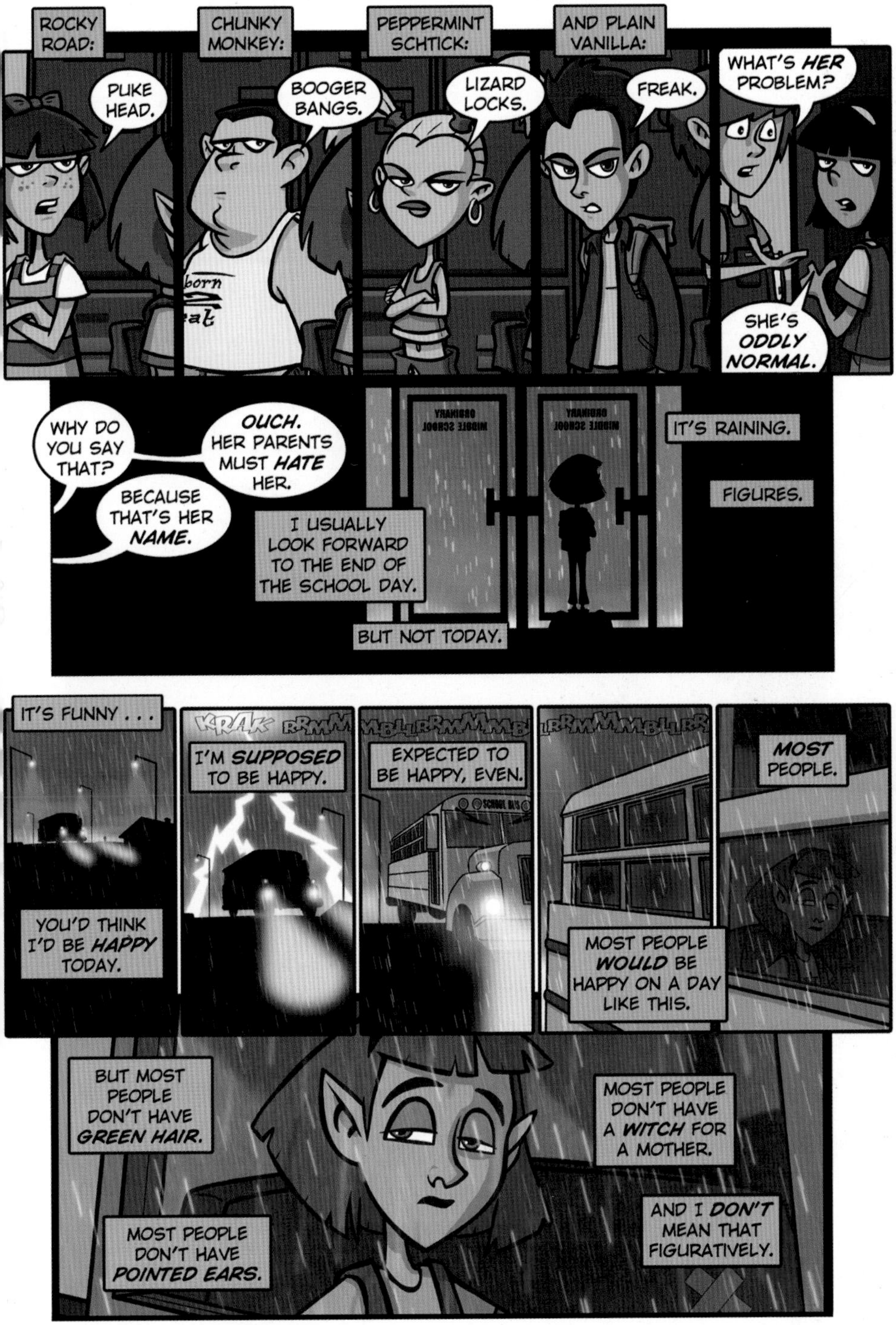
ROCKY ROAD:
PUKE HEAD.
CHUNKY MONKEY:
BOOGER BANGS.
PEPPERMINT SCHTICK:
LIZARD LOCKS.
AND PLAIN VANILLA:
FREAK.
WHAT'S *HER* PROBLEM?
SHE'S *ODDLY NORMAL.*
WHY DO YOU SAY THAT?
BECAUSE THAT'S HER *NAME.*
OUCH. HER PARENTS MUST *HATE* HER.
I USUALLY LOOK FORWARD TO THE END OF THE SCHOOL DAY.
BUT NOT TODAY.
IT'S RAINING.
FIGURES.
IT'S FUNNY . . .
YOU'D THINK I'D BE *HAPPY* TODAY.
KRAK
RRMMMMBLLRRMMMMBLLRRMMMMBLLRR
I'M *SUPPOSED* TO BE HAPPY.
EXPECTED TO BE HAPPY, EVEN.
MOST PEOPLE *WOULD* BE HAPPY ON A DAY LIKE THIS.
MOST PEOPLE.
BUT MOST PEOPLE DON'T HAVE *GREEN HAIR.*
MOST PEOPLE DON'T HAVE *POINTED EARS.*
MOST PEOPLE DON'T HAVE A *WITCH* FOR A MOTHER.
AND I *DON'T* MEAN THAT FIGURATIVELY.

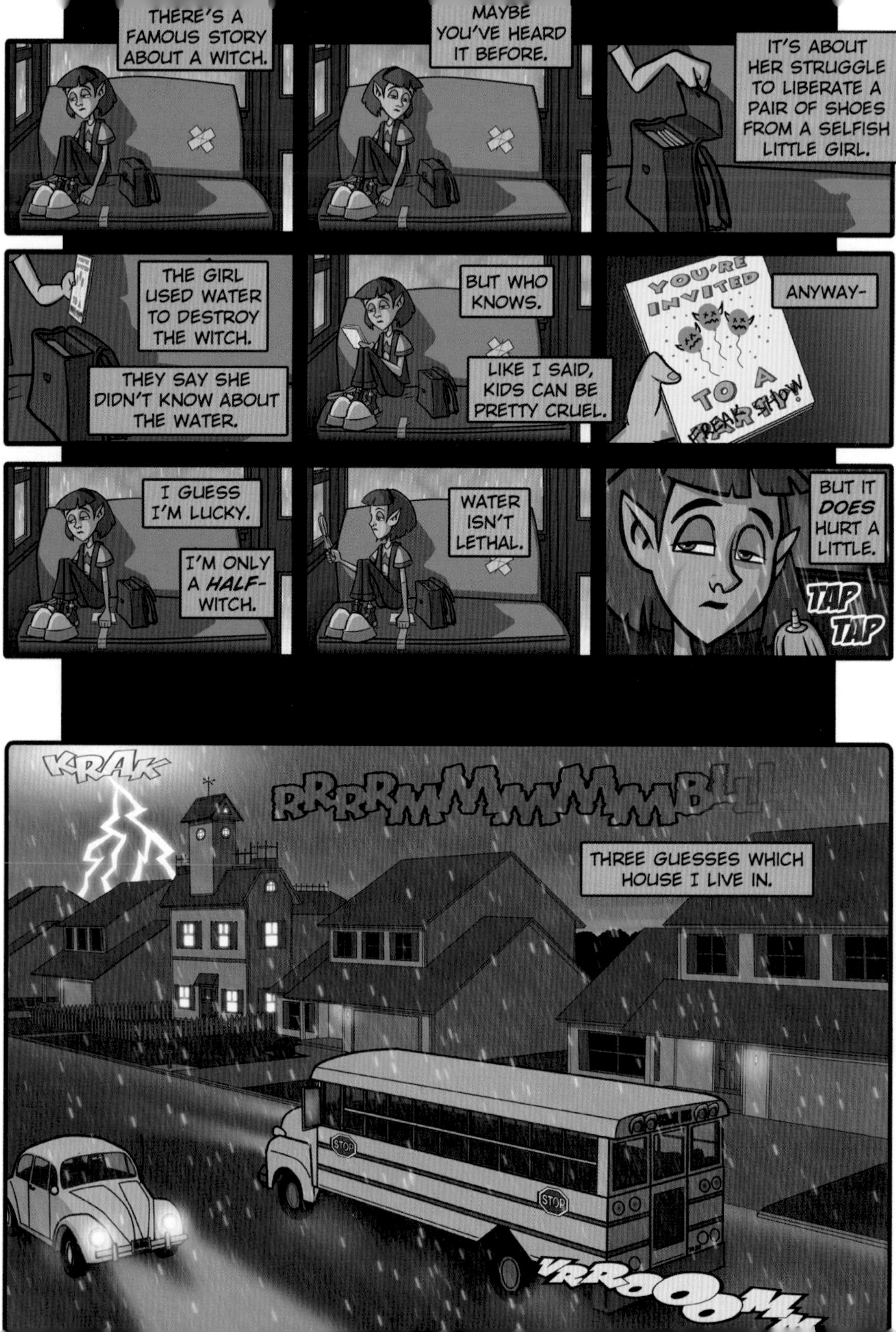
THERE'S A FAMOUS STORY ABOUT A WITCH.
MAYBE YOU'VE HEARD IT BEFORE.
IT'S ABOUT HER STRUGGLE TO LIBERATE A PAIR OF SHOES FROM A SELFISH LITTLE GIRL.
THE GIRL USED WATER TO DESTROY THE WITCH.
THEY SAY SHE DIDN'T KNOW ABOUT THE WATER.
BUT WHO KNOWS.
LIKE I SAID, KIDS CAN BE PRETTY CRUEL.
YOU'RE INVITED TO A FREAK SHOW
ANYWAY-
I GUESS I'M LUCKY.
I'M ONLY A *HALF*-WITCH.
WATER ISN'T LETHAL.
BUT IT *DOES* HURT A LITTLE.
TAP TAP
KRAK
RRRRMMMMMMMBL
THREE GUESSES WHICH HOUSE I LIVE IN.
STOP
STOP
VRROOOM

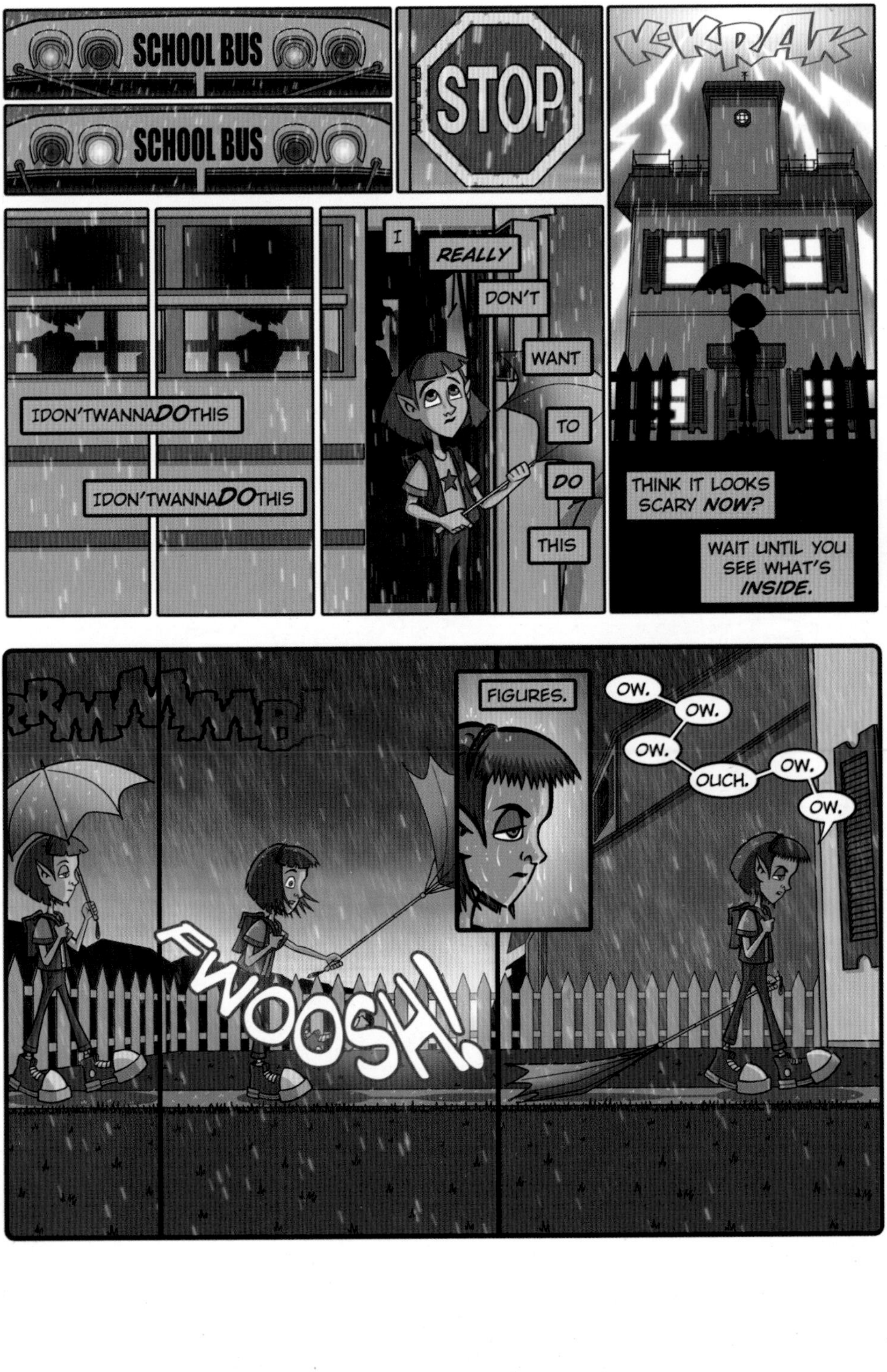
SCHOOL BUS
SCHOOL BUS
STOP
K-KRAK
IDON'TWANNADOTHIS
IDON'TWANNADOTHIS
I
REALLY
DON'T
WANT
TO
DO
THIS
THINK IT LOOKS SCARY NOW?
WAIT UNTIL YOU SEE WHAT'S INSIDE.
FWOOSH!
FIGURES.
OW.
OW.
OW.
OUCH.
OW.
OW.

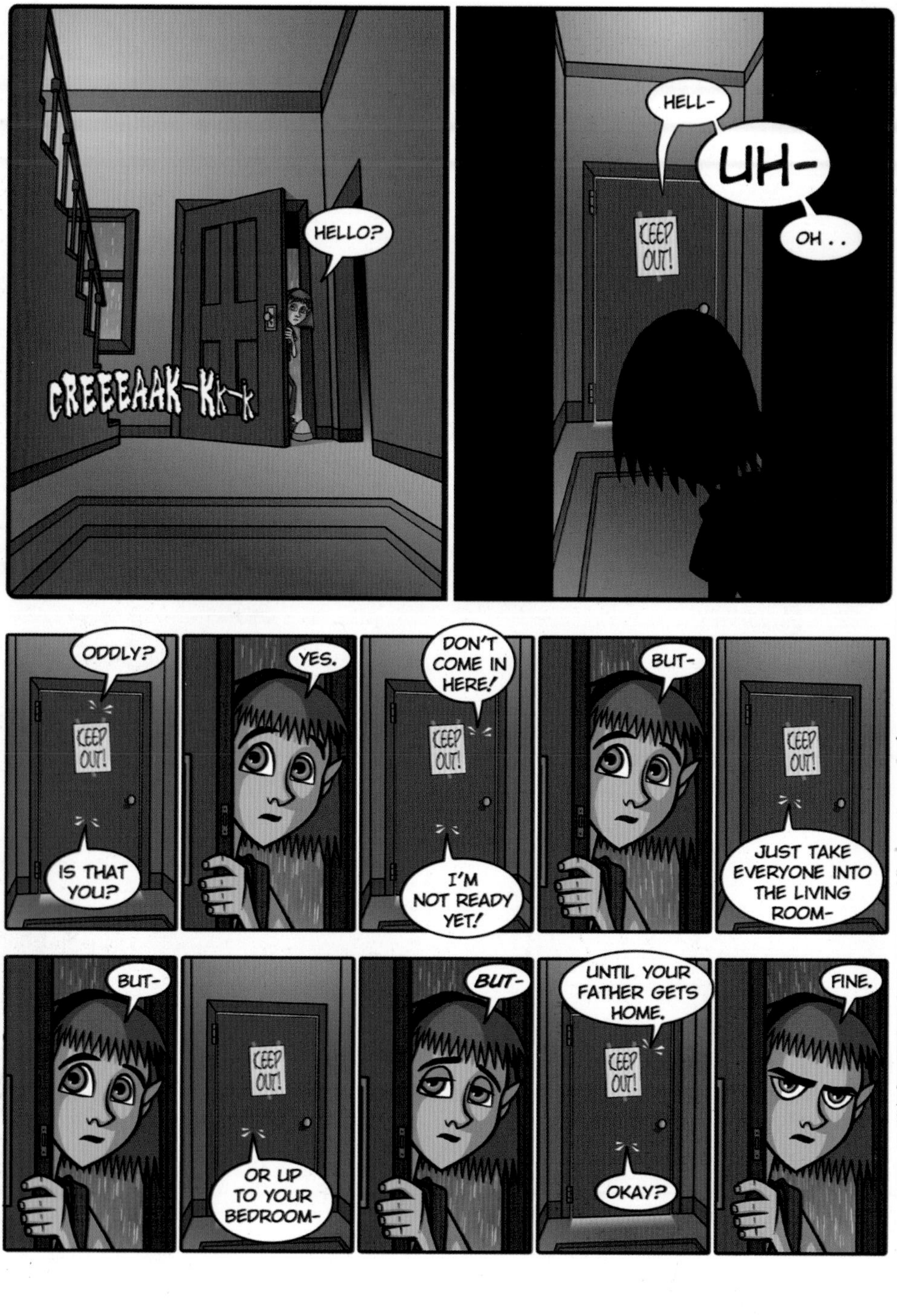
HELLO?
CREEEAAK-Kk-k
HELL-
UH-
OH . .
KEEP OUT!
ODDLY?
IS THAT YOU?
YES.
DON'T COME IN HERE!
I'M NOT READY YET!
BUT-
JUST TAKE EVERYONE INTO THE LIVING ROOM-
BUT-
OR UP TO YOUR BEDROOM-
BUT-
UNTIL YOUR FATHER GETS HOME.
OKAY?
FINE.

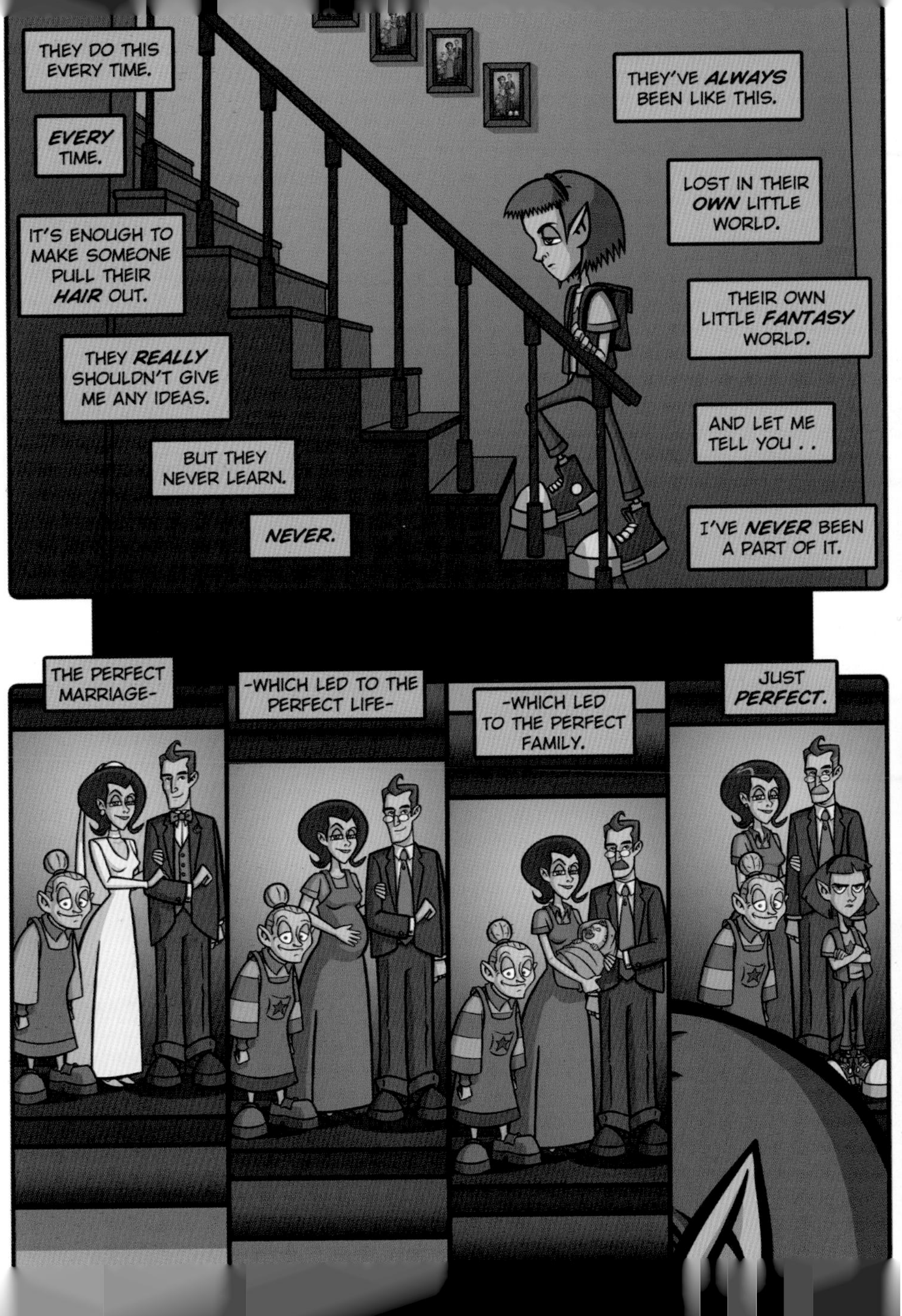
THEY DO THIS EVERY TIME.
EVERY TIME.
IT'S ENOUGH TO MAKE SOMEONE PULL THEIR HAIR OUT.
THEY REALLY SHOULDN'T GIVE ME ANY IDEAS.
BUT THEY NEVER LEARN.
NEVER.
THEY'VE ALWAYS BEEN LIKE THIS.
LOST IN THEIR OWN LITTLE WORLD.
THEIR OWN LITTLE FANTASY WORLD.
AND LET ME TELL YOU . .
I'VE NEVER BEEN A PART OF IT.
THE PERFECT MARRIAGE-
-WHICH LED TO THE PERFECT LIFE-
-WHICH LED TO THE PERFECT FAMILY.
JUST PERFECT.

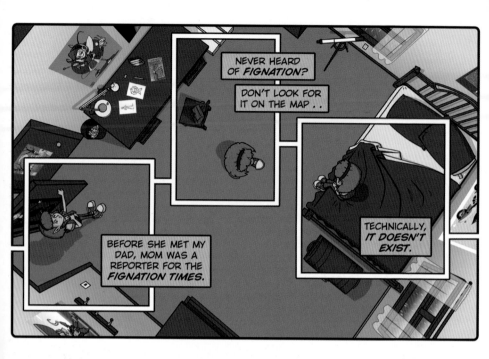

NEVER HEARD OF *FIGNATION?*

DON'T LOOK FOR IT ON THE MAP . .

BEFORE SHE MET MY DAD, MOM WAS A REPORTER FOR THE *FIGNATION TIMES.*

TECHNICALLY, *IT DOESN'T EXIST.*

THE *CITIZENS* OF FIGNATION ARE CURIOUS—

VERY CURIOUS ABOUT THE *REAL WORLD.*

MY MOM WAS SENT OUT TO DO SOME *SNOOPING.*

A *COMMON* ASSIGNMENT.

WITCHES ARE VERY GOOD AT BLENDING IN WHEN THEY *NEED* TO.

WAVE YOUR *WAND—*

—CAST A *SPELL—*

CREATE A *NEW LOOK.*

SO MY MOM CAME *HERE—*

—TO *ORDINARY,* VIRGINIA—

ON ASSIGNMENT FROM THE WORLD OF *FICTION* TO REPORT ON THE *AVERAGE* HUMAN.

SHE LOOKED FOR AN *EVERYMAN—*

—A REAL *NOBODY—*

—"MR. NORMAL".

AND WHO DID SHE *FIND?*

HONEY, I'M *HOME!*

WHERE'S MY SPECIAL GIRL?

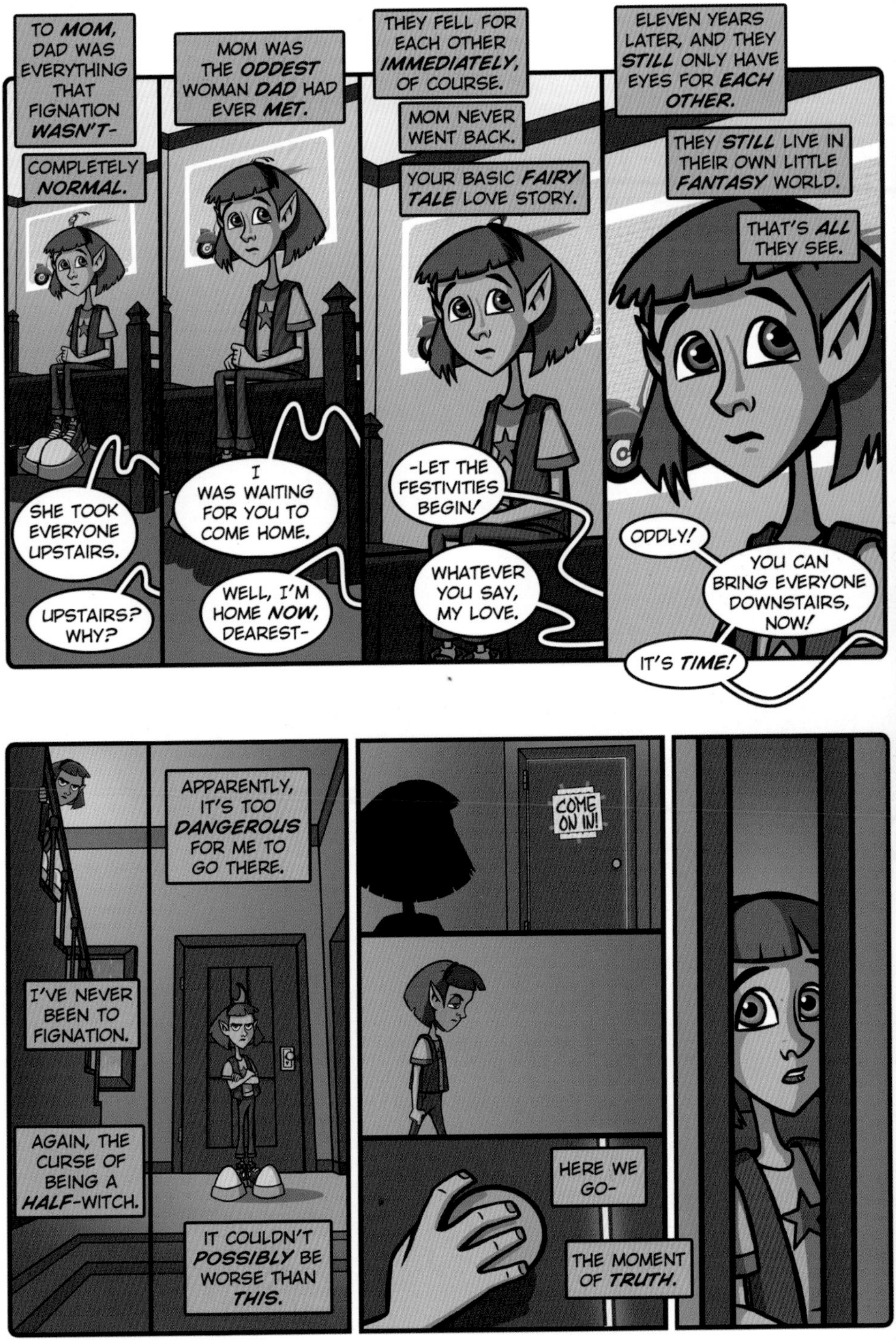
TO MOM, DAD WAS EVERYTHING THAT FIGNATION WASN'T-
COMPLETELY NORMAL.
SHE TOOK EVERYONE UPSTAIRS.
UPSTAIRS? WHY?
MOM WAS THE ODDEST WOMAN DAD HAD EVER MET.
I WAS WAITING FOR YOU TO COME HOME.
WELL, I'M HOME NOW, DEAREST-
THEY FELL FOR EACH OTHER IMMEDIATELY, OF COURSE.
MOM NEVER WENT BACK.
YOUR BASIC FAIRY TALE LOVE STORY.
-LET THE FESTIVITIES BEGIN!
WHATEVER YOU SAY, MY LOVE.
ELEVEN YEARS LATER, AND THEY STILL ONLY HAVE EYES FOR EACH OTHER.
THEY STILL LIVE IN THEIR OWN LITTLE FANTASY WORLD.
THAT'S ALL THEY SEE.
ODDLY!
YOU CAN BRING EVERYONE DOWNSTAIRS, NOW!
IT'S TIME!
APPARENTLY, IT'S TOO DANGEROUS FOR ME TO GO THERE.
I'VE NEVER BEEN TO FIGNATION.
AGAIN, THE CURSE OF BEING A HALF-WITCH.
IT COULDN'T POSSIBLY BE WORSE THAN THIS.
COME ON IN!
HERE WE GO-
THE MOMENT OF TRUTH.

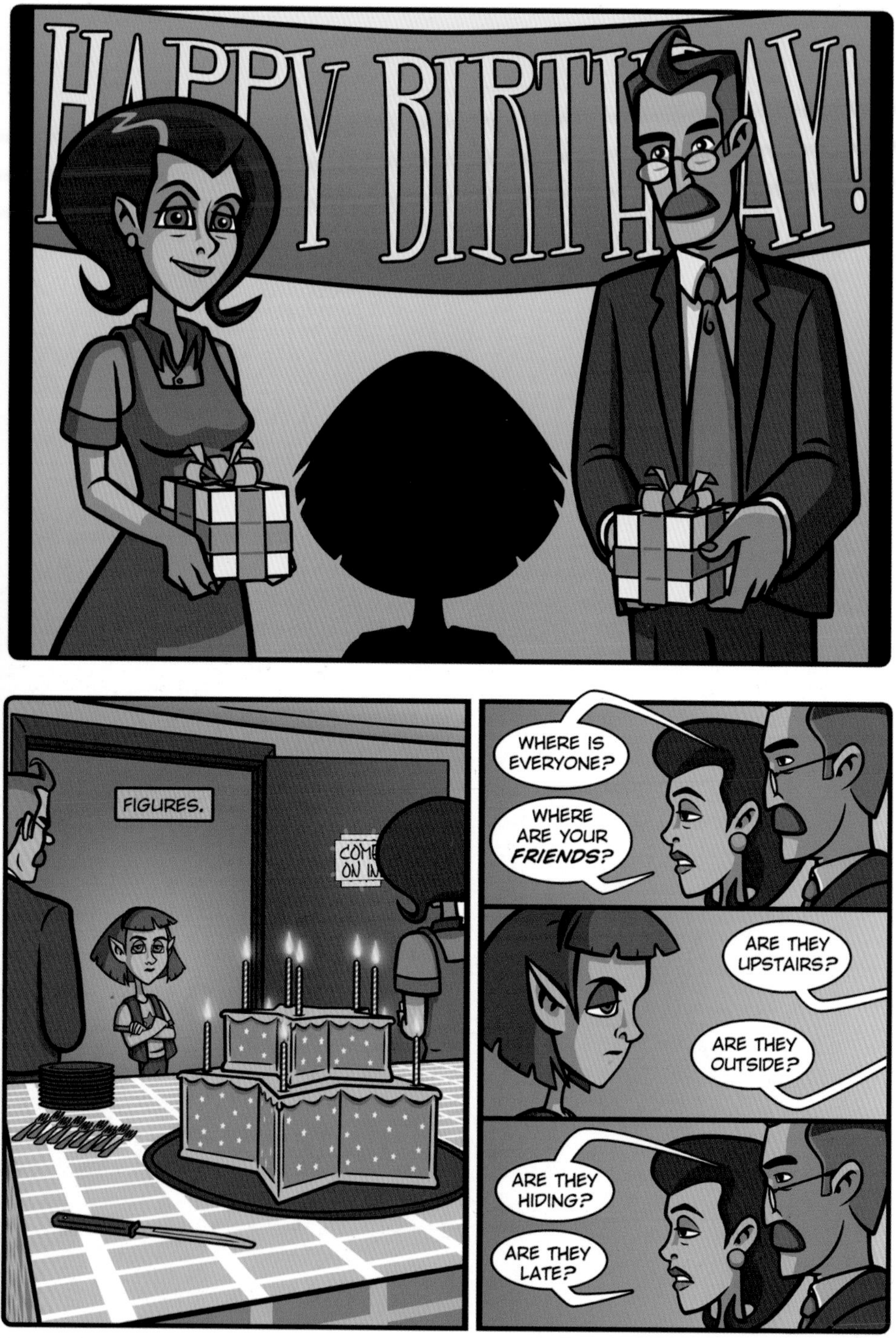
HAPPY BIRTHDAY!
FIGURES.
WHERE IS EVERYONE?
WHERE ARE YOUR *FRIENDS?*
ARE THEY UPSTAIRS?
ARE THEY OUTSIDE?
ARE THEY HIDING?
ARE THEY LATE?

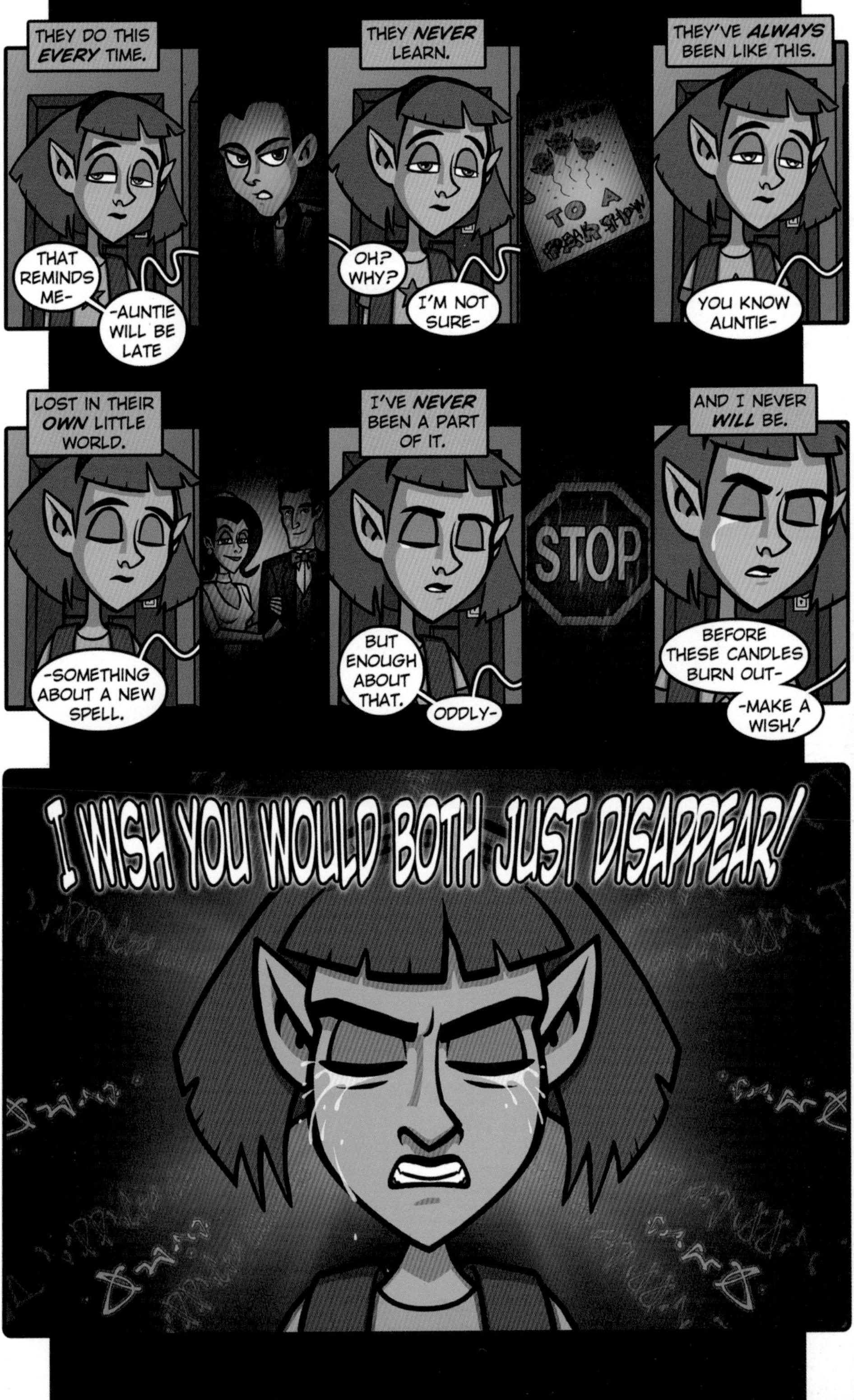
THEY DO THIS EVERY TIME.
THAT REMINDS ME-
-AUNTIE WILL BE LATE
THEY NEVER LEARN.
OH? WHY?
I'M NOT SURE-
TO A
THEY'VE ALWAYS BEEN LIKE THIS.
YOU KNOW AUNTIE-
LOST IN THEIR OWN LITTLE WORLD.
-SOMETHING ABOUT A NEW SPELL.
I'VE NEVER BEEN A PART OF IT.
BUT ENOUGH ABOUT THAT.
ODDLY-
STOP
AND I NEVER WILL BE.
BEFORE THESE CANDLES BURN OUT-
-MAKE A WISH!
I WISH YOU WOULD BOTH JUST DISAPPEAR!

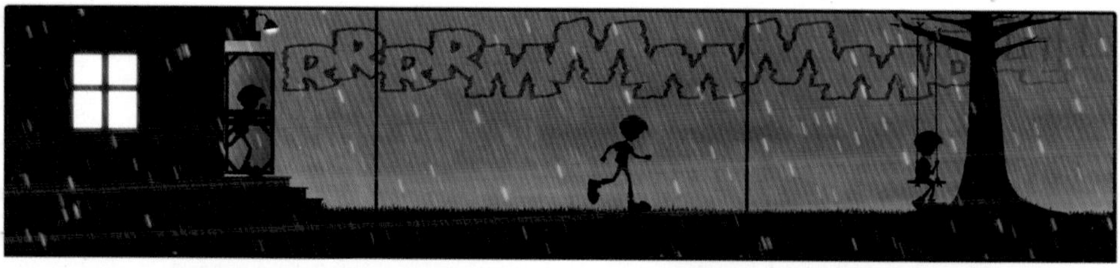
RRRRMMMMMMMMM

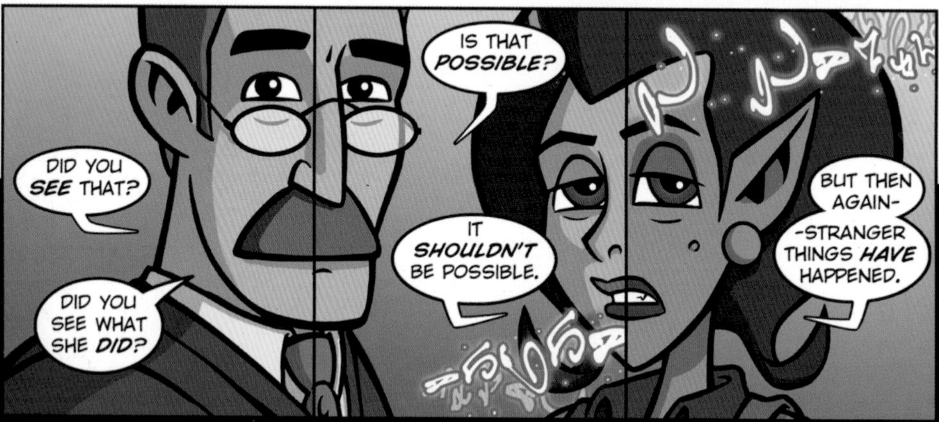
DID YOU SEE THAT?
DID YOU SEE WHAT SHE DID?
IS THAT POSSIBLE?
IT SHOULDN'T BE POSSIBLE.
BUT THEN AGAIN-
-STRANGER THINGS HAVE HAPPENED.

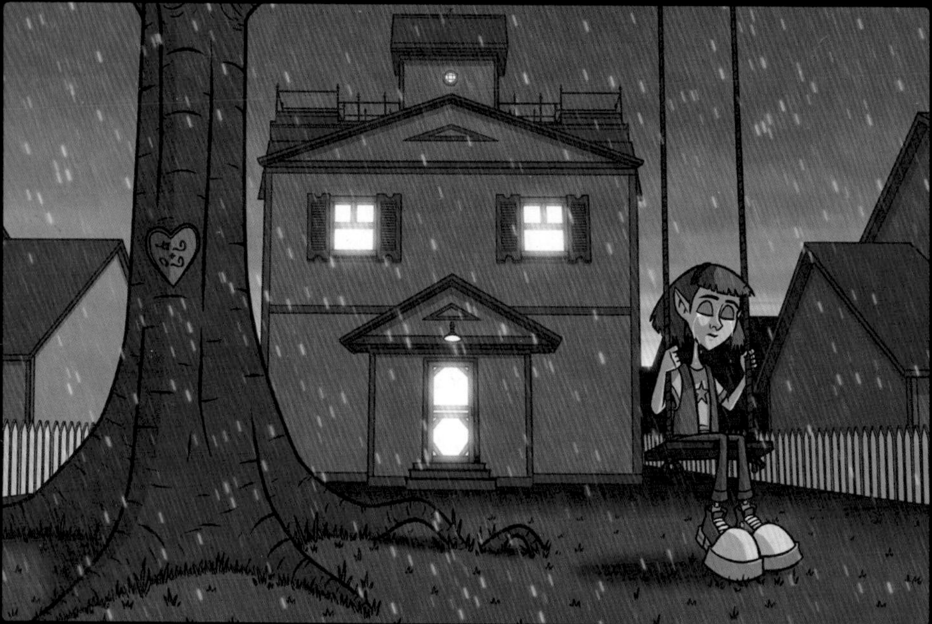

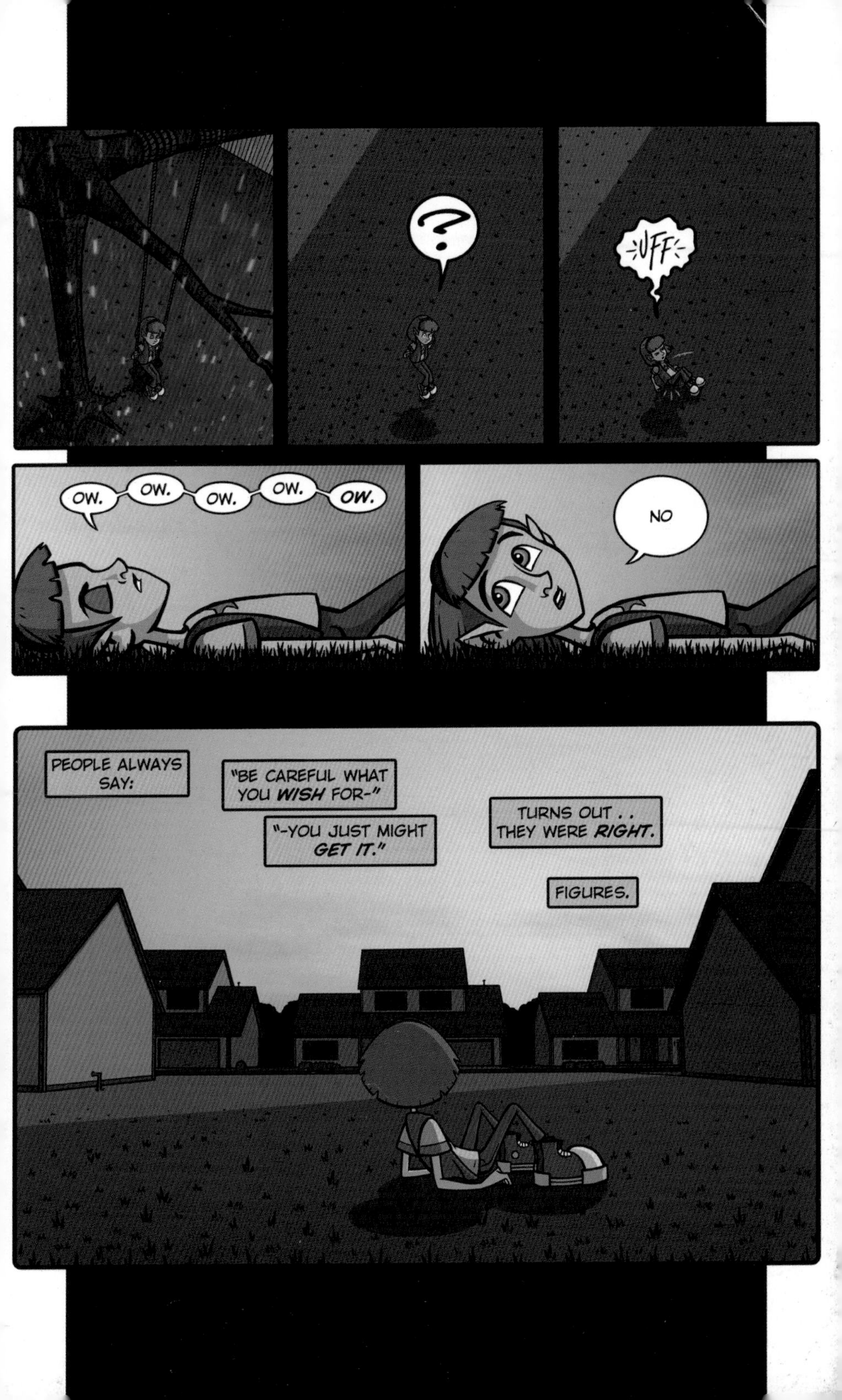

?
UFF
OW.
OW.
OW.
OW.
OW.
NO
PEOPLE ALWAYS SAY:
"BE CAREFUL WHAT YOU *WISH* FOR-"
"-YOU JUST MIGHT *GET IT.*"
TURNS OUT . . THEY WERE *RIGHT*.
FIGURES.

Chapter 2

A Figment Of Your Imagination

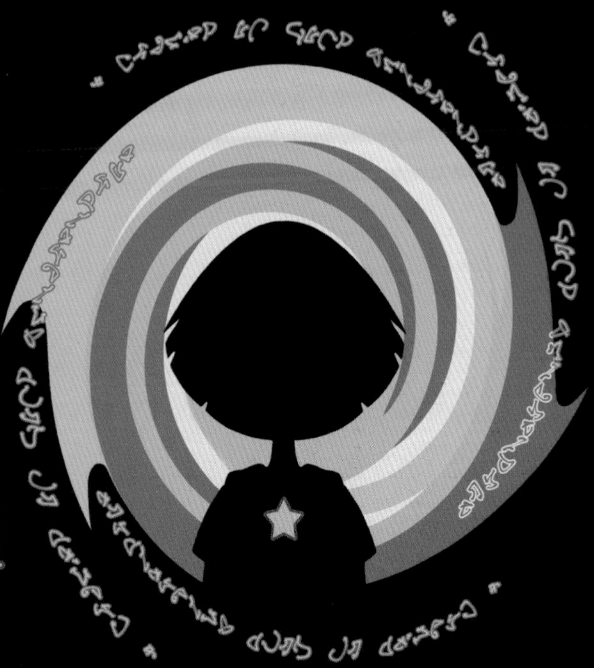

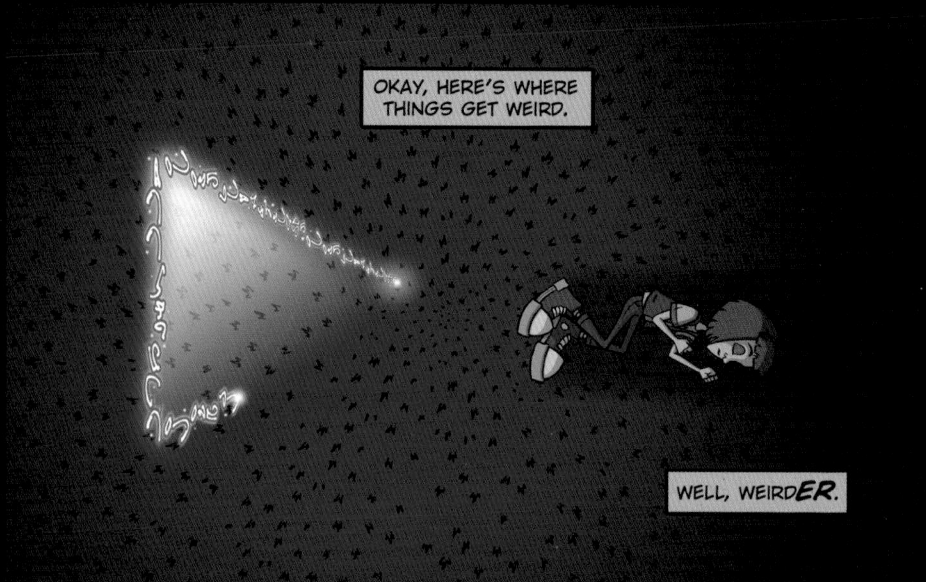

OKAY, HERE'S WHERE THINGS GET WEIRD.
WELL, WEIRDER.

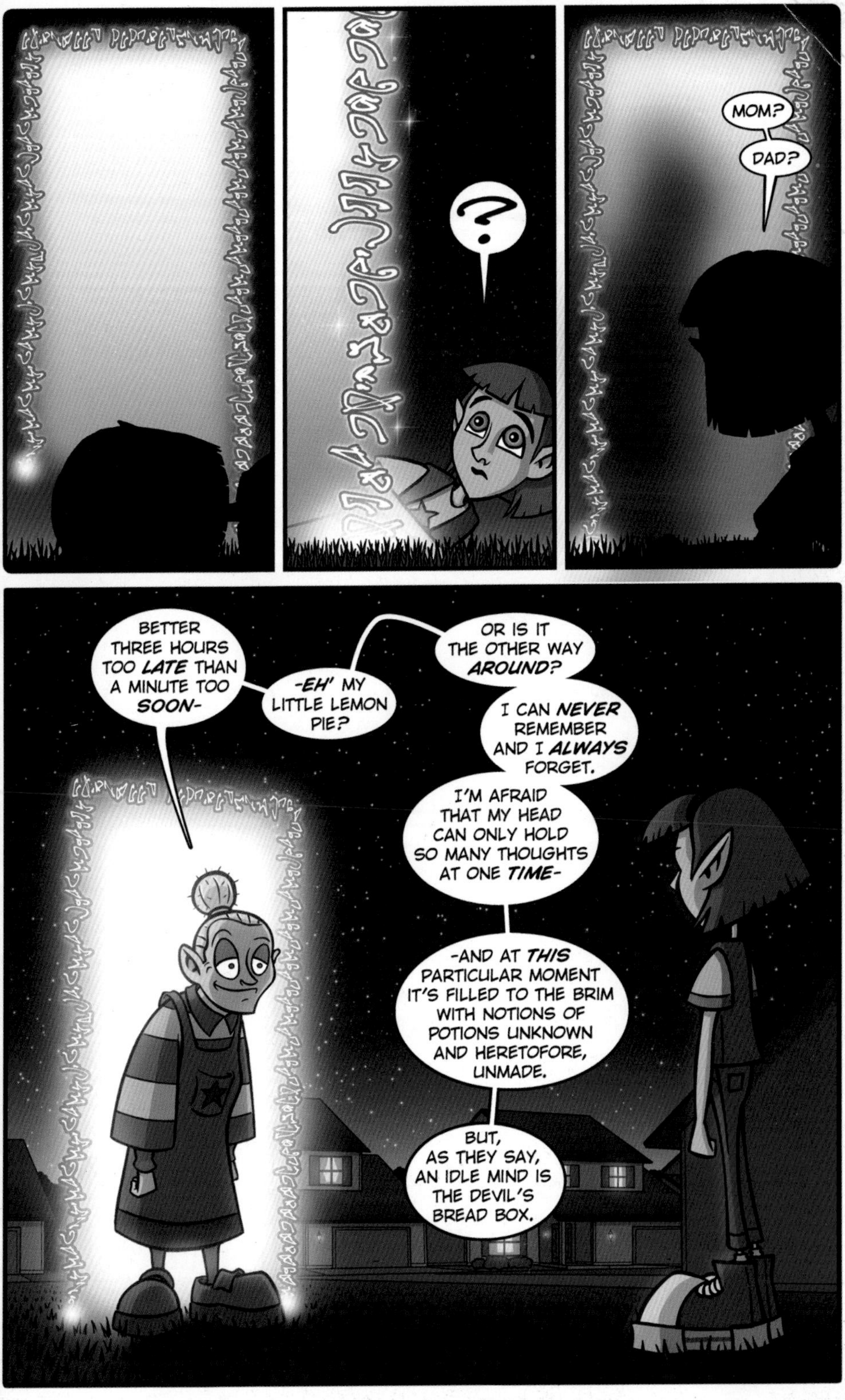
?
MOM?
DAD?
BETTER THREE HOURS TOO LATE THAN A MINUTE TOO SOON-
-EH' MY LITTLE LEMON PIE?
OR IS IT THE OTHER WAY AROUND?
I CAN NEVER REMEMBER AND I ALWAYS FORGET.
I'M AFRAID THAT MY HEAD CAN ONLY HOLD SO MANY THOUGHTS AT ONE TIME-
-AND AT THIS PARTICULAR MOMENT IT'S FILLED TO THE BRIM WITH NOTIONS OF POTIONS UNKNOWN AND HERETOFORE, UNMADE.
BUT, AS THEY SAY, AN IDLE MIND IS THE DEVIL'S BREAD BOX.

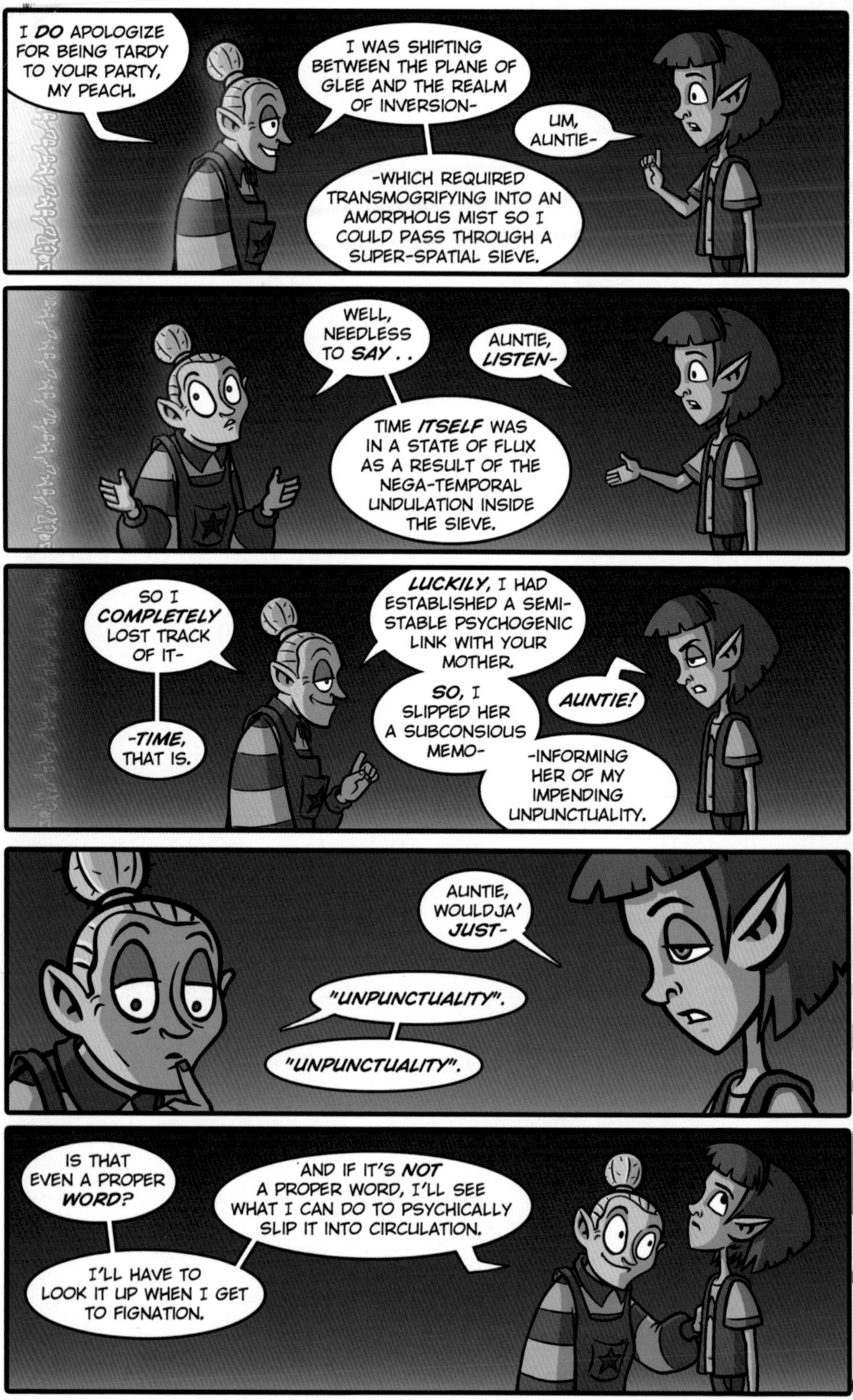

I DO APOLOGIZE FOR BEING TARDY TO YOUR PARTY, MY PEACH.
I WAS SHIFTING BETWEEN THE PLANE OF GLEE AND THE REALM OF INVERSION-
-WHICH REQUIRED TRANSMOGRIFYING INTO AN AMORPHOUS MIST SO I COULD PASS THROUGH A SUPER-SPATIAL SIEVE.
UM, AUNTIE-
WELL, NEEDLESS TO SAY . .
AUNTIE, LISTEN-
TIME ITSELF WAS IN A STATE OF FLUX AS A RESULT OF THE NEGA-TEMPORAL UNDULATION INSIDE THE SIEVE.
SO I COMPLETELY LOST TRACK OF IT-
-TIME, THAT IS.
LUCKILY, I HAD ESTABLISHED A SEMI-STABLE PSYCHOGENIC LINK WITH YOUR MOTHER.
SO, I SLIPPED HER A SUBCONSIOUS MEMO-
AUNTIE!
-INFORMING HER OF MY IMPENDING UNPUNCTUALITY.
AUNTIE, WOULDJA' JUST-
"UNPUNCTUALITY".
"UNPUNCTUALITY".
IS THAT EVEN A PROPER WORD?
I'LL HAVE TO LOOK IT UP WHEN I GET TO FIGNATION.
AND IF IT'S NOT A PROPER WORD, I'LL SEE WHAT I CAN DO TO PSYCHICALLY SLIP IT INTO CIRCULATION.

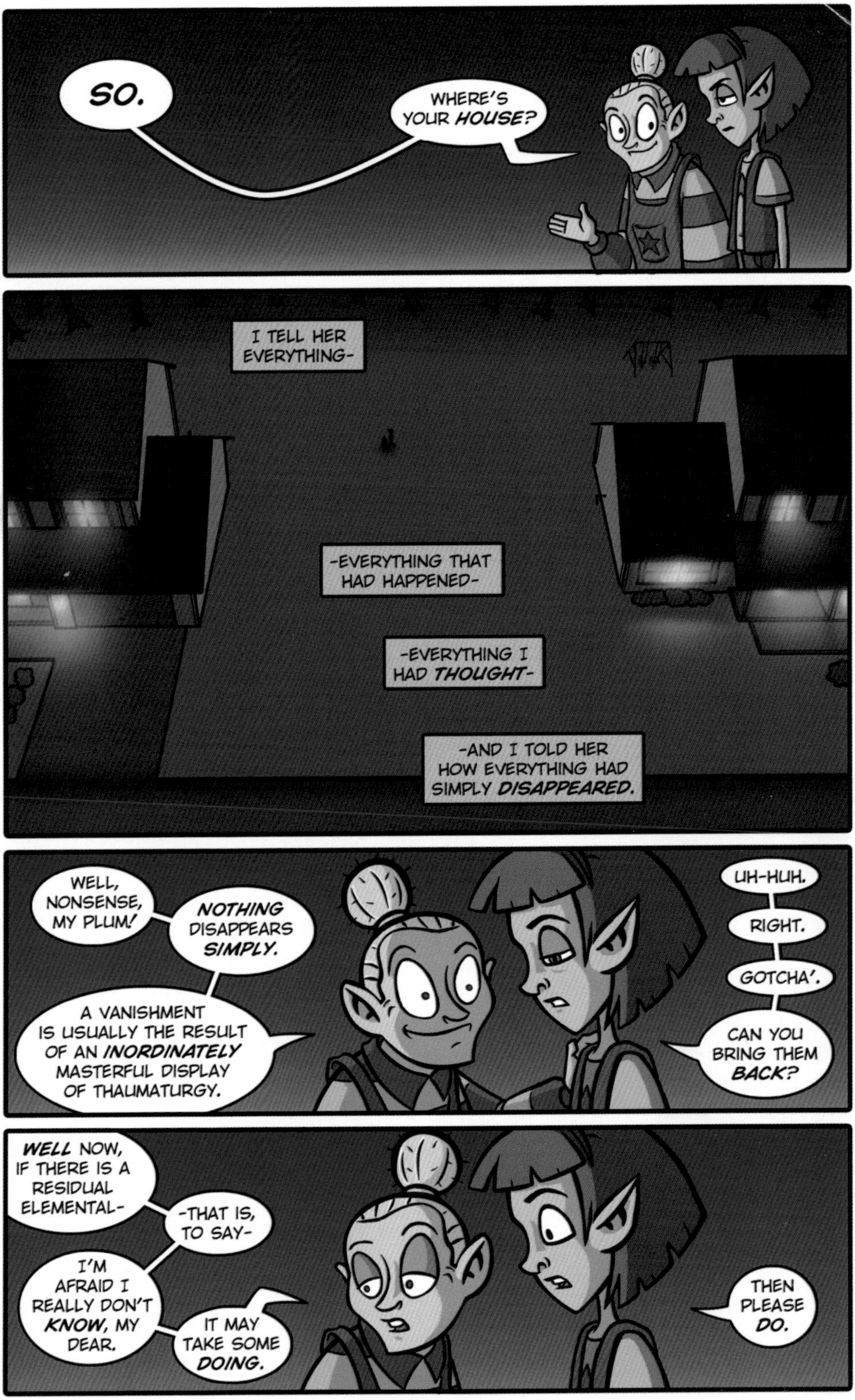
SO.
WHERE'S YOUR HOUSE?
I TELL HER EVERYTHING-
-EVERYTHING THAT HAD HAPPENED-
-EVERYTHING I HAD THOUGHT-
-AND I TOLD HER HOW EVERYTHING HAD SIMPLY DISAPPEARED.
WELL, NONSENSE, MY PLUM!
NOTHING DISAPPEARS SIMPLY.
A VANISHMENT IS USUALLY THE RESULT OF AN INORDINATELY MASTERFUL DISPLAY OF THAUMATURGY.
UH-HUH.
RIGHT.
GOTCHA'.
CAN YOU BRING THEM BACK?
WELL NOW, IF THERE IS A RESIDUAL ELEMENTAL-
-THAT IS, TO SAY-
I'M AFRAID I REALLY DON'T KNOW, MY DEAR.
IT MAY TAKE SOME DOING.
THEN PLEASE DO.

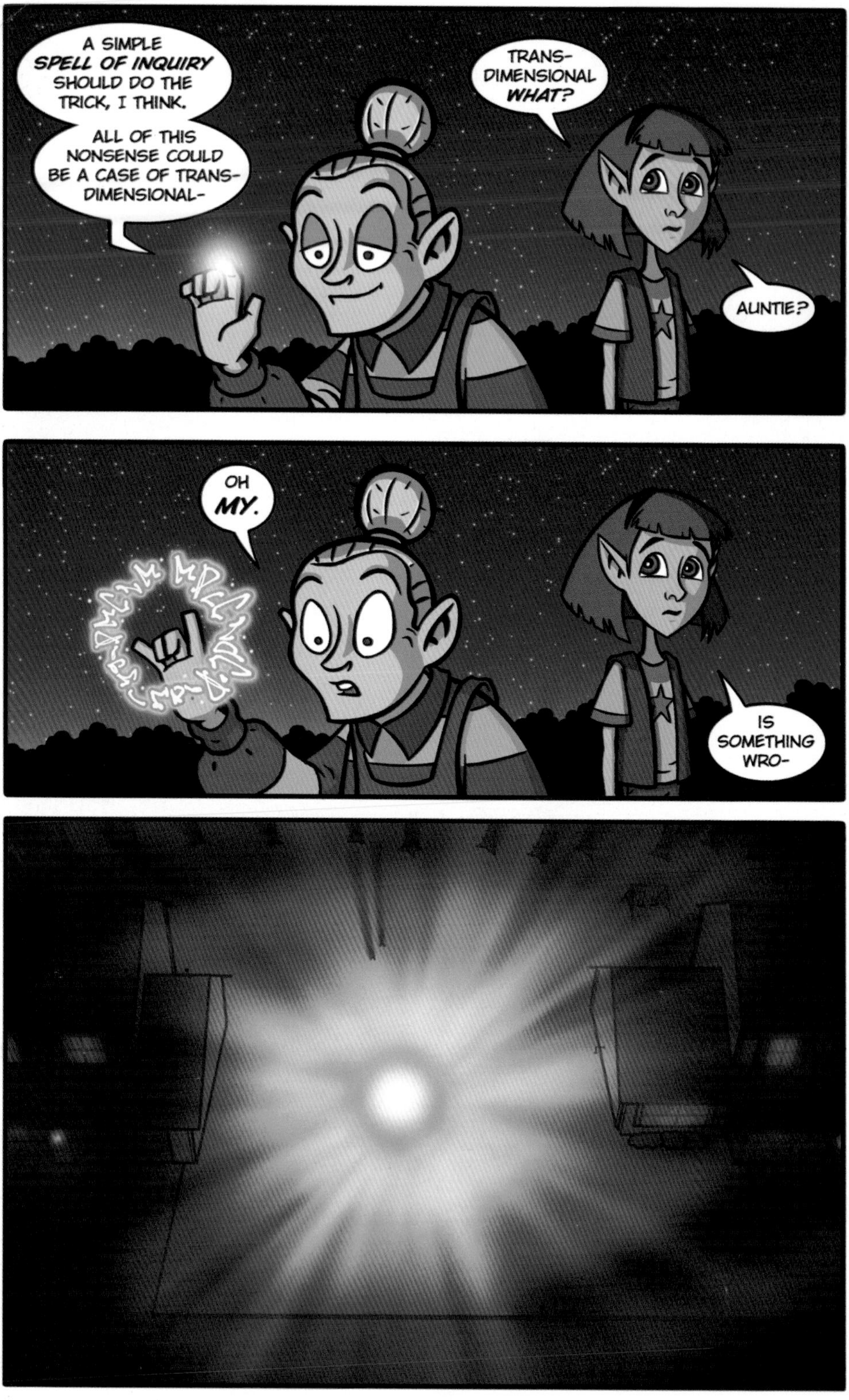
A SIMPLE SPELL OF INQUIRY SHOULD DO THE TRICK, I THINK.
ALL OF THIS NONSENSE COULD BE A CASE OF TRANS-DIMENSIONAL-
TRANS-DIMENSIONAL WHAT?
AUNTIE?
OH MY.
IS SOMETHING WRO-

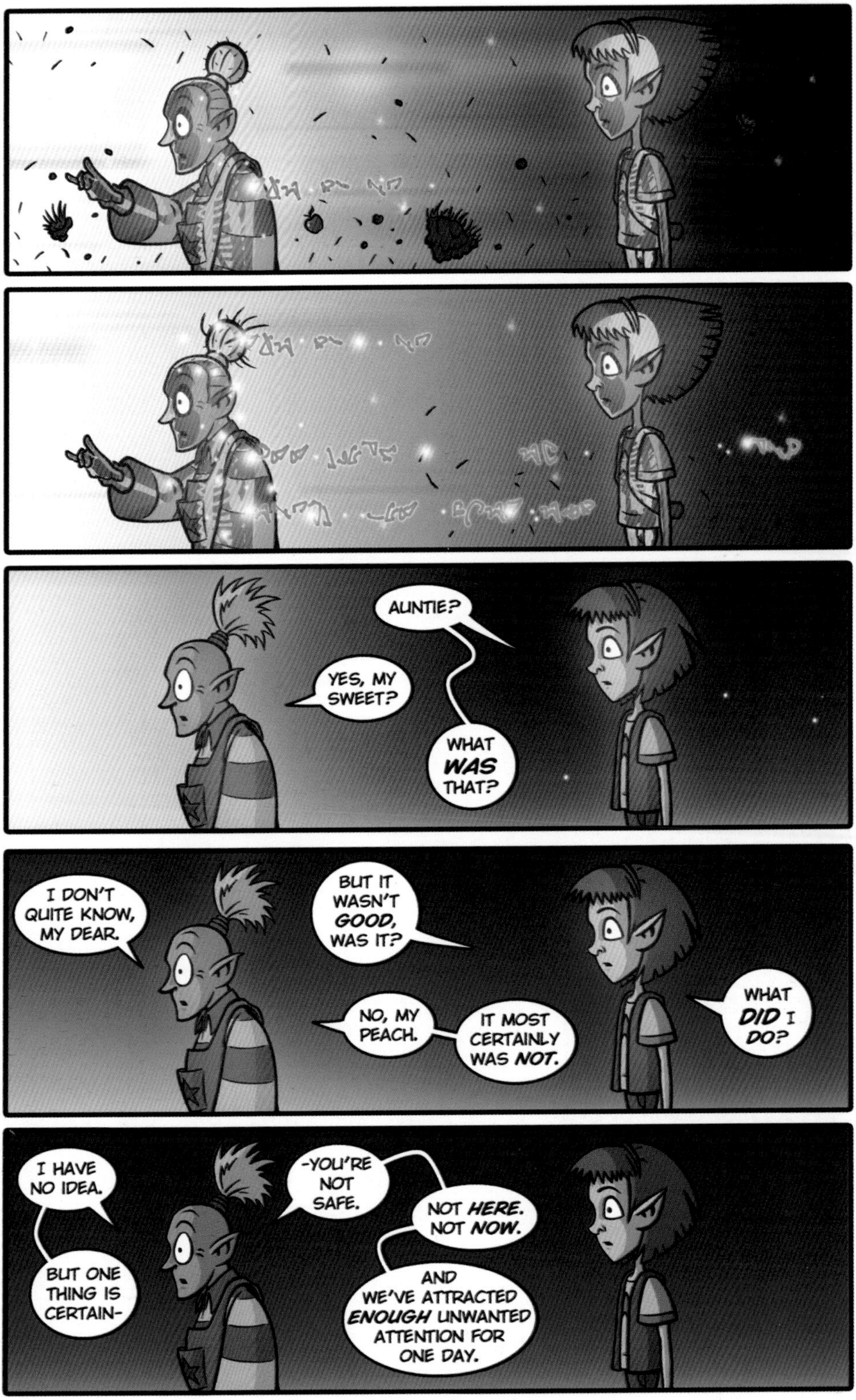
AUNTIE?
YES, MY SWEET?
WHAT *WAS* THAT?
I DON'T QUITE KNOW, MY DEAR.
BUT IT WASN'T *GOOD*, WAS IT?
NO, MY PEACH.
IT MOST CERTAINLY WAS *NOT*.
WHAT *DID* I DO?
I HAVE NO IDEA.
BUT ONE THING IS CERTAIN-
-YOU'RE NOT SAFE.
NOT *HERE*. NOT *NOW*.
AND WE'VE ATTRACTED *ENOUGH* UNWANTED ATTENTION FOR ONE DAY.

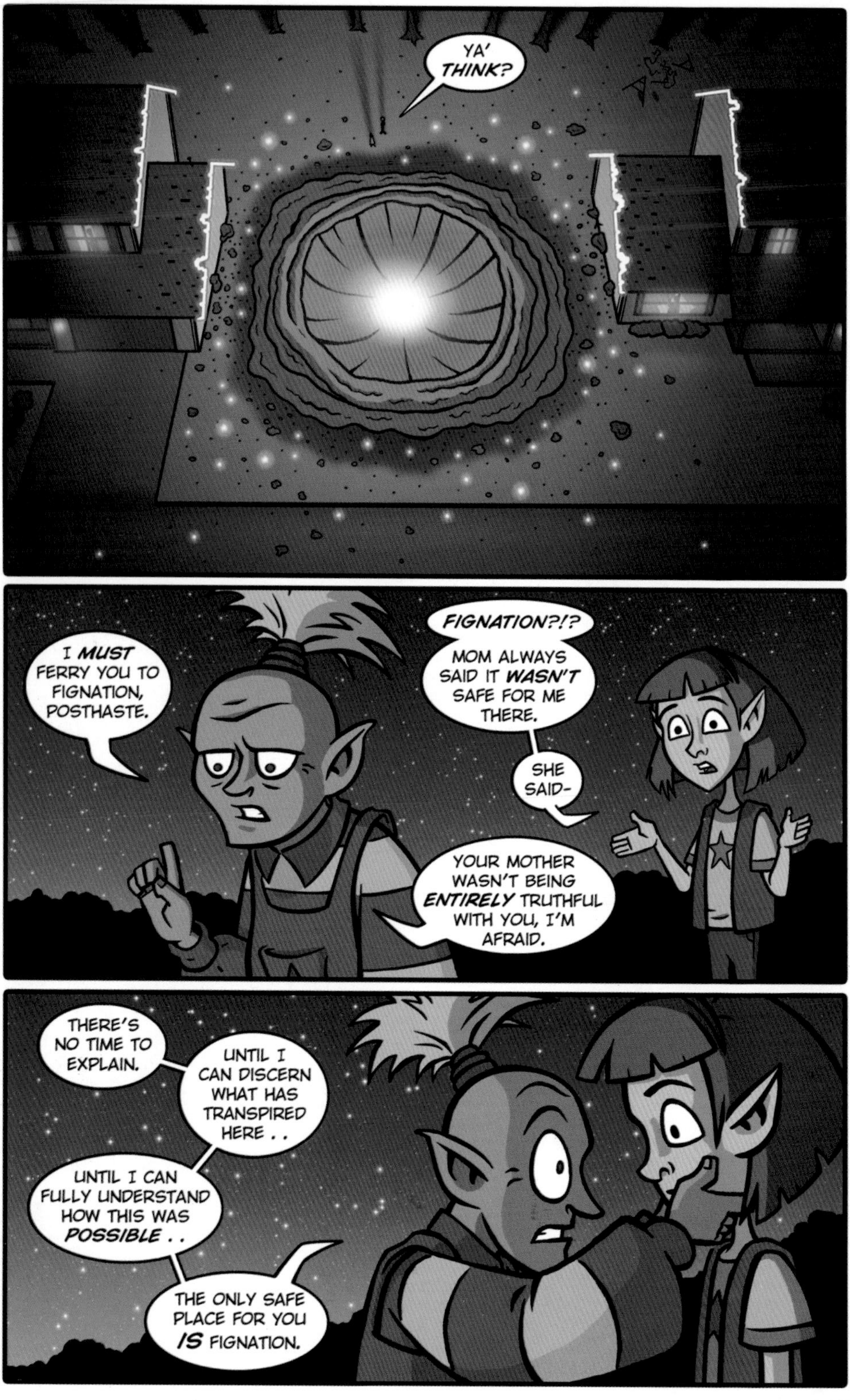
YA' THINK?
I MUST FERRY YOU TO FIGNATION, POSTHASTE.
FIGNATION?!?
MOM ALWAYS SAID IT WASN'T SAFE FOR ME THERE.
SHE SAID-
YOUR MOTHER WASN'T BEING ENTIRELY TRUTHFUL WITH YOU, I'M AFRAID.
THERE'S NO TIME TO EXPLAIN.
UNTIL I CAN DISCERN WHAT HAS TRANSPIRED HERE . .
UNTIL I CAN FULLY UNDERSTAND HOW THIS WAS POSSIBLE . .
THE ONLY SAFE PLACE FOR YOU IS FIGNATION.

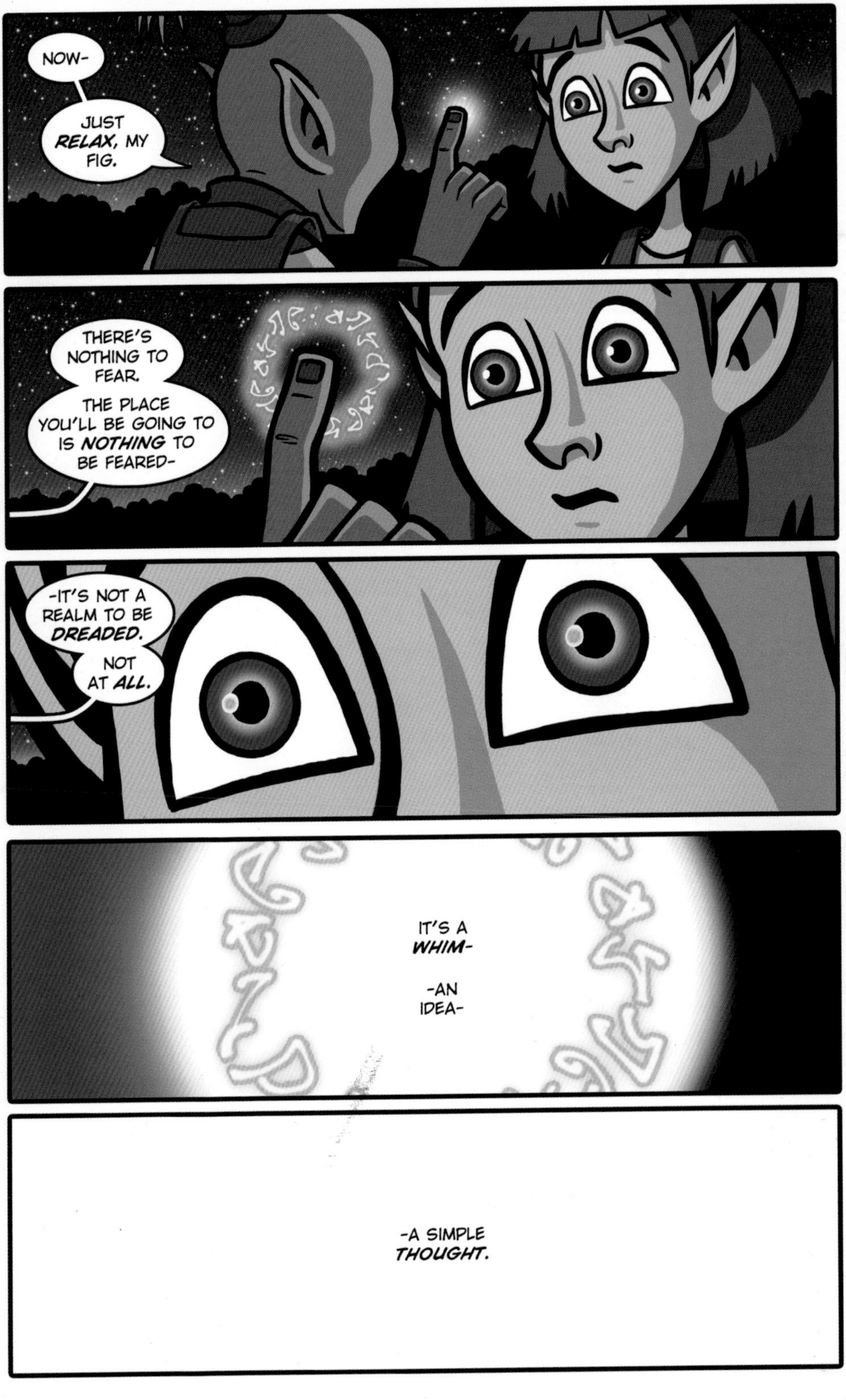
NOW-
JUST RELAX, MY FIG.
THERE'S NOTHING TO FEAR.
THE PLACE YOU'LL BE GOING TO IS NOTHING TO BE FEARED-
-IT'S NOT A REALM TO BE DREADED.
NOT AT ALL.
IT'S A WHIM-
-AN IDEA-
-A SIMPLE THOUGHT.

IN *FACT-*

-IT'S REALLY JUST A *FIGMENT OF YOUR IMAGINATION.*

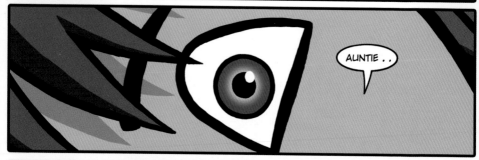

AUNTIE . .

I'M . .

HOME.

MOM.

DAD.

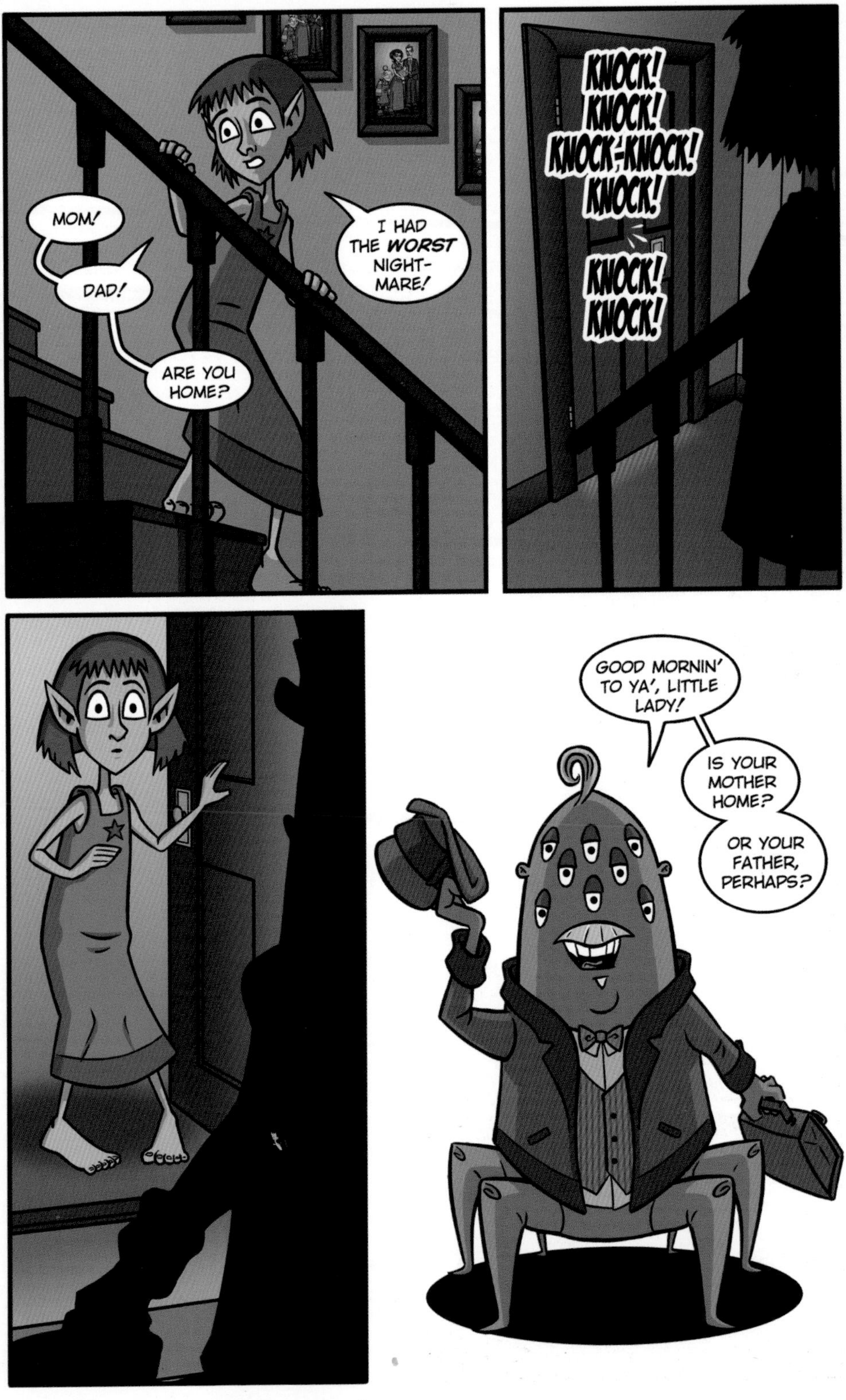
MOM!
DAD!
ARE YOU HOME?
I HAD THE WORST NIGHT-MARE!
KNOCK! KNOCK! KNOCK-KNOCK! KNOCK!
KNOCK! KNOCK!
GOOD MORNIN' TO YA', LITTLE LADY!
IS YOUR MOTHER HOME?
OR YOUR FATHER, PERHAPS?

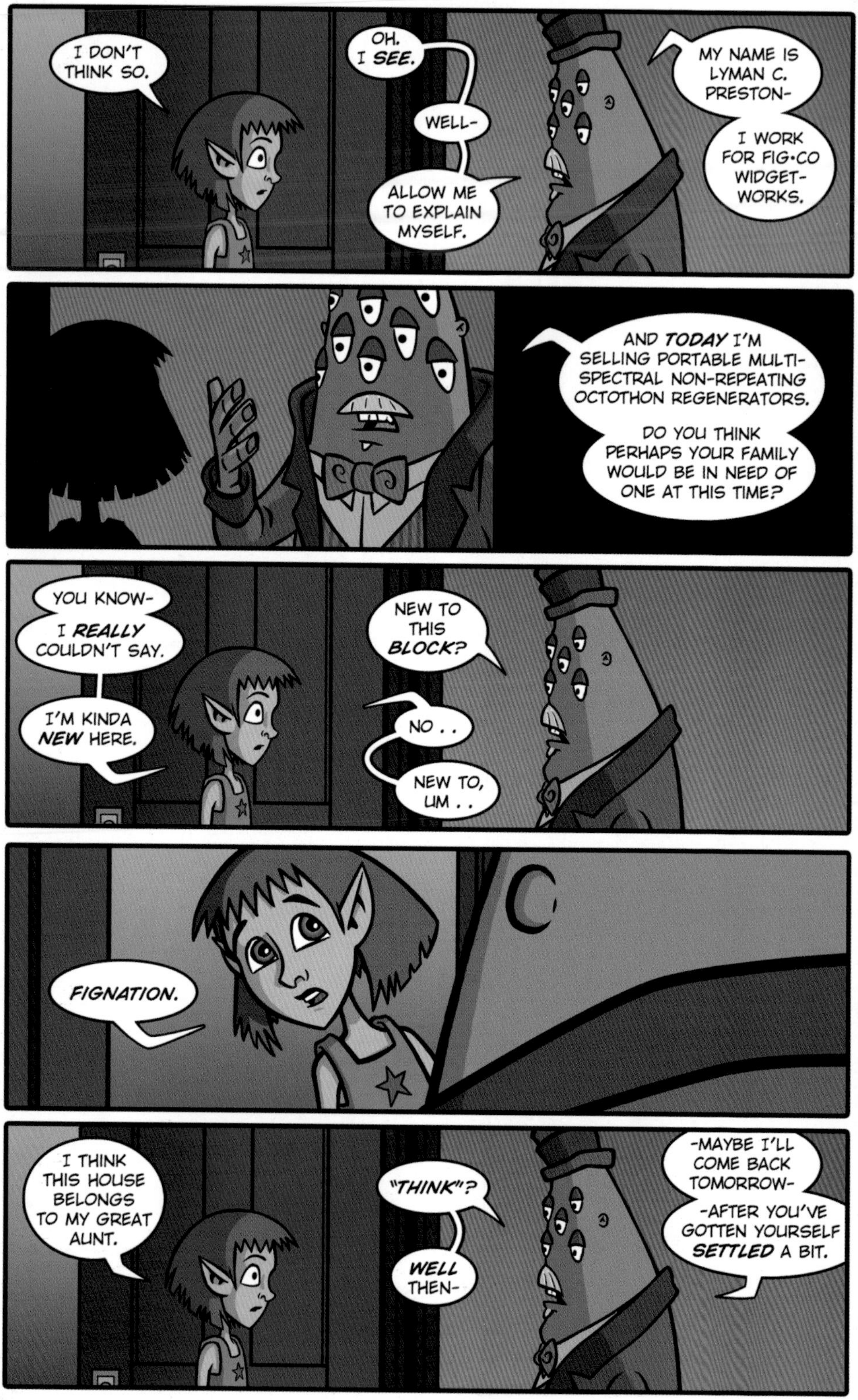
I DON'T THINK SO.
OH. I **SEE.**
WELL-
ALLOW ME TO EXPLAIN MYSELF.
MY NAME IS LYMAN C. PRESTON-
I WORK FOR FIG•CO WIDGET-WORKS.
AND **TODAY** I'M SELLING PORTABLE MULTI-SPECTRAL NON-REPEATING OCTOTHON REGENERATORS.
DO YOU THINK PERHAPS YOUR FAMILY WOULD BE IN NEED OF ONE AT THIS TIME?
YOU KNOW-
I **REALLY** COULDN'T SAY.
I'M KINDA **NEW** HERE.
NEW TO THIS **BLOCK?**
NO . .
NEW TO, UM . .
FIGNATION.
I THINK THIS HOUSE BELONGS TO MY GREAT AUNT.
"**THINK**"?
WELL THEN-
-MAYBE I'LL COME BACK TOMORROW-
-AFTER YOU'VE GOTTEN YOURSELF **SETTLED** A BIT.

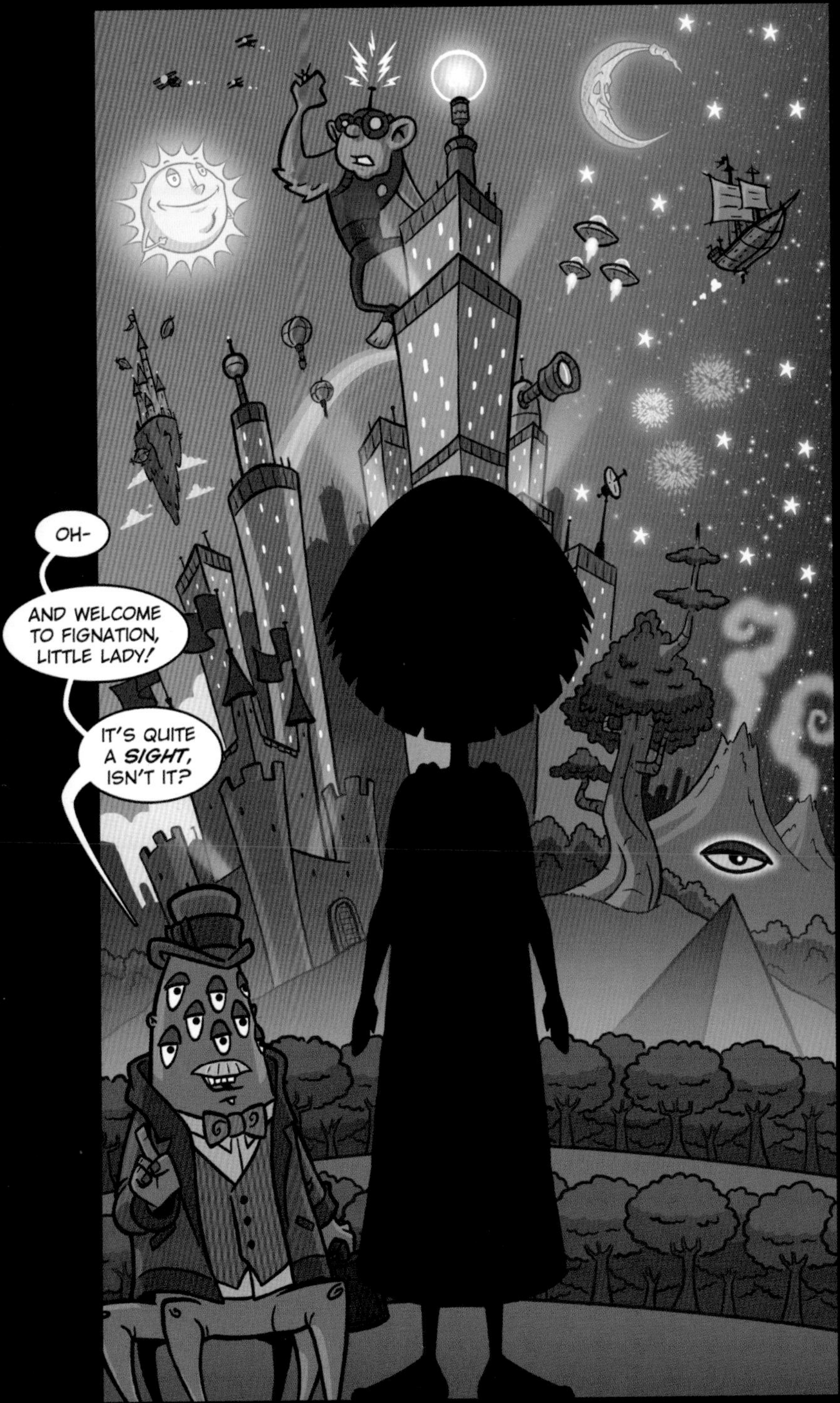
OH-
AND WELCOME TO FIGNATION, LITTLE LADY!
IT'S QUITE A *SIGHT*, ISN'T IT?

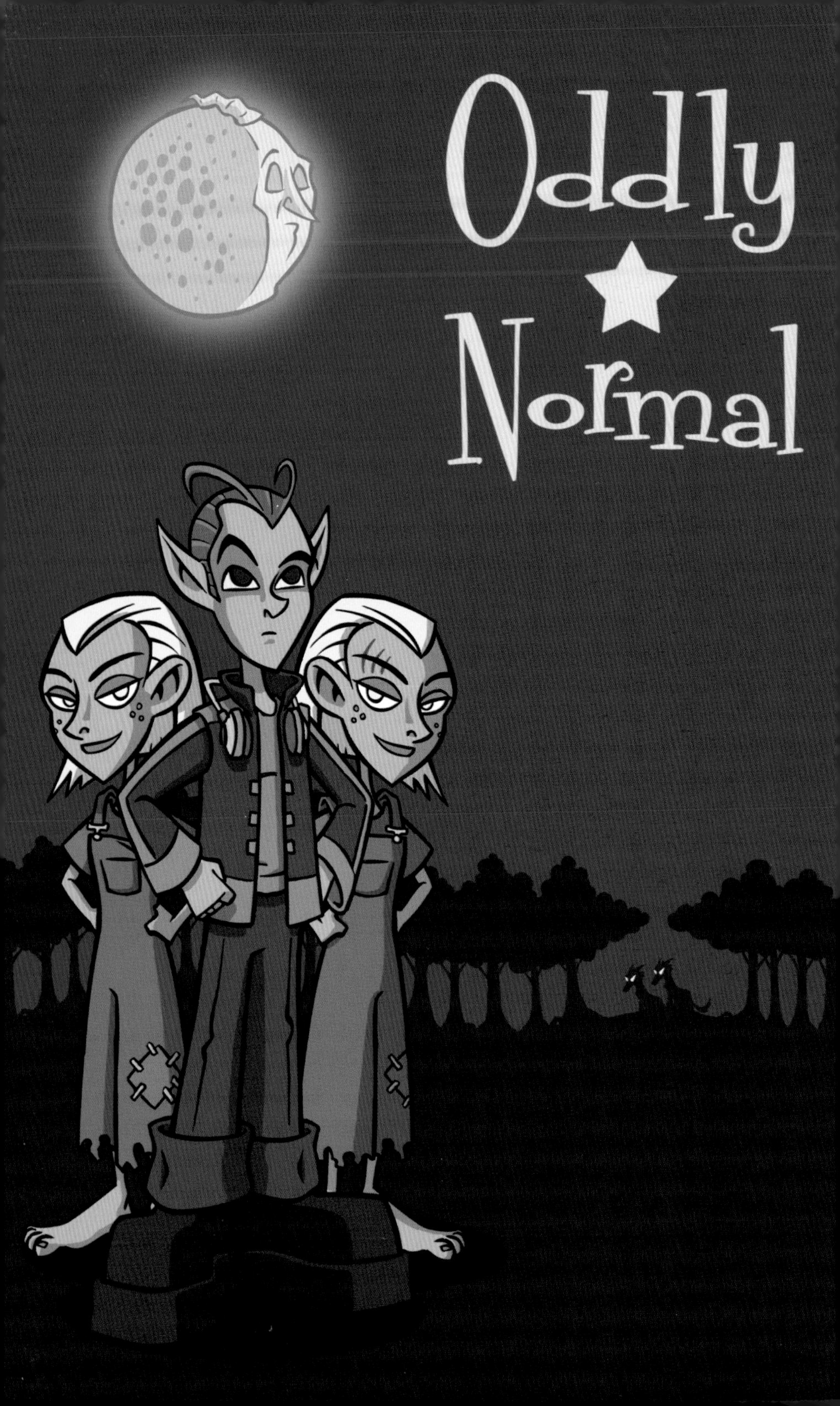
Oddly
Normal

Chapter 3

The Class ★ Menagerie

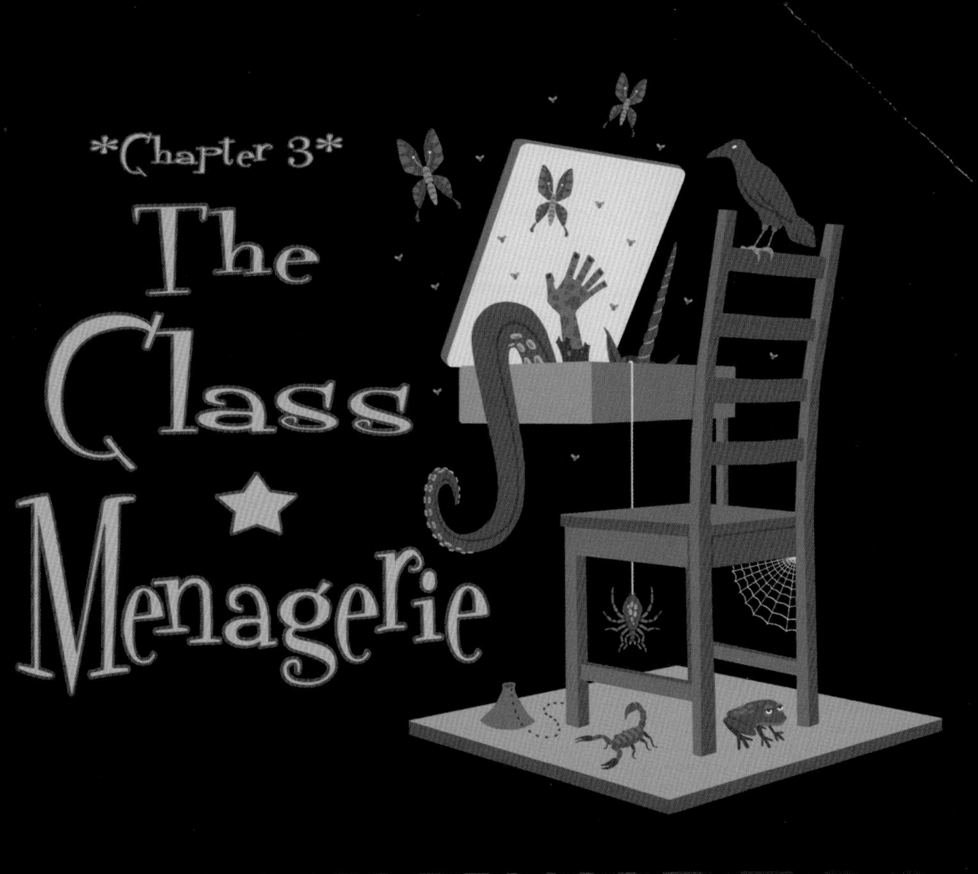

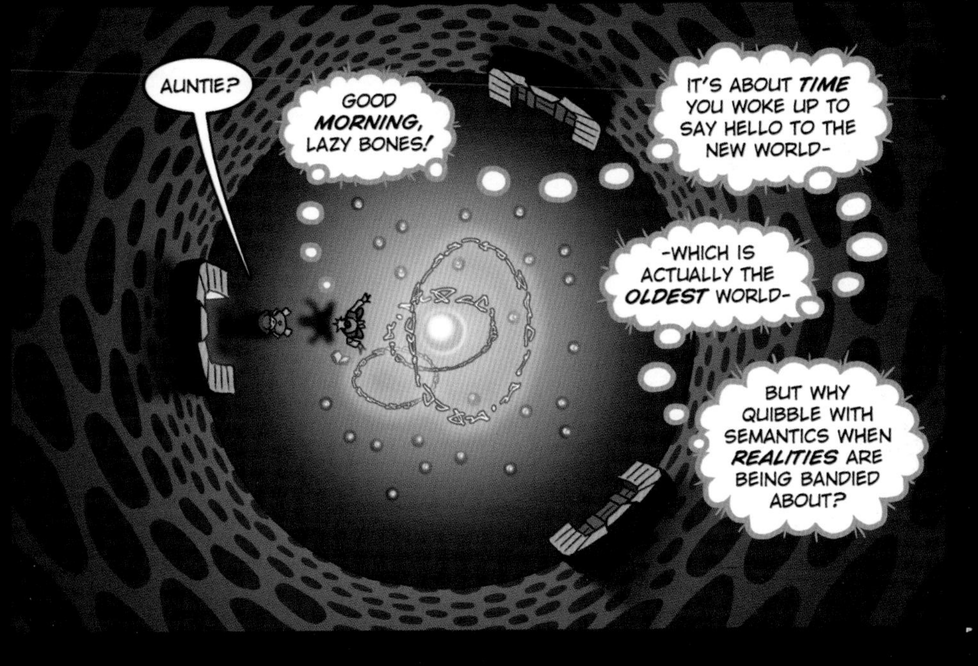
AUNTIE?
GOOD MORNING, LAZY BONES!
IT'S ABOUT TIME YOU WOKE UP TO SAY HELLO TO THE NEW WORLD-
-WHICH IS ACTUALLY THE OLDEST WORLD-
BUT WHY QUIBBLE WITH SEMANTICS WHEN REALITIES ARE BEING BANDIED ABOUT?

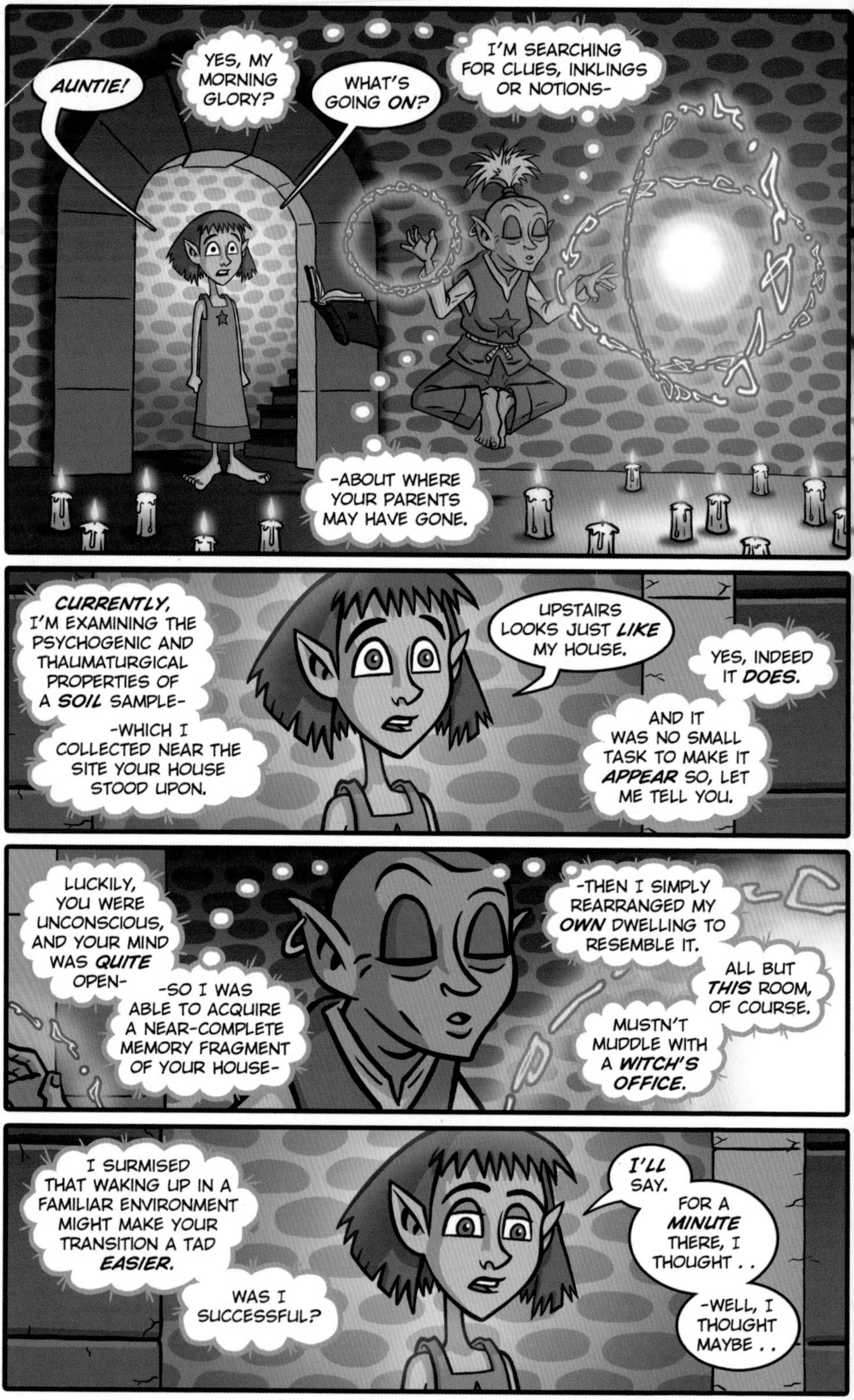
AUNTIE!
YES, MY MORNING GLORY?
WHAT'S GOING ON?
I'M SEARCHING FOR CLUES, INKLINGS OR NOTIONS-
-ABOUT WHERE YOUR PARENTS MAY HAVE GONE.
CURRENTLY, I'M EXAMINING THE PSYCHOGENIC AND THAUMATURGICAL PROPERTIES OF A SOIL SAMPLE-
-WHICH I COLLECTED NEAR THE SITE YOUR HOUSE STOOD UPON.
UPSTAIRS LOOKS JUST LIKE MY HOUSE.
YES, INDEED IT DOES.
AND IT WAS NO SMALL TASK TO MAKE IT APPEAR SO, LET ME TELL YOU.
LUCKILY, YOU WERE UNCONSCIOUS, AND YOUR MIND WAS QUITE OPEN-
-SO I WAS ABLE TO ACQUIRE A NEAR-COMPLETE MEMORY FRAGMENT OF YOUR HOUSE-
-THEN I SIMPLY REARRANGED MY OWN DWELLING TO RESEMBLE IT.
ALL BUT THIS ROOM, OF COURSE.
MUSTN'T MUDDLE WITH A WITCH'S OFFICE.
I SURMISED THAT WAKING UP IN A FAMILIAR ENVIRONMENT MIGHT MAKE YOUR TRANSITION A TAD EASIER.
WAS I SUCCESSFUL?
I'LL SAY.
FOR A MINUTE THERE, I THOUGHT . .
-WELL, I THOUGHT MAYBE . .

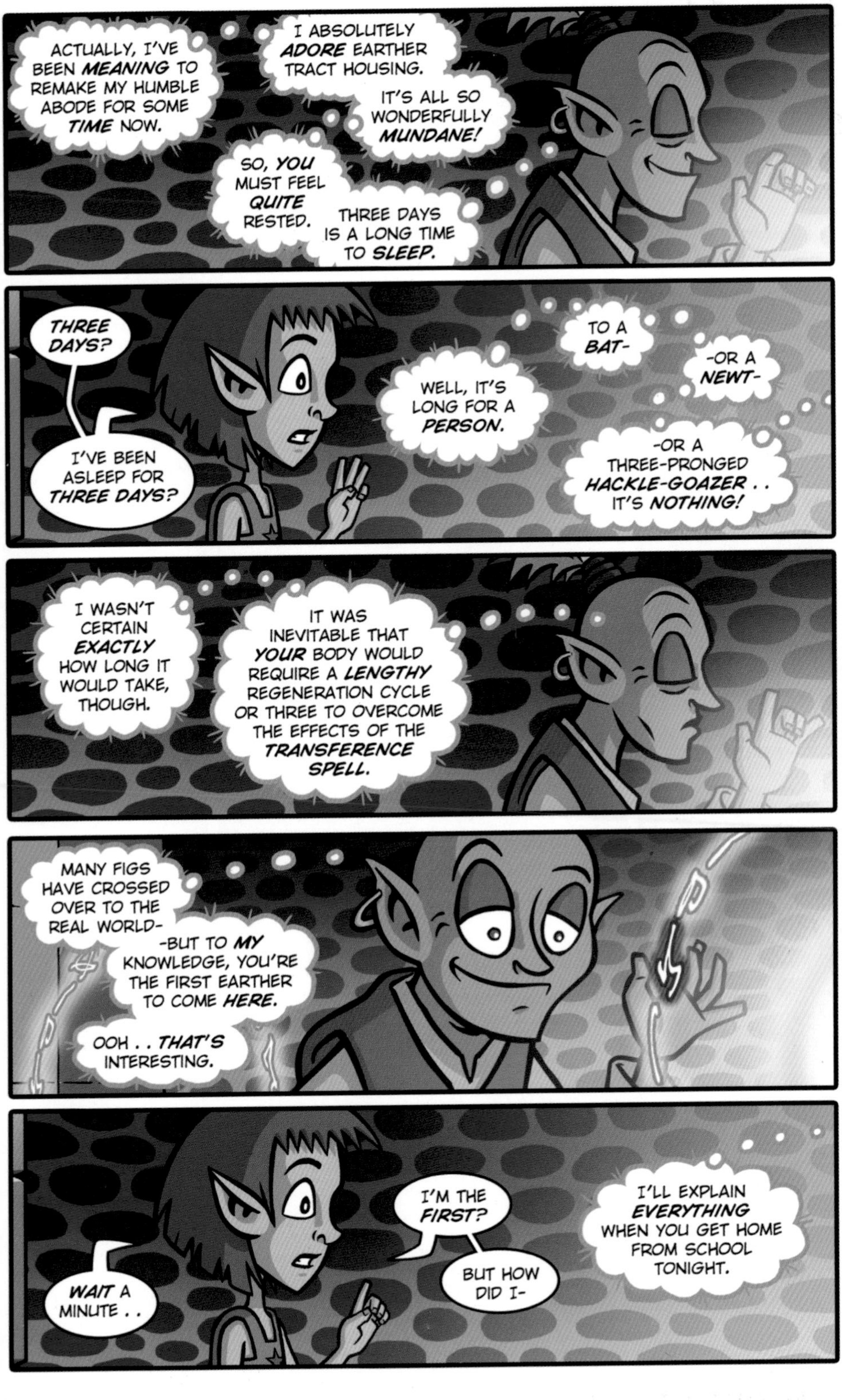
ACTUALLY, I'VE BEEN MEANING TO REMAKE MY HUMBLE ABODE FOR SOME TIME NOW.
I ABSOLUTELY ADORE EARTHER TRACT HOUSING.
IT'S ALL SO WONDERFULLY MUNDANE!
SO, YOU MUST FEEL QUITE RESTED.
THREE DAYS IS A LONG TIME TO SLEEP.
THREE DAYS?
I'VE BEEN ASLEEP FOR THREE DAYS?
WELL, IT'S LONG FOR A PERSON.
TO A BAT-
-OR A NEWT-
-OR A THREE-PRONGED HACKLE-GOAZER . . IT'S NOTHING!
I WASN'T CERTAIN EXACTLY HOW LONG IT WOULD TAKE, THOUGH.
IT WAS INEVITABLE THAT YOUR BODY WOULD REQUIRE A LENGTHY REGENERATION CYCLE OR THREE TO OVERCOME THE EFFECTS OF THE TRANSFERENCE SPELL.
MANY FIGS HAVE CROSSED OVER TO THE REAL WORLD-
-BUT TO MY KNOWLEDGE, YOU'RE THE FIRST EARTHER TO COME HERE.
OOH . . THAT'S INTERESTING.
WAIT A MINUTE . .
I'M THE FIRST?
BUT HOW DID I-
I'LL EXPLAIN EVERYTHING WHEN YOU GET HOME FROM SCHOOL TONIGHT.

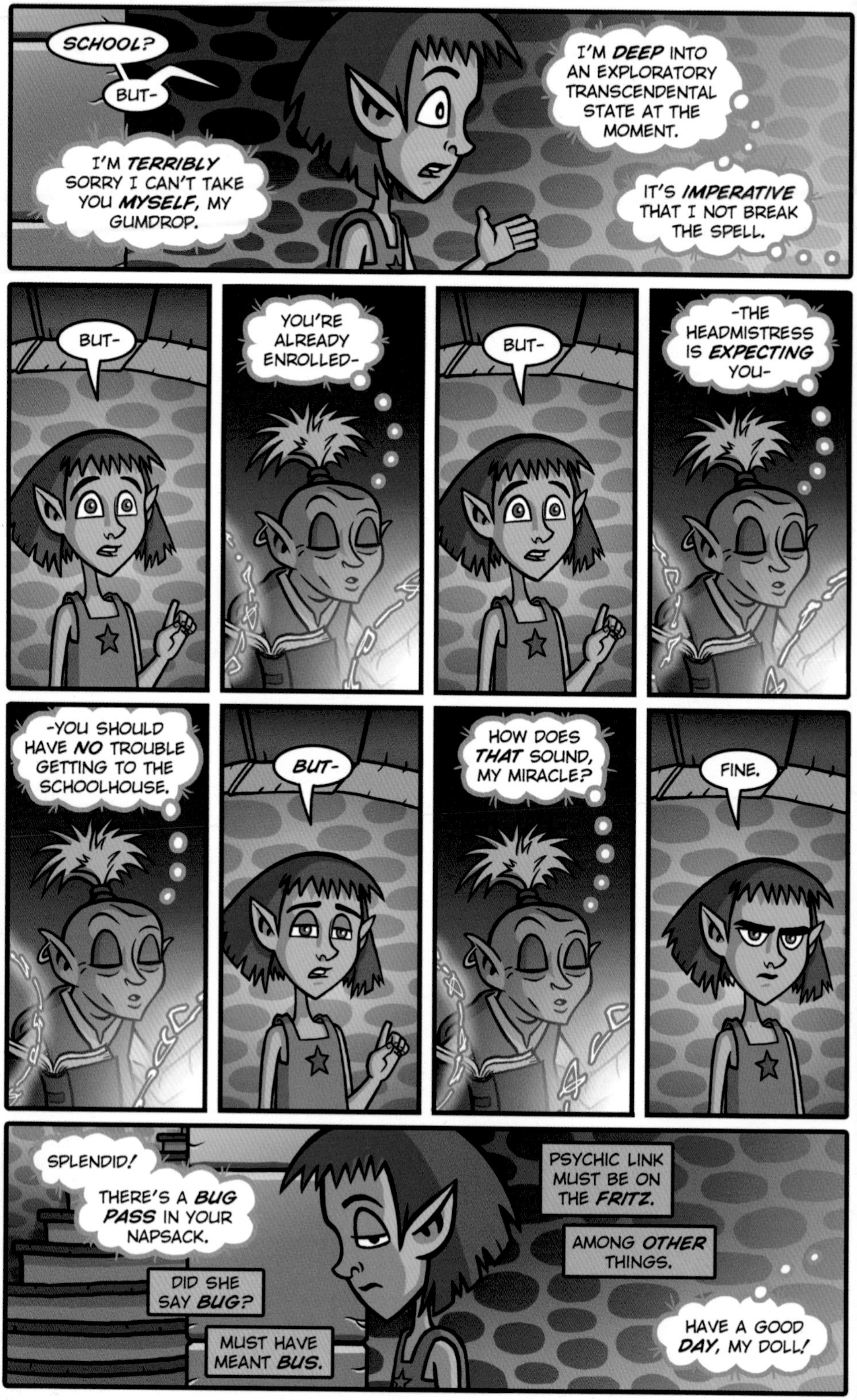
SCHOOL?
BUT-
I'M TERRIBLY SORRY I CAN'T TAKE YOU MYSELF, MY GUMDROP.
I'M DEEP INTO AN EXPLORATORY TRANSCENDENTAL STATE AT THE MOMENT.
IT'S IMPERATIVE THAT I NOT BREAK THE SPELL.
BUT-
YOU'RE ALREADY ENROLLED-
BUT-
-THE HEADMISTRESS IS EXPECTING YOU-
-YOU SHOULD HAVE NO TROUBLE GETTING TO THE SCHOOLHOUSE.
BUT-
HOW DOES THAT SOUND, MY MIRACLE?
FINE.
SPLENDID!
THERE'S A BUG PASS IN YOUR NAPSACK.
DID SHE SAY BUG?
MUST HAVE MEANT BUS.
PSYCHIC LINK MUST BE ON THE FRITZ.
AMONG OTHER THINGS.
HAVE A GOOD DAY, MY DOLL!

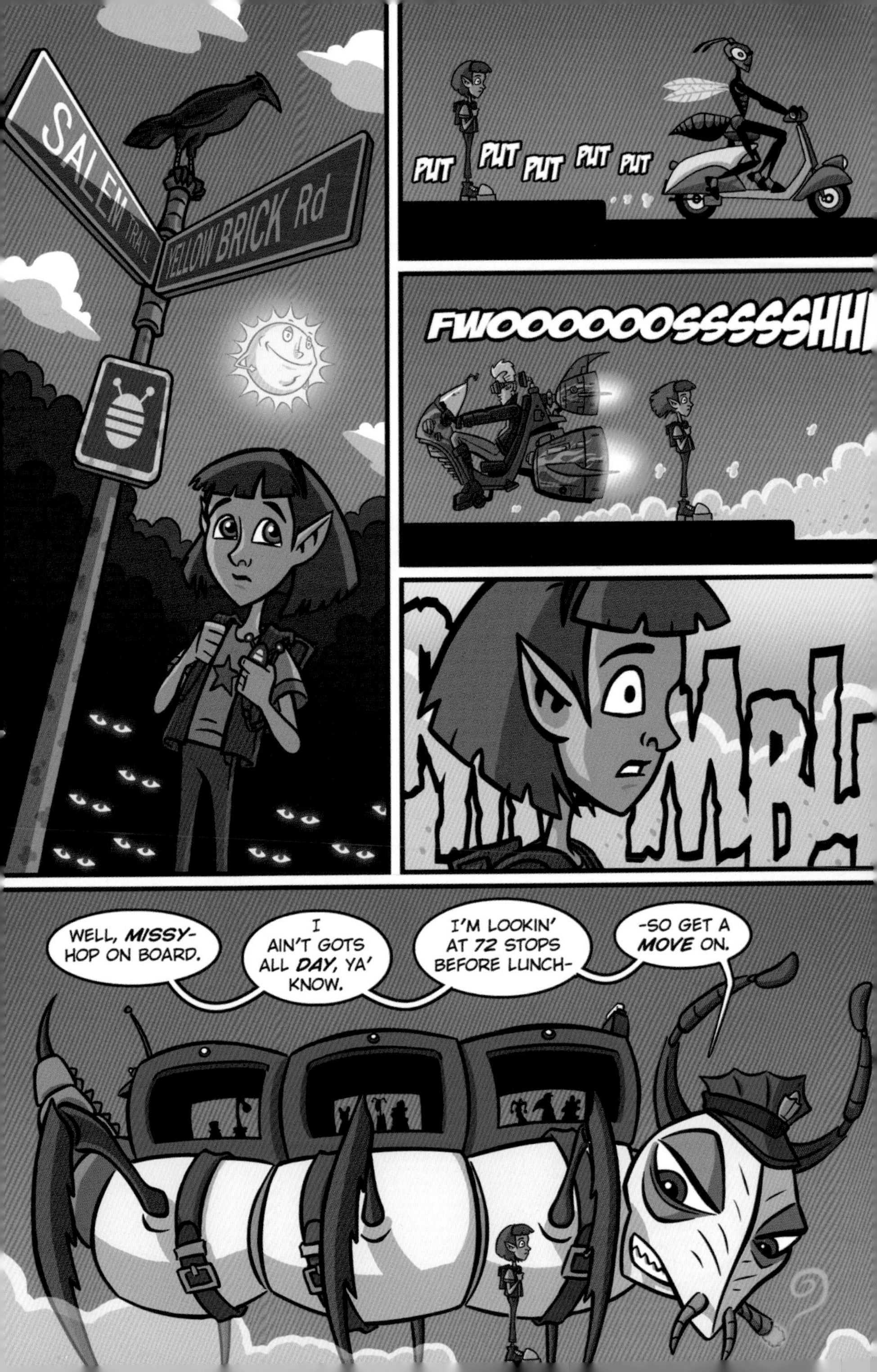
SALEM TRAIL
YELLOW BRICK Rd
PUT PUT PUT PUT PUT
FWOOOOOOOSSSSSHH
WELL, MISSY-
HOP ON BOARD.
I AIN'T GOTS ALL DAY, YA' KNOW.
I'M LOOKIN' AT 72 STOPS BEFORE LUNCH-
-SO GET A MOVE ON.

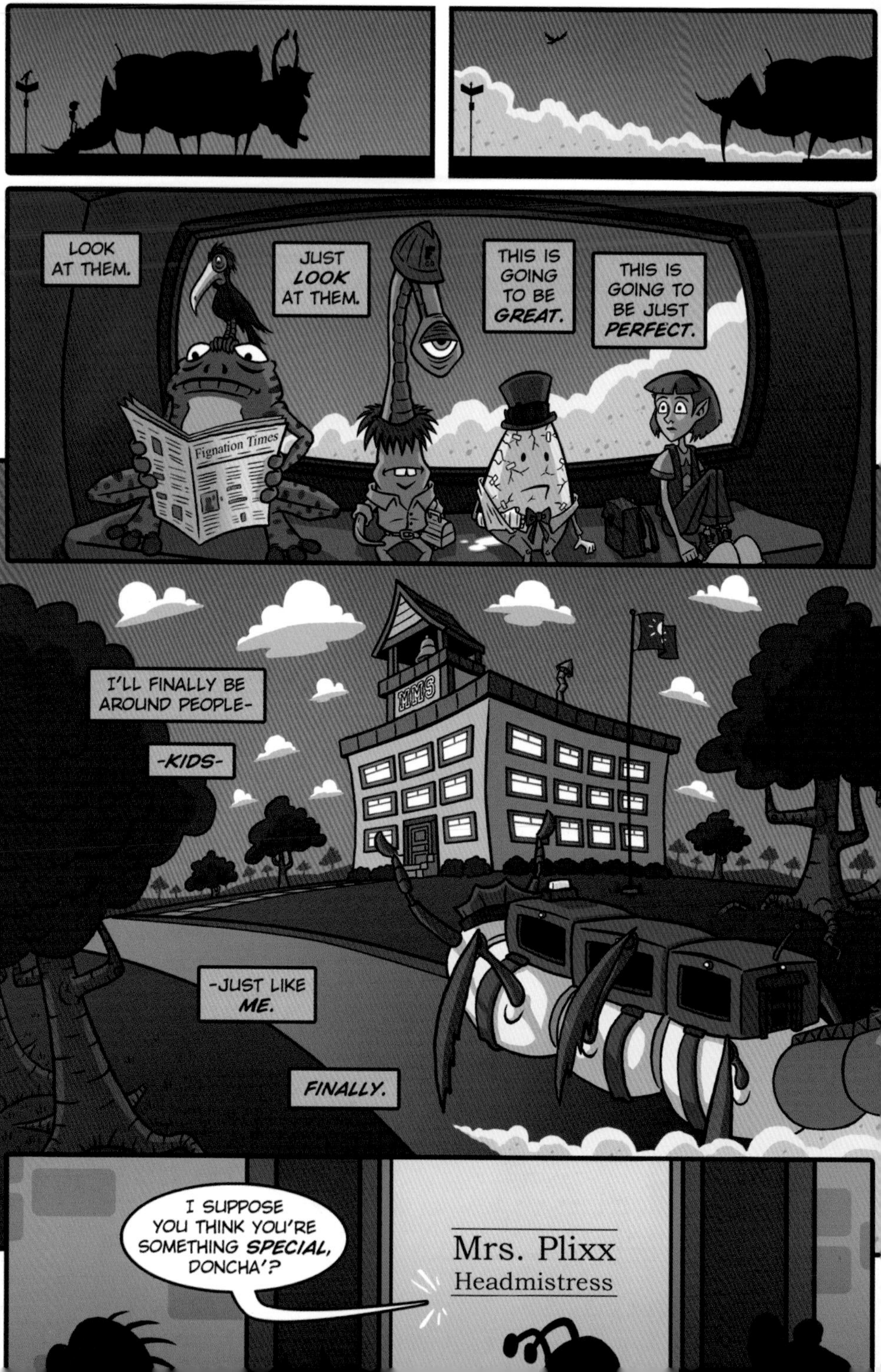

LOOK AT THEM.
JUST LOOK AT THEM.
THIS IS GOING TO BE GREAT.
THIS IS GOING TO BE JUST PERFECT.
Fignation Times
MMS
I'LL FINALLY BE AROUND PEOPLE-
-KIDS-
-JUST LIKE ME.
FINALLY.
I SUPPOSE YOU THINK YOU'RE SOMETHING SPECIAL, DONCHA'?
Mrs. Plixx
Headmistress

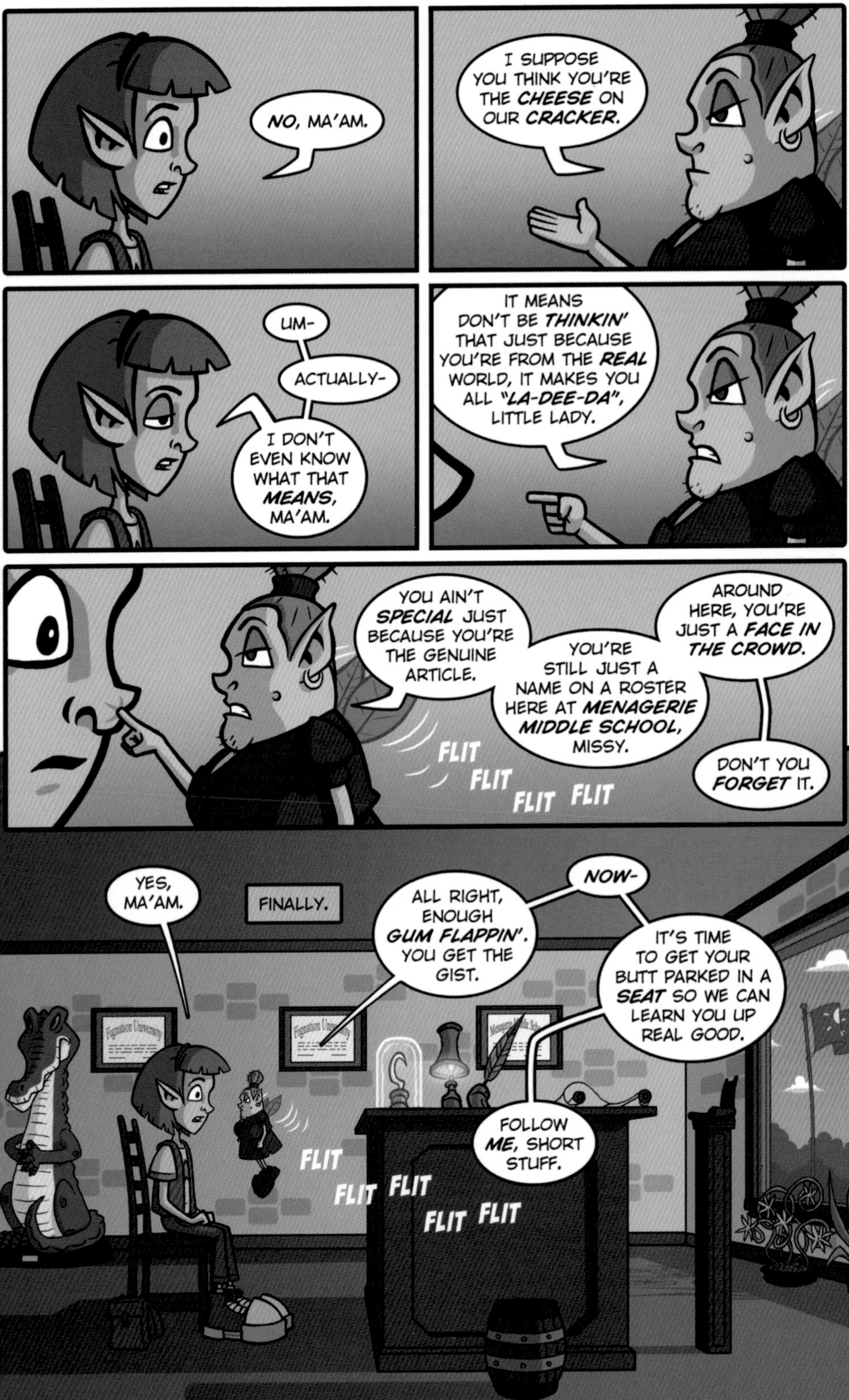
NO, MA'AM.
I SUPPOSE YOU THINK YOU'RE THE CHEESE ON OUR CRACKER.
UM-
ACTUALLY-
I DON'T EVEN KNOW WHAT THAT MEANS, MA'AM.
IT MEANS DON'T BE THINKIN' THAT JUST BECAUSE YOU'RE FROM THE REAL WORLD, IT MAKES YOU ALL "LA-DEE-DA", LITTLE LADY.
YOU AIN'T SPECIAL JUST BECAUSE YOU'RE THE GENUINE ARTICLE.
YOU'RE STILL JUST A NAME ON A ROSTER HERE AT MENAGERIE MIDDLE SCHOOL, MISSY.
AROUND HERE, YOU'RE JUST A FACE IN THE CROWD.
DON'T YOU FORGET IT.
FLIT FLIT FLIT FLIT
YES, MA'AM.
FINALLY.
ALL RIGHT, ENOUGH GUM FLAPPIN'. YOU GET THE GIST.
NOW-
IT'S TIME TO GET YOUR BUTT PARKED IN A SEAT SO WE CAN LEARN YOU UP REAL GOOD.
FOLLOW ME, SHORT STUFF.
FLIT FLIT FLIT FLIT FLIT
Fignation University
Fignation University

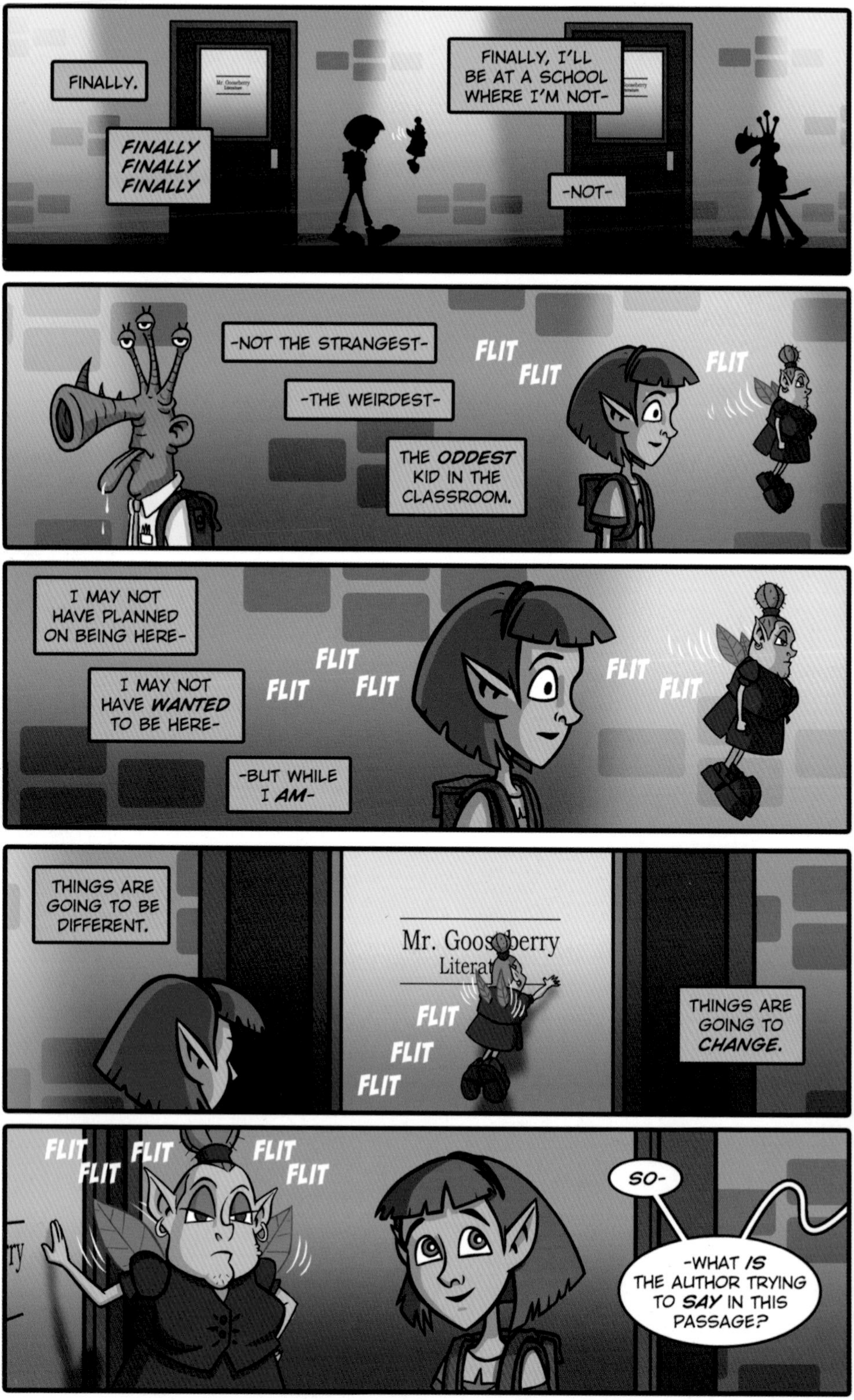
FINALLY.
FINALLY FINALLY FINALLY
Mr. Gooseberry
FINALLY, I'LL BE AT A SCHOOL WHERE I'M NOT-
-NOT-
-NOT THE STRANGEST-
-THE WEIRDEST-
THE ODDEST KID IN THE CLASSROOM.
FLIT
FLIT
FLIT
I MAY NOT HAVE PLANNED ON BEING HERE-
I MAY NOT HAVE WANTED TO BE HERE-
-BUT WHILE I AM-
FLIT FLIT FLIT
FLIT FLIT
THINGS ARE GOING TO BE DIFFERENT.
Mr. Goos berry
Literat
FLIT FLIT FLIT
THINGS ARE GOING TO CHANGE.
FLIT FLIT FLIT FLIT FLIT
SO-
-WHAT IS THE AUTHOR TRYING TO SAY IN THIS PASSAGE?

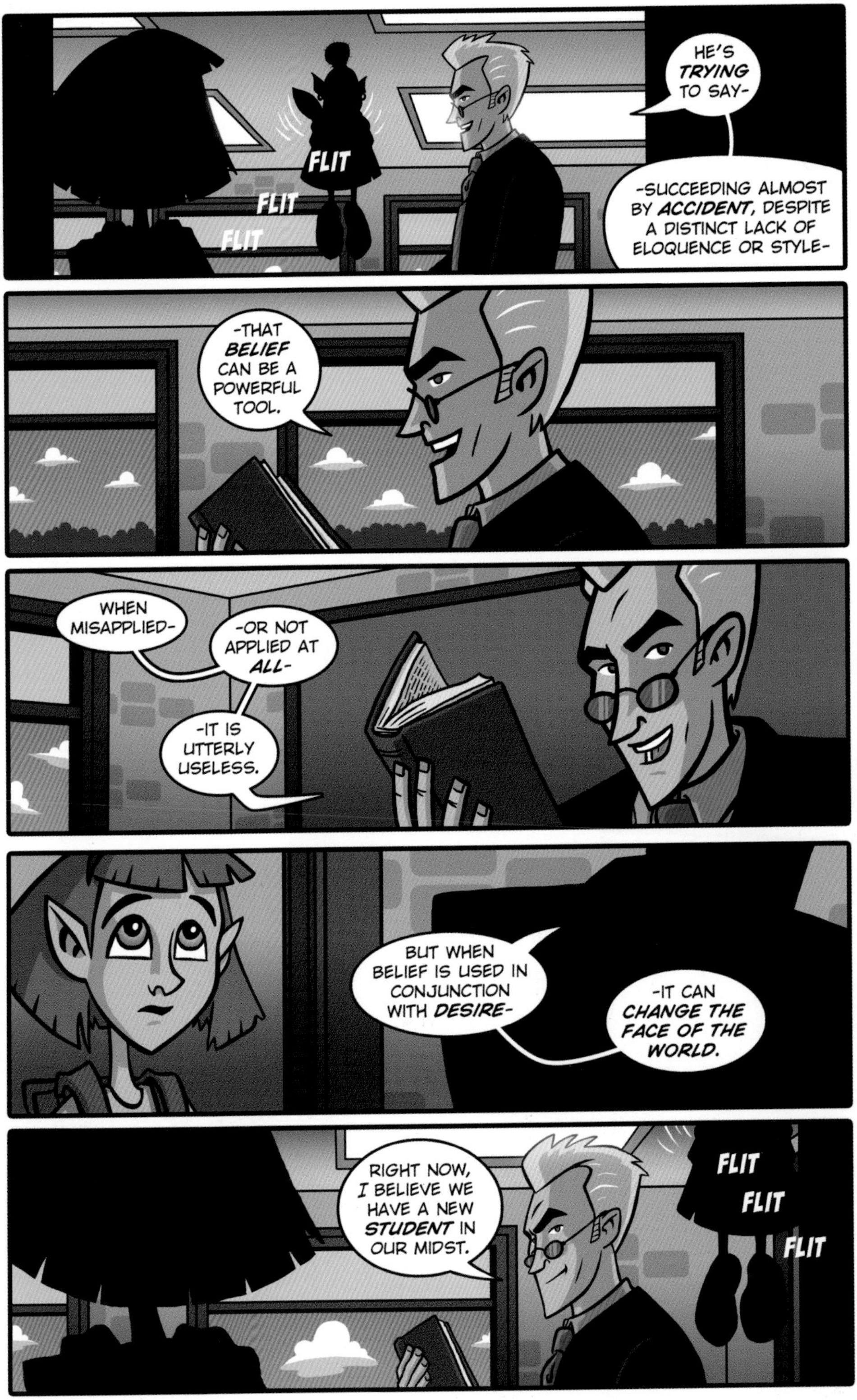
HE'S *TRYING* TO SAY-
FLIT
FLIT
FLIT
-SUCCEEDING ALMOST BY *ACCIDENT*, DESPITE A DISTINCT LACK OF ELOQUENCE OR STYLE-
-THAT *BELIEF* CAN BE A POWERFUL TOOL.
WHEN MISAPPLIED-
-OR NOT APPLIED AT *ALL*-
-IT IS UTTERLY USELESS.
BUT WHEN BELIEF IS USED IN CONJUNCTION WITH *DESIRE*-
-IT CAN *CHANGE THE FACE OF THE WORLD*.
RIGHT NOW, *I* BELIEVE WE HAVE A NEW *STUDENT* IN OUR MIDST.
FLIT
FLIT
FLIT

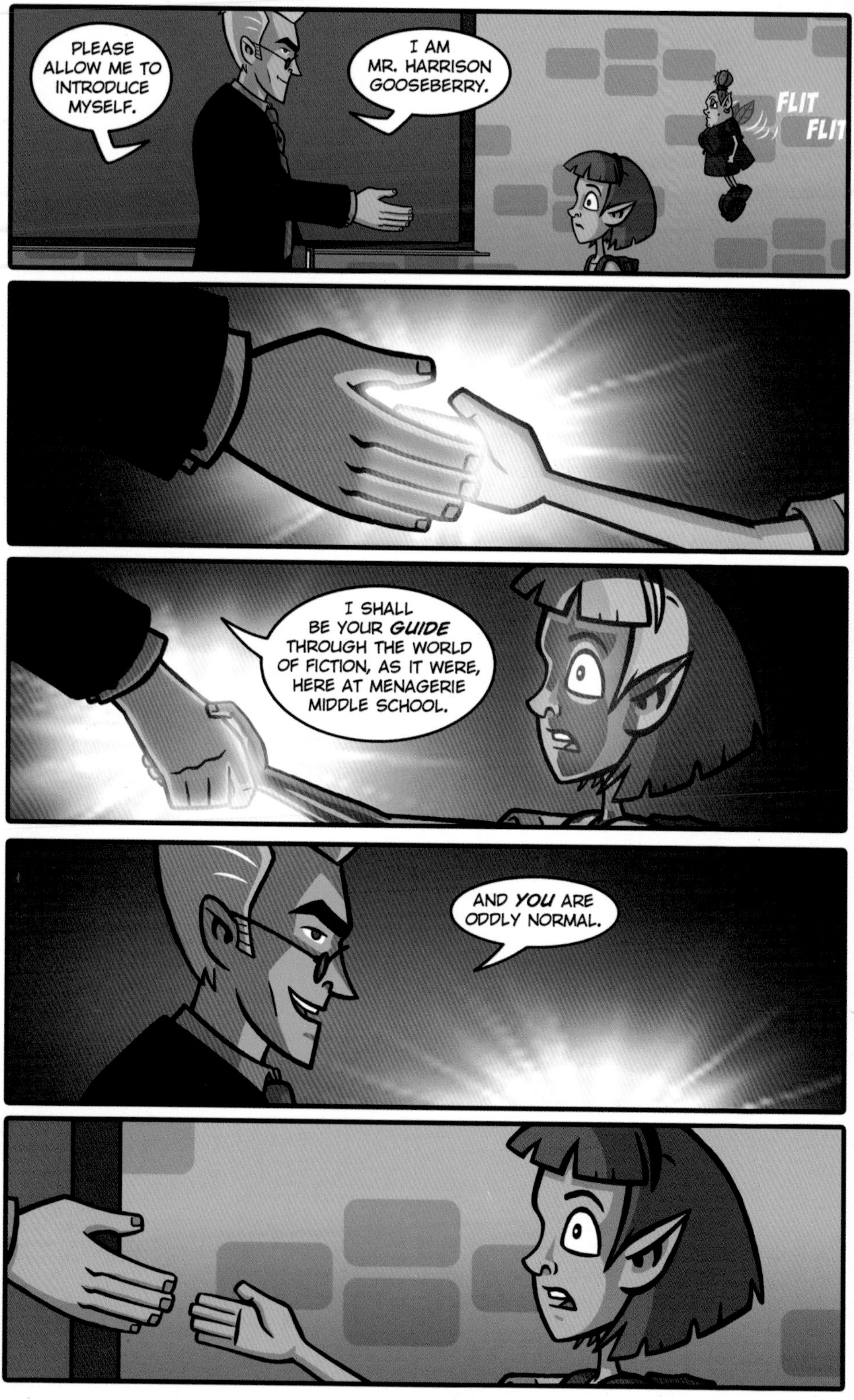
PLEASE ALLOW ME TO INTRODUCE MYSELF.
I AM MR. HARRISON GOOSEBERRY.
FLIT FLIT
I SHALL BE YOUR GUIDE THROUGH THE WORLD OF FICTION, AS IT WERE, HERE AT MENAGERIE MIDDLE SCHOOL.
AND YOU ARE ODDLY NORMAL.

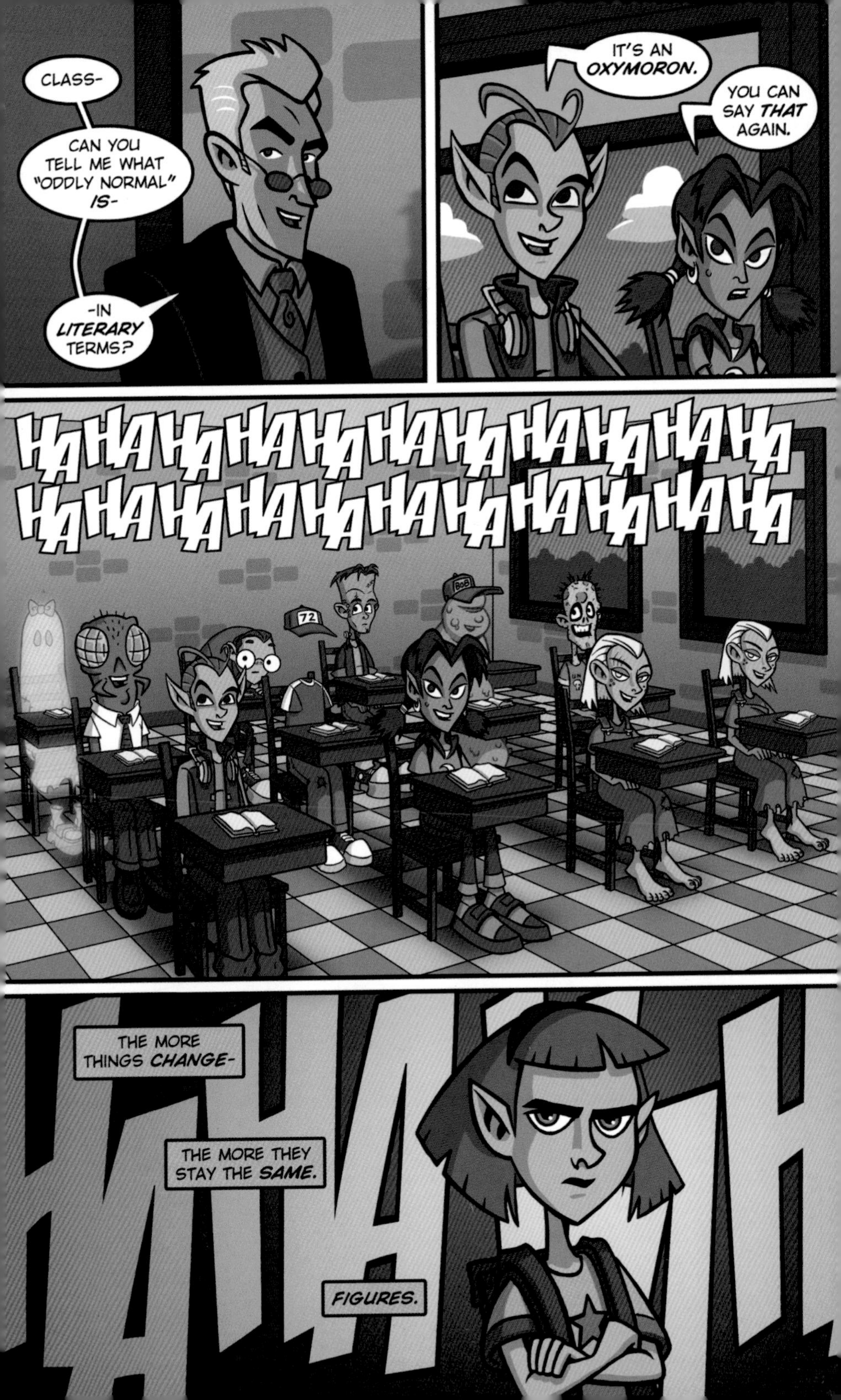

CLASS-
CAN YOU TELL ME WHAT "ODDLY NORMAL" IS-
-IN LITERARY TERMS?
IT'S AN OXYMORON.
YOU CAN SAY THAT AGAIN.
HAHAHAHAHAHAHAHAHAHAHAHAHAHAHAHAHAHAHAHAHAHA
HAHAHAHAHAHAHAHAHAHAHAHAHAHAHAHAHAHAHAHAHAHA
THE MORE THINGS CHANGE-
THE MORE THEY STAY THE SAME.
FIGURES.

Chapter 4

Sticks, Stones, Words & Bones

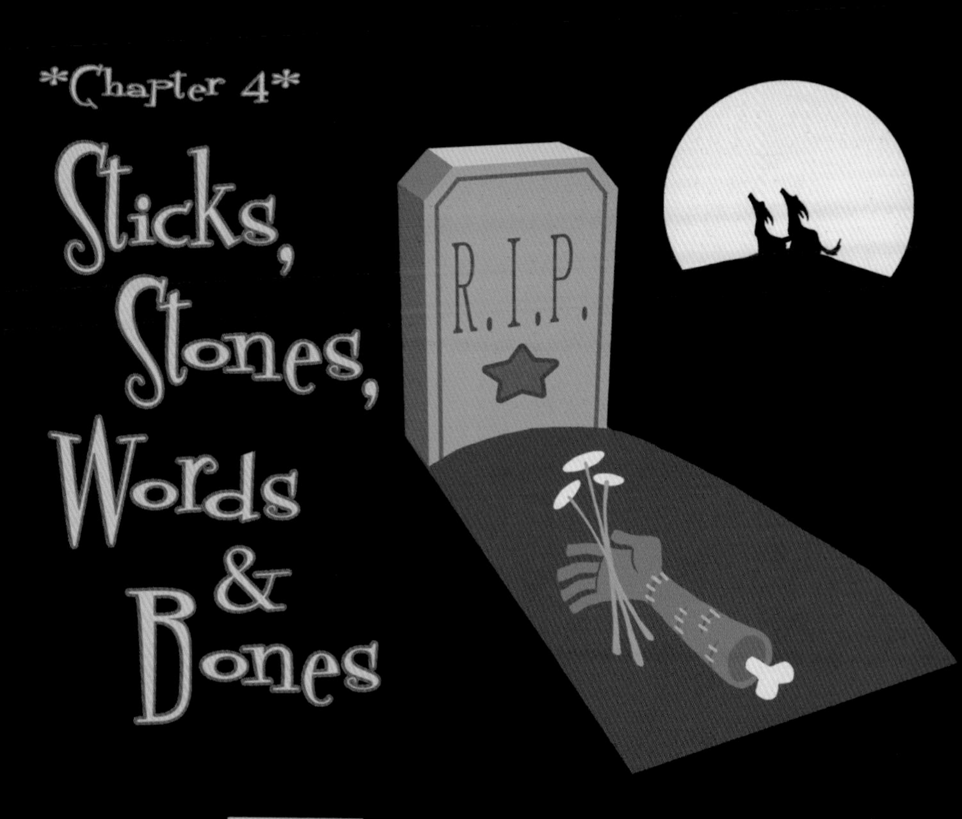
R.I.P.

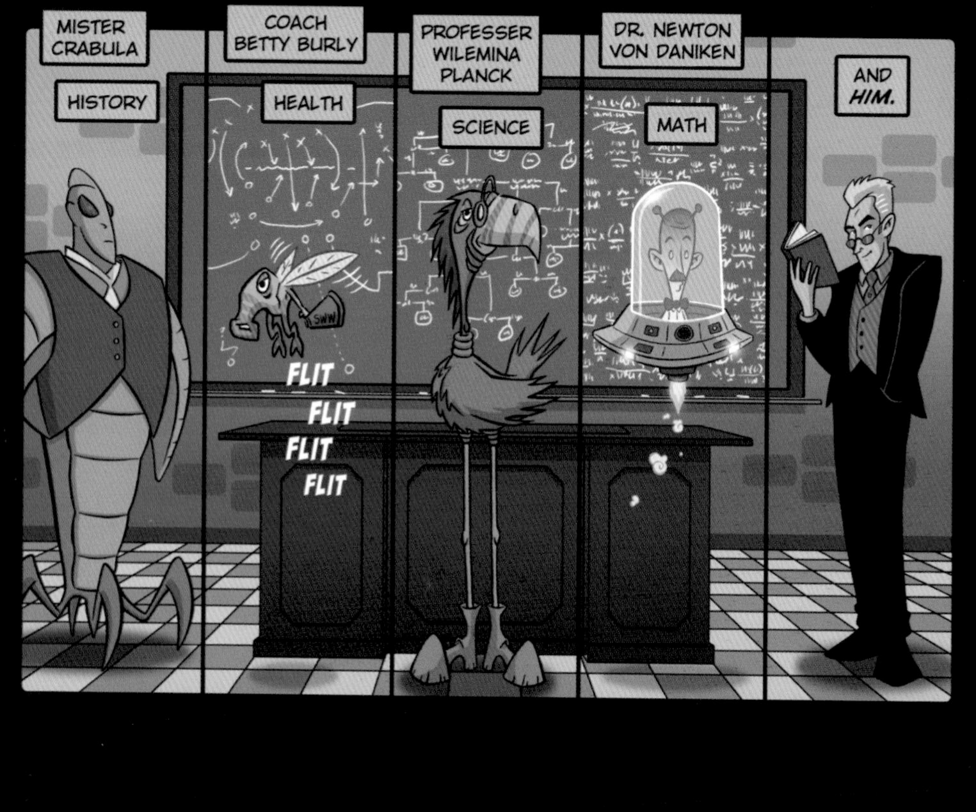
MISTER CRABULA
HISTORY
COACH BETTY BURLY
HEALTH
PROFESSER WILEMINA PLANCK
SCIENCE
DR. NEWTON VON DANIKEN
MATH
AND HIM.
SWW
FLIT
FLIT
FLIT
FLIT

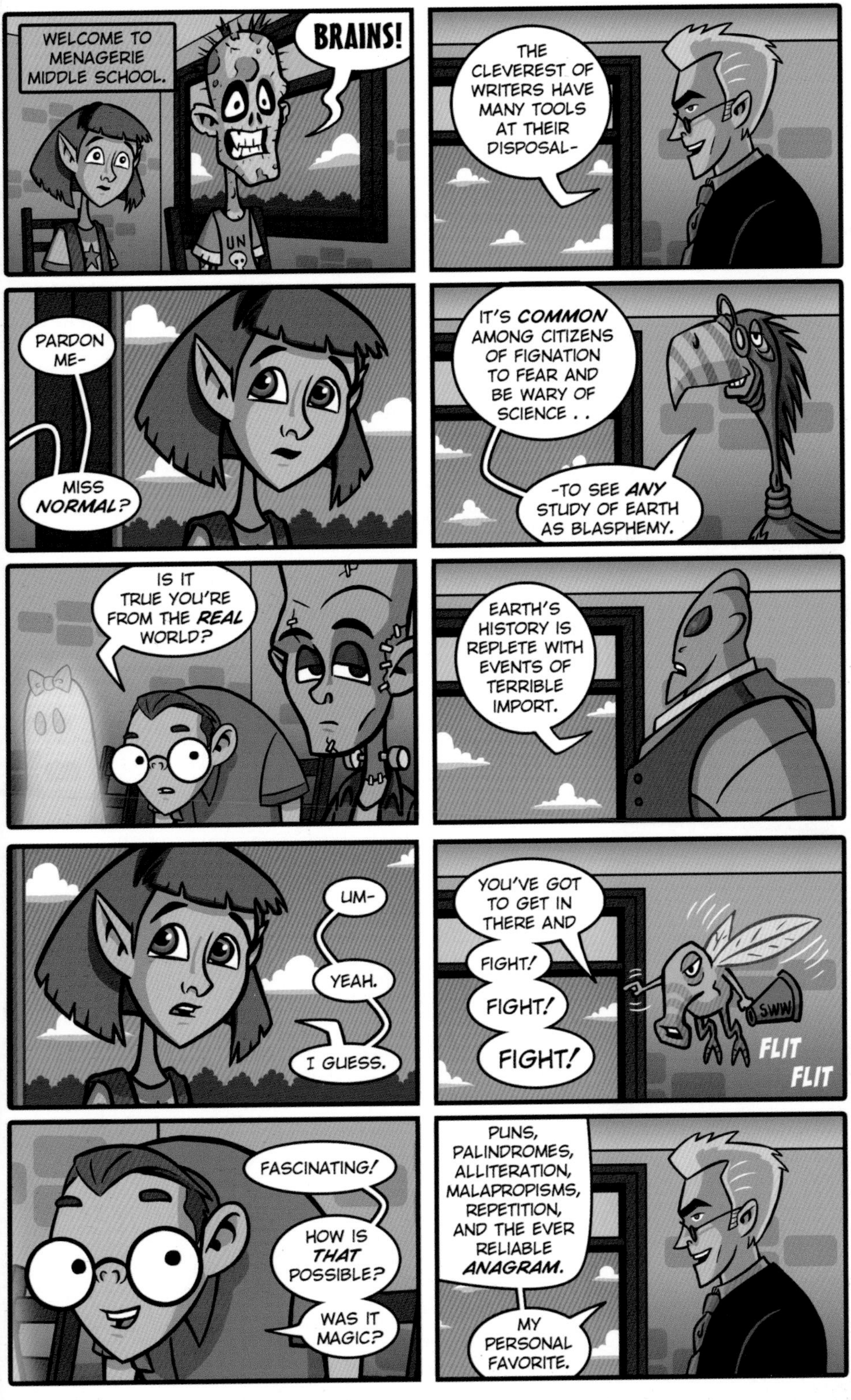
WELCOME TO MENAGERIE MIDDLE SCHOOL.
BRAINS!
UN
THE CLEVEREST OF WRITERS HAVE MANY TOOLS AT THEIR DISPOSAL-
PARDON ME-
MISS *NORMAL?*
IT'S *COMMON* AMONG CITIZENS OF FIGNATION TO FEAR AND BE WARY OF SCIENCE . .
-TO SEE *ANY* STUDY OF EARTH AS BLASPHEMY.
IS IT TRUE YOU'RE FROM THE *REAL* WORLD?
EARTH'S HISTORY IS REPLETE WITH EVENTS OF TERRIBLE IMPORT.
UM-
YEAH.
I GUESS.
YOU'VE GOT TO GET IN THERE AND
FIGHT!
FIGHT!
FIGHT!
SWW
FLIT
FLIT
FASCINATING!
HOW IS *THAT* POSSIBLE?
WAS IT MAGIC?
PUNS, PALINDROMES, ALLITERATION, MALAPROPISMS, REPETITION, AND THE EVER RELIABLE ***ANAGRAM.***
MY PERSONAL FAVORITE.

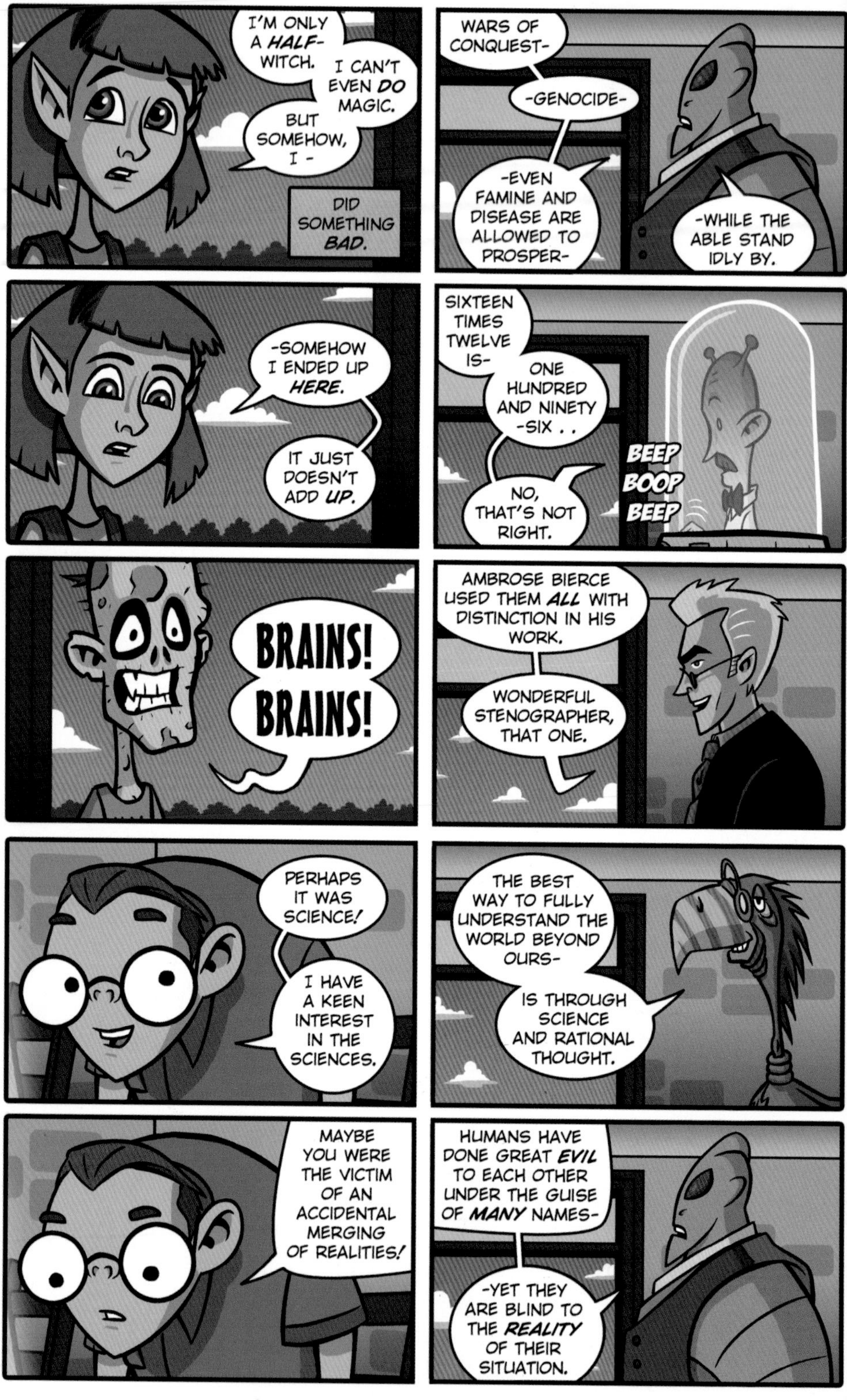
I'M ONLY A HALF-WITCH.
I CAN'T EVEN DO MAGIC.
BUT SOMEHOW, I -
DID SOMETHING BAD.
WARS OF CONQUEST-
-GENOCIDE-
-EVEN FAMINE AND DISEASE ARE ALLOWED TO PROSPER-
-WHILE THE ABLE STAND IDLY BY.
-SOMEHOW I ENDED UP HERE.
IT JUST DOESN'T ADD UP.
SIXTEEN TIMES TWELVE IS-
ONE HUNDRED AND NINETY -SIX . .
NO, THAT'S NOT RIGHT.
BEEP
BOOP
BEEP
BRAINS!
BRAINS!
AMBROSE BIERCE USED THEM ALL WITH DISTINCTION IN HIS WORK.
WONDERFUL STENOGRAPHER, THAT ONE.
PERHAPS IT WAS SCIENCE!
I HAVE A KEEN INTEREST IN THE SCIENCES.
THE BEST WAY TO FULLY UNDERSTAND THE WORLD BEYOND OURS-
IS THROUGH SCIENCE AND RATIONAL THOUGHT.
MAYBE YOU WERE THE VICTIM OF AN ACCIDENTAL MERGING OF REALITIES!
HUMANS HAVE DONE GREAT EVIL TO EACH OTHER UNDER THE GUISE OF MANY NAMES-
-YET THEY ARE BLIND TO THE REALITY OF THEIR SITUATION.

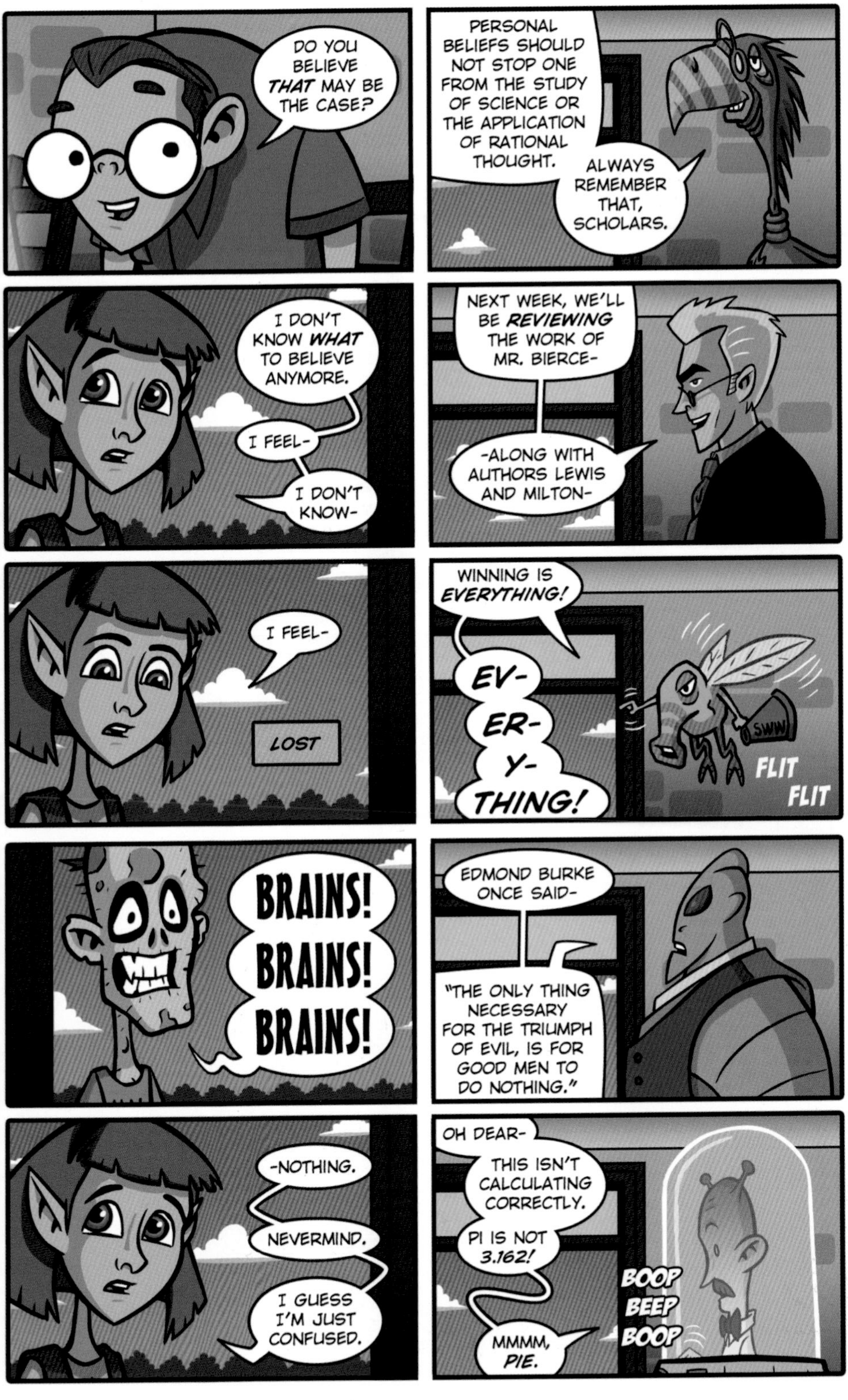
DO YOU BELIEVE THAT MAY BE THE CASE?
PERSONAL BELIEFS SHOULD NOT STOP ONE FROM THE STUDY OF SCIENCE OR THE APPLICATION OF RATIONAL THOUGHT.
ALWAYS REMEMBER THAT, SCHOLARS.
I DON'T KNOW WHAT TO BELIEVE ANYMORE.
I FEEL-
I DON'T KNOW-
NEXT WEEK, WE'LL BE REVIEWING THE WORK OF MR. BIERCE-
-ALONG WITH AUTHORS LEWIS AND MILTON-
I FEEL-
LOST
WINNING IS EVERYTHING!
EV-
ER-
Y-
THING!
SWW
FLIT
FLIT
BRAINS!
BRAINS!
BRAINS!
EDMOND BURKE ONCE SAID-
"THE ONLY THING NECESSARY FOR THE TRIUMPH OF EVIL, IS FOR GOOD MEN TO DO NOTHING."
-NOTHING.
NEVERMIND.
I GUESS I'M JUST CONFUSED.
OH DEAR-
THIS ISN'T CALCULATING CORRECTLY.
PI IS NOT 3.162!
MMMM, PIE.
BOOP
BEEP
BOOP

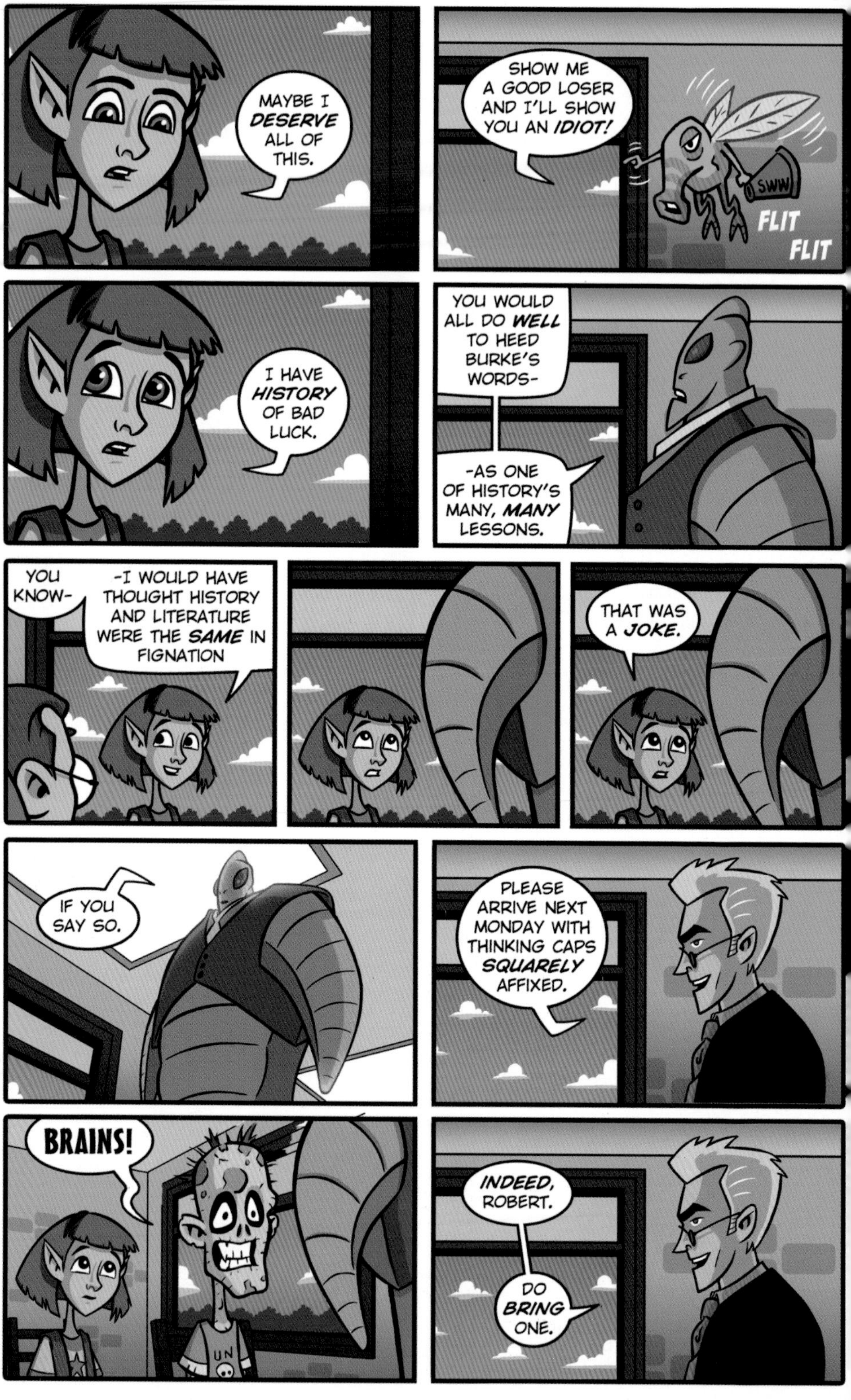

MAYBE I DESERVE ALL OF THIS.
SHOW ME A GOOD LOSER AND I'LL SHOW YOU AN IDIOT!
SWW
FLIT
FLIT
I HAVE HISTORY OF BAD LUCK.
YOU WOULD ALL DO WELL TO HEED BURKE'S WORDS-
-AS ONE OF HISTORY'S MANY, MANY LESSONS.
YOU KNOW-
-I WOULD HAVE THOUGHT HISTORY AND LITERATURE WERE THE SAME IN FIGNATION
THAT WAS A JOKE.
IF YOU SAY SO.
PLEASE ARRIVE NEXT MONDAY WITH THINKING CAPS SQUARELY AFFIXED.
BRAINS!
UN
INDEED, ROBERT.
DO BRING ONE.

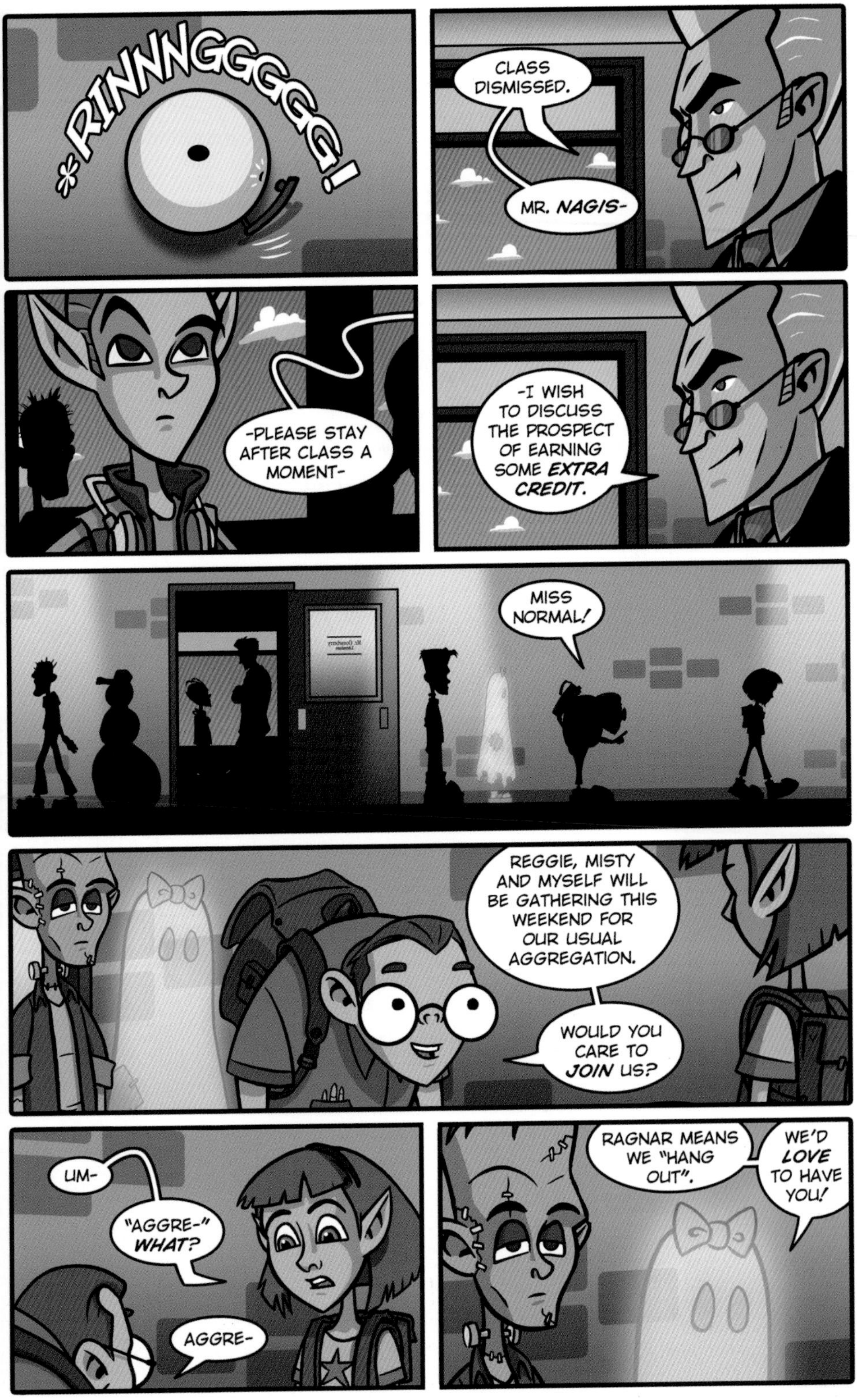
*RINNNGGGGG!
CLASS DISMISSED.
MR. NAGIS-
-PLEASE STAY AFTER CLASS A MOMENT-
-I WISH TO DISCUSS THE PROSPECT OF EARNING SOME EXTRA CREDIT.
MISS NORMAL!
REGGIE, MISTY AND MYSELF WILL BE GATHERING THIS WEEKEND FOR OUR USUAL AGGREGATION.
WOULD YOU CARE TO JOIN US?
UM-
"AGGRE-" WHAT?
AGGRE-
RAGNAR MEANS WE "HANG OUT".
WE'D LOVE TO HAVE YOU!

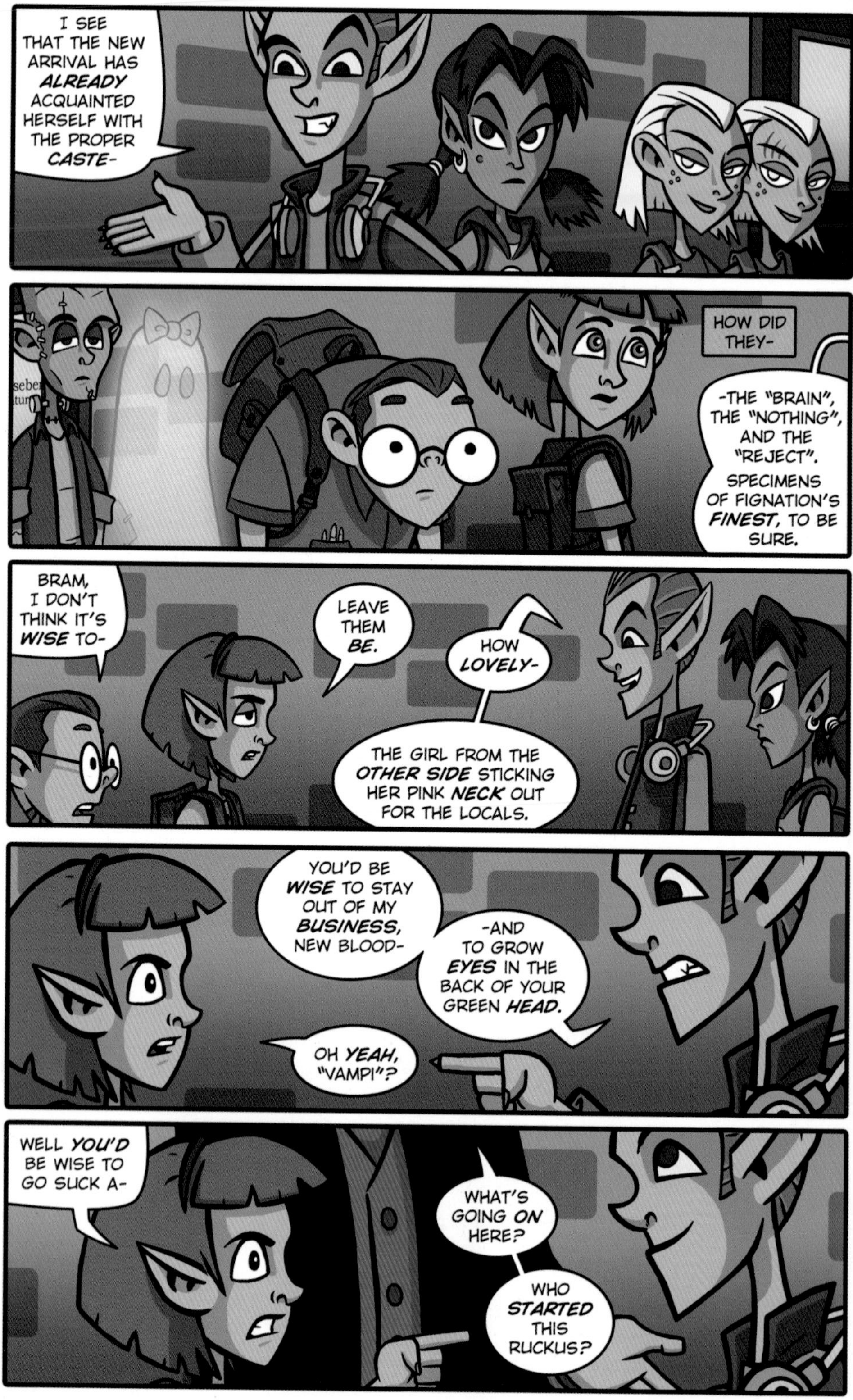

I SEE THAT THE NEW ARRIVAL HAS ALREADY ACQUAINTED HERSELF WITH THE PROPER CASTE-
HOW DID THEY-
-THE "BRAIN", THE "NOTHING", AND THE "REJECT".
SPECIMENS OF FIGNATION'S FINEST, TO BE SURE.
BRAM, I DON'T THINK IT'S WISE TO-
LEAVE THEM BE.
HOW LOVELY-
THE GIRL FROM THE OTHER SIDE STICKING HER PINK NECK OUT FOR THE LOCALS.
YOU'D BE WISE TO STAY OUT OF MY BUSINESS, NEW BLOOD-
-AND TO GROW EYES IN THE BACK OF YOUR GREEN HEAD.
OH YEAH, "VAMPI"?
WELL YOU'D BE WISE TO GO SUCK A-
WHAT'S GOING ON HERE?
WHO STARTED THIS RUCKUS?

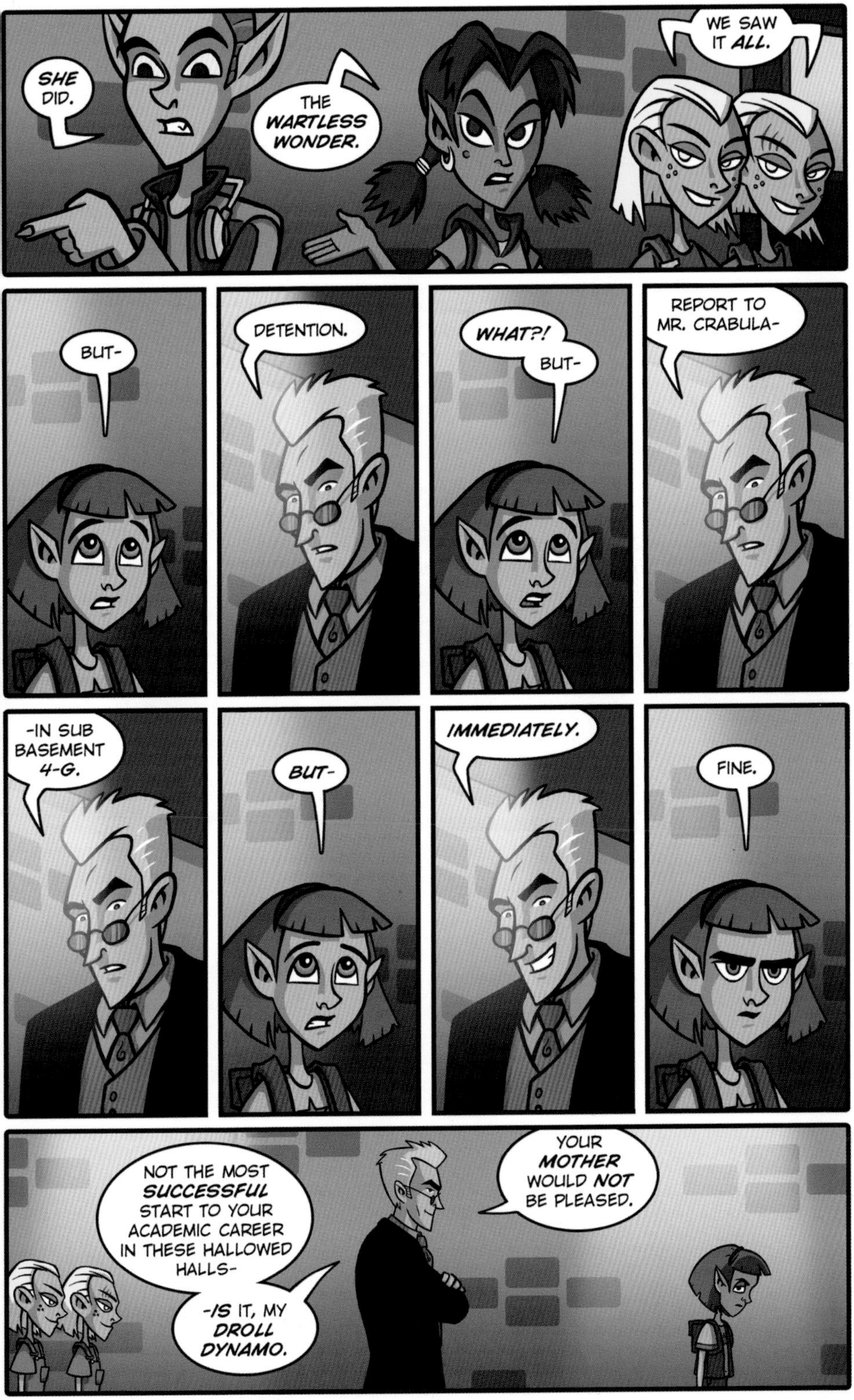
SHE DID.
THE WARTLESS WONDER.
WE SAW IT ALL.
BUT-
DETENTION.
WHAT?!
BUT-
REPORT TO MR. CRABULA-
-IN SUB BASEMENT 4-G.
BUT-
IMMEDIATELY.
FINE.
NOT THE MOST SUCCESSFUL START TO YOUR ACADEMIC CAREER IN THESE HALLOWED HALLS-
-IS IT, MY DROLL DYNAMO.
YOUR MOTHER WOULD NOT BE PLEASED.

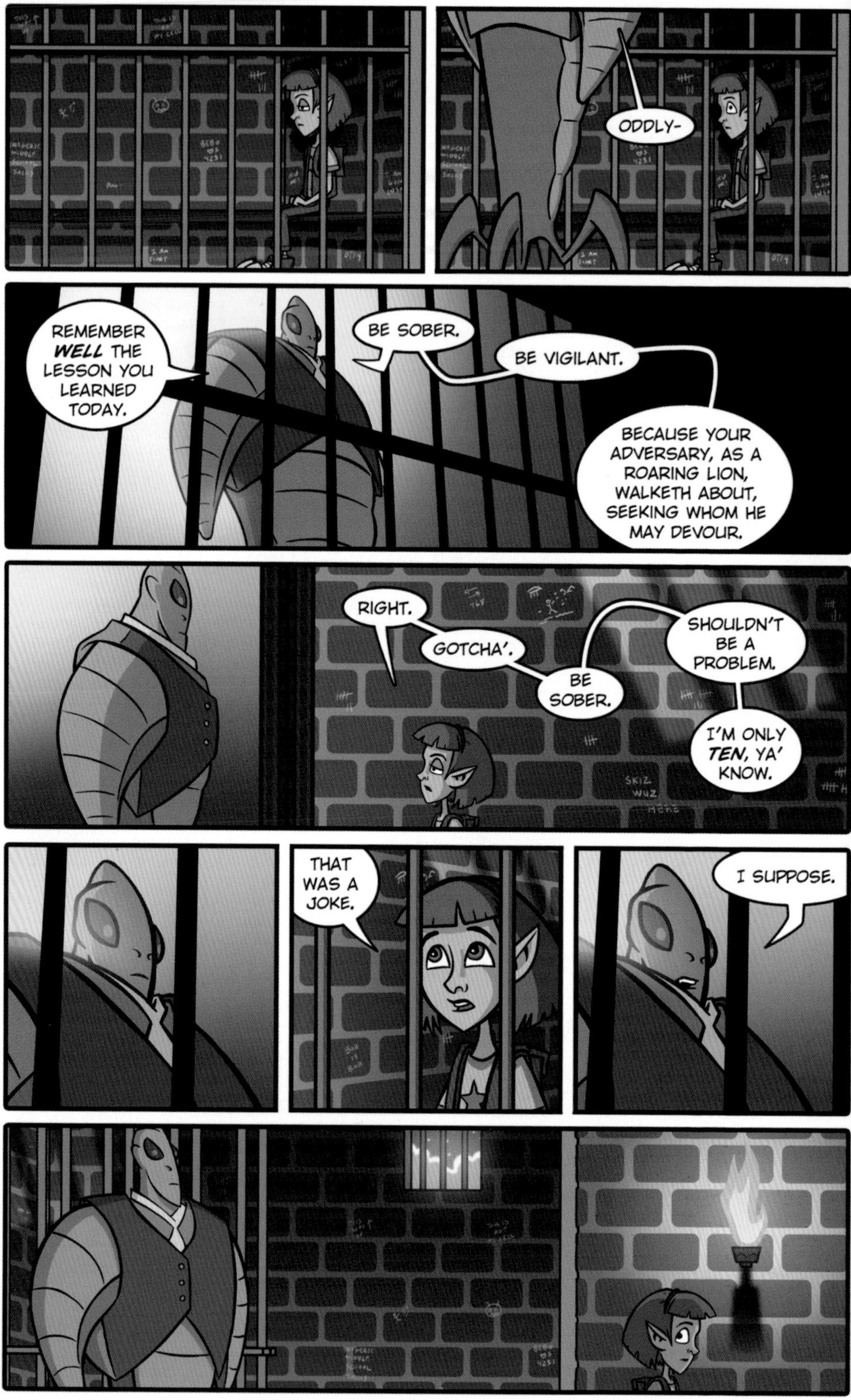
ODDLY-
REMEMBER WELL THE LESSON YOU LEARNED TODAY.
BE SOBER.
BE VIGILANT.
BECAUSE YOUR ADVERSARY, AS A ROARING LION, WALKETH ABOUT, SEEKING WHOM HE MAY DEVOUR.
RIGHT.
GOTCHA'.
BE SOBER.
SHOULDN'T BE A PROBLEM.
I'M ONLY TEN, YA' KNOW.
THAT WAS A JOKE.
I SUPPOSE.

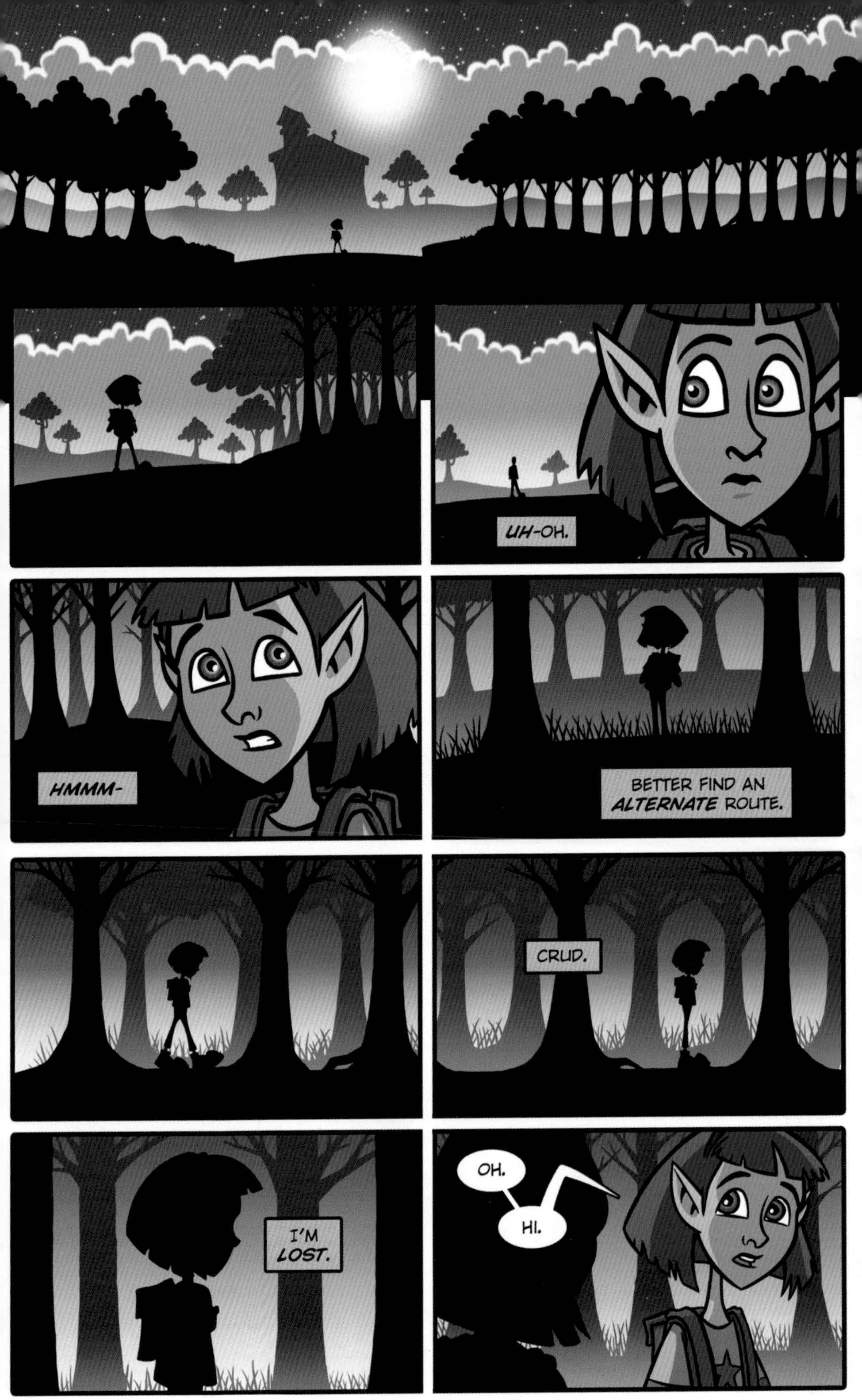
UH-OH.
HMMM-
BETTER FIND AN ALTERNATE ROUTE.
CRUD.
I'M LOST.
OH.
HI.

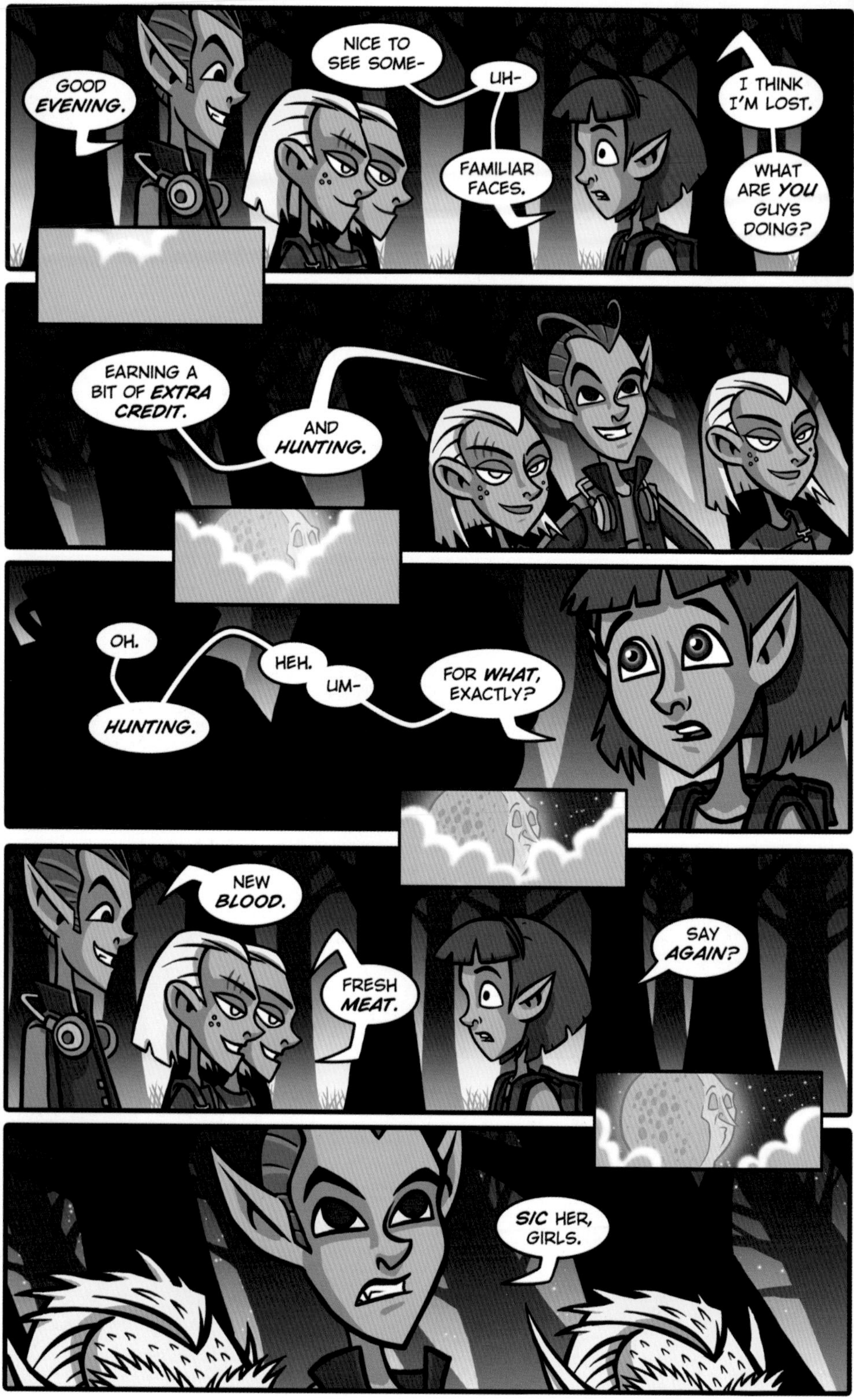
GOOD EVENING.
NICE TO SEE SOME-
UH-
FAMILIAR FACES.
I THINK I'M LOST.
WHAT ARE YOU GUYS DOING?
EARNING A BIT OF EXTRA CREDIT.
AND HUNTING.
OH.
HUNTING.
HEH.
UM-
FOR WHAT, EXACTLY?
NEW BLOOD.
FRESH MEAT.
SAY AGAIN?
SIC HER, GIRLS.

*GGGGRRRRRR
*GGGGRRRRRR

IIIIIIEEE!

LISTEN TO THEM—

—THE *CHILDREN* OF THE NIGHT.

WHAT SWEET *MUSIC* THEY MAKE.

SPEAKING OF WHICH—

AH!

"*DIE FLEDERMAUS*"!

UFF!

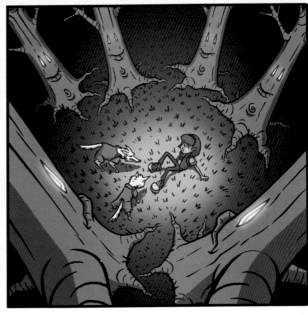

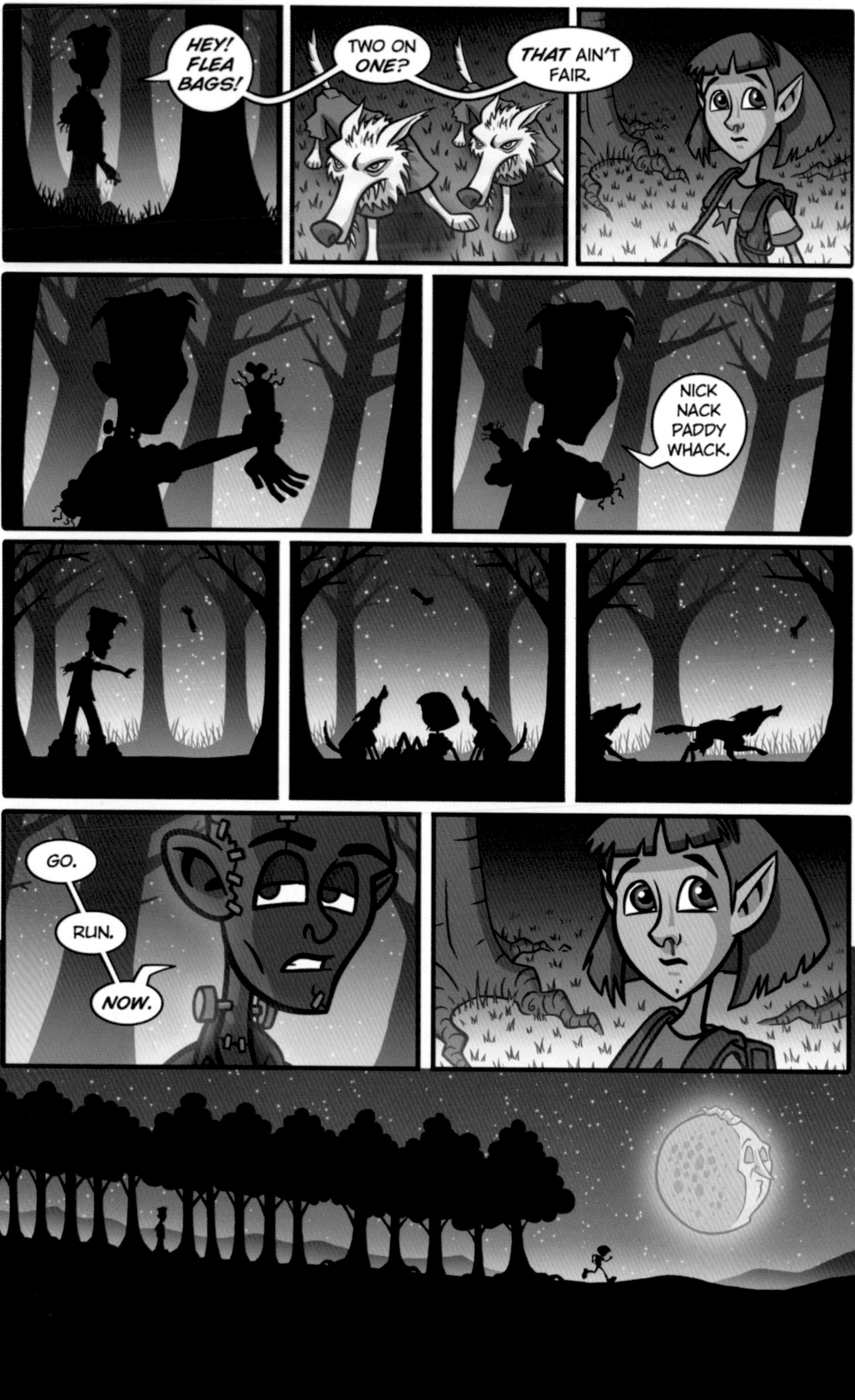
HEY! FLEA BAGS!
TWO ON ONE?
THAT AIN'T FAIR.
NICK NACK PADDY WHACK.
GO.
RUN.
NOW.

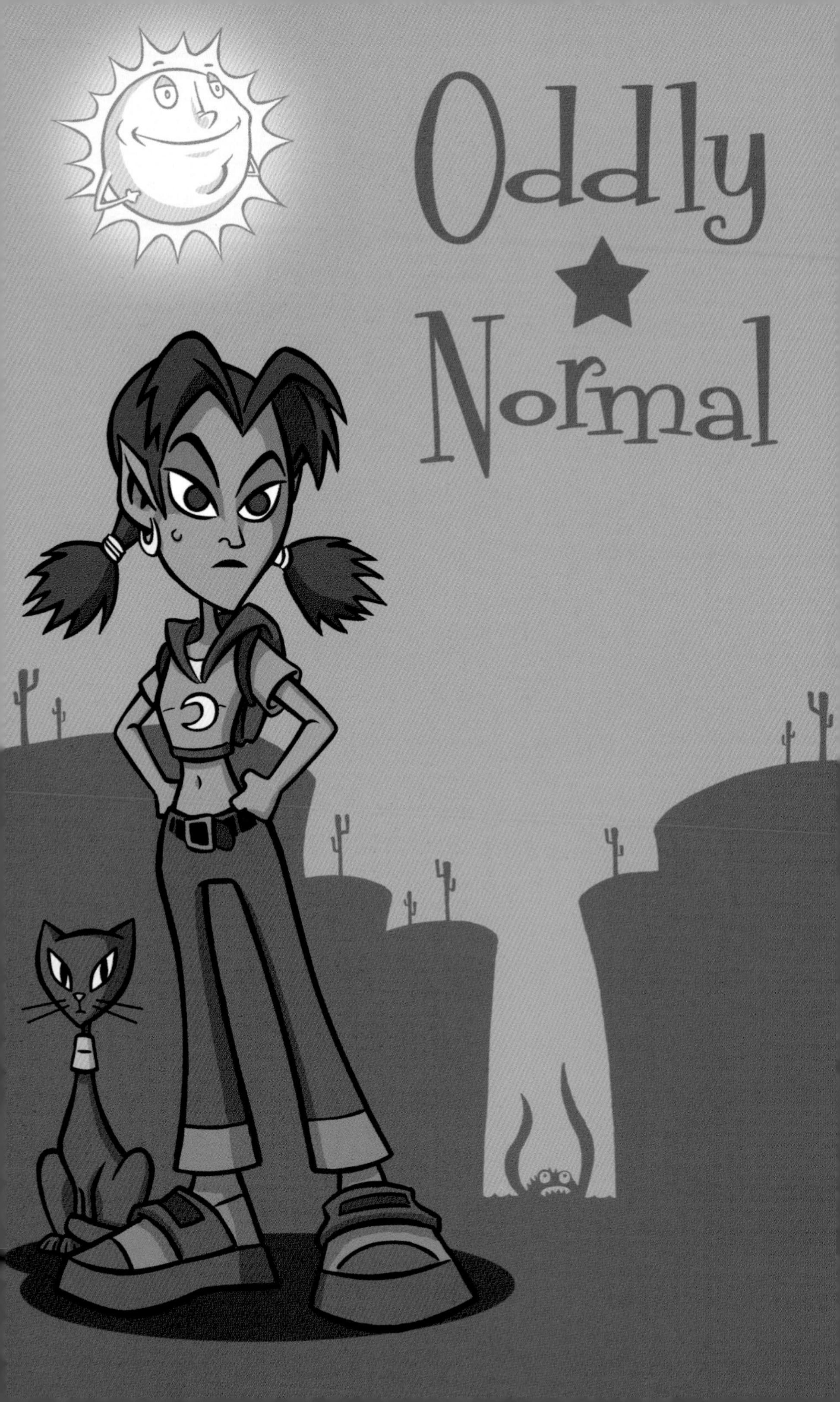
Oddly
Normal

Chapter 5
Kindred
Spirits

"MY DEAREST FIG . . ."

"IN MY HASTE TO FERRY YOU OFF TO YOUR MOTHER'S HOMELAND, I FORGOT TO GIVE YOU THE BIRTHDAY PRESENT I HAD MADE FOR YOU."

"NOW THAT YOU'RE *HERE*, I HAVE DECIDED TO SAVE MY INTENDED GIFT FOR NEXT YEAR AND PRESENT YOU WITH THE *WITCH'S BROOM* UPON WHICH YOUR BELOVED MOTHER ONCE SOARED."

"I AM *CERTAIN* THAT SHE WOULD WANT YOU TO HAVE IT. I REALIZE THAT YOUR NATURE PRECLUDES YOU FROM *USING* IT AT THIS TIME . . ."

"BUT WHO *KNOWS* WHAT THE FUTURE MAY BRING DURING YOUR STAY HERE IN FIGNATION?"

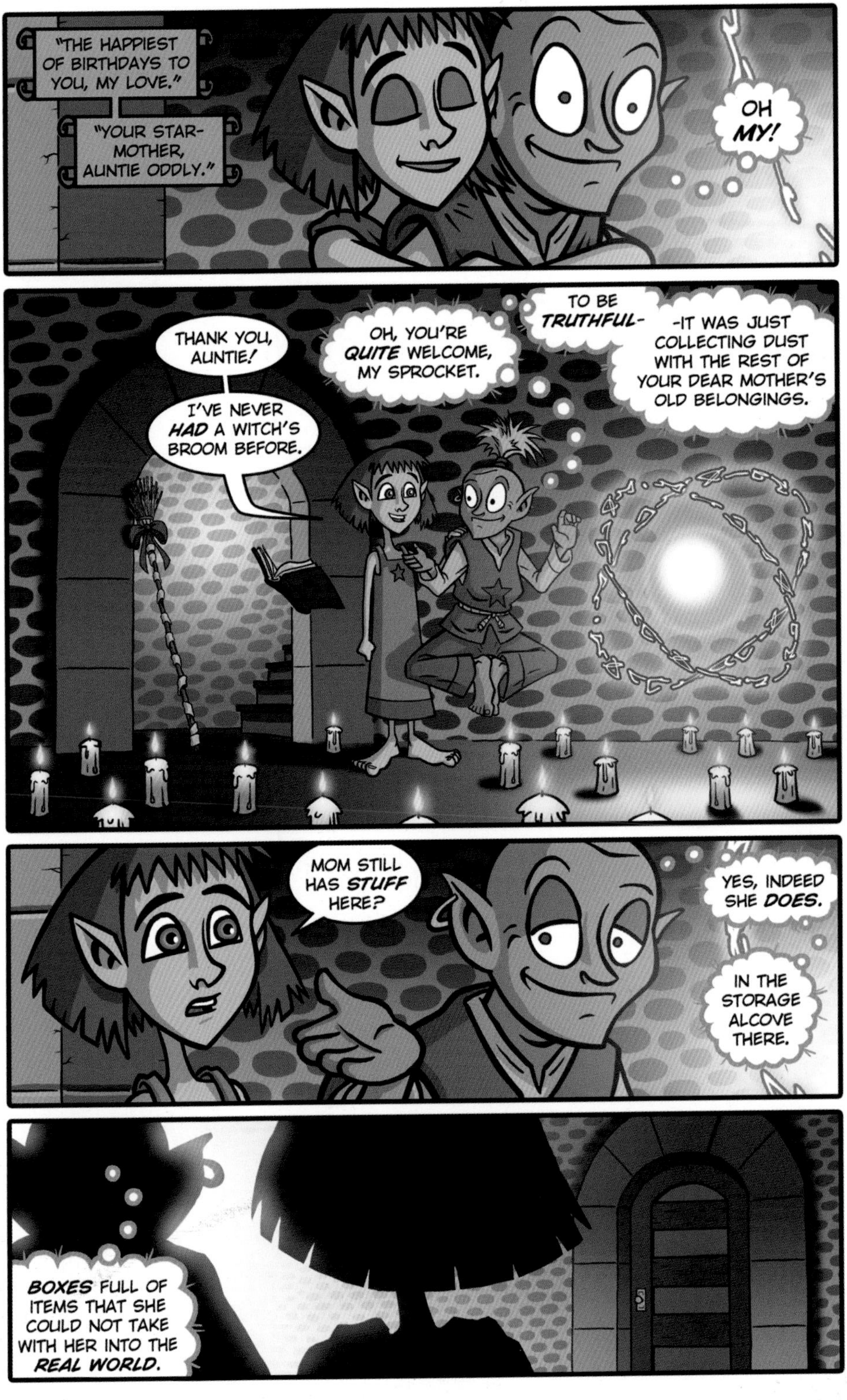
"THE HAPPIEST OF BIRTHDAYS TO YOU, MY LOVE."
"YOUR STAR-MOTHER, AUNTIE ODDLY."
OH MY!
THANK YOU, AUNTIE!
I'VE NEVER HAD A WITCH'S BROOM BEFORE.
OH, YOU'RE QUITE WELCOME, MY SPROCKET.
TO BE TRUTHFUL-
-IT WAS JUST COLLECTING DUST WITH THE REST OF YOUR DEAR MOTHER'S OLD BELONGINGS.
MOM STILL HAS STUFF HERE?
YES, INDEED SHE DOES.
IN THE STORAGE ALCOVE THERE.
BOXES FULL OF ITEMS THAT SHE COULD NOT TAKE WITH HER INTO THE REAL WORLD.

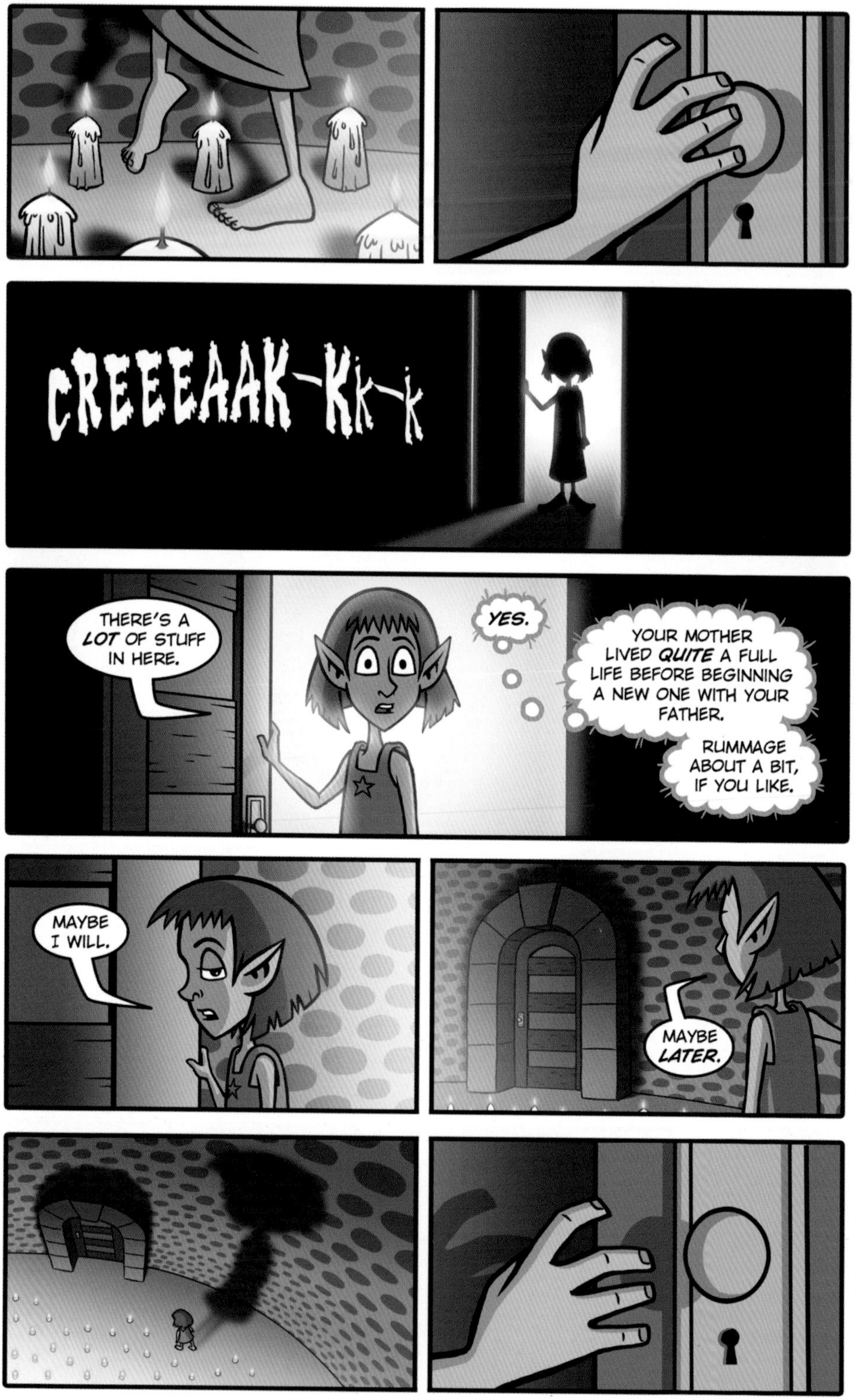
CREEEAAK-Kk-k
THERE'S A LOT OF STUFF IN HERE.
YES.
YOUR MOTHER LIVED QUITE A FULL LIFE BEFORE BEGINNING A NEW ONE WITH YOUR FATHER.
RUMMAGE ABOUT A BIT, IF YOU LIKE.
MAYBE I WILL.
MAYBE LATER.

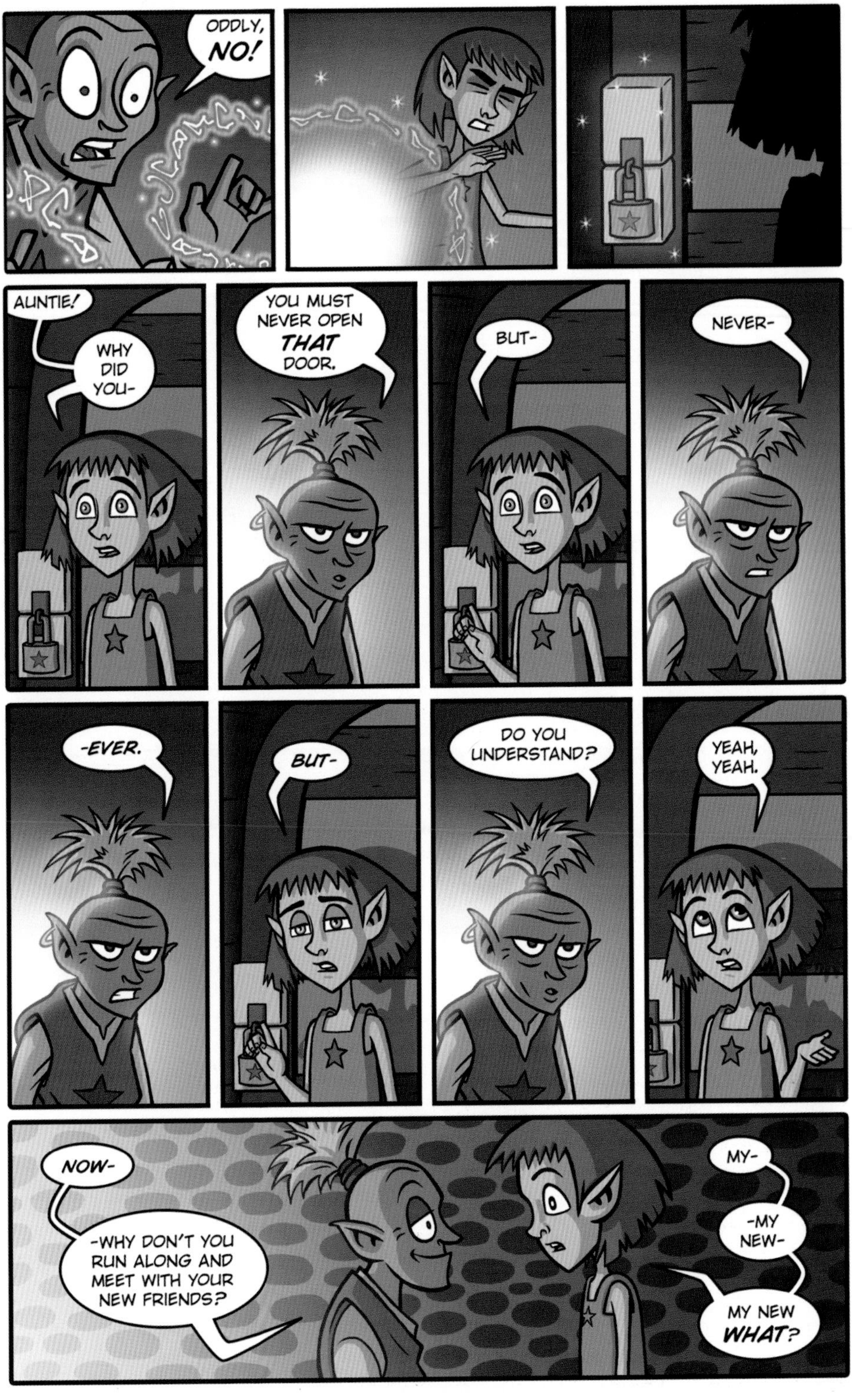
ODDLY, NO!
AUNTIE!
WHY DID YOU-
YOU MUST NEVER OPEN THAT DOOR.
BUT-
NEVER-
-EVER.
BUT-
DO YOU UNDERSTAND?
YEAH, YEAH.
NOW-
-WHY DON'T YOU RUN ALONG AND MEET WITH YOUR NEW FRIENDS?
MY-
-MY NEW-
MY NEW WHAT?

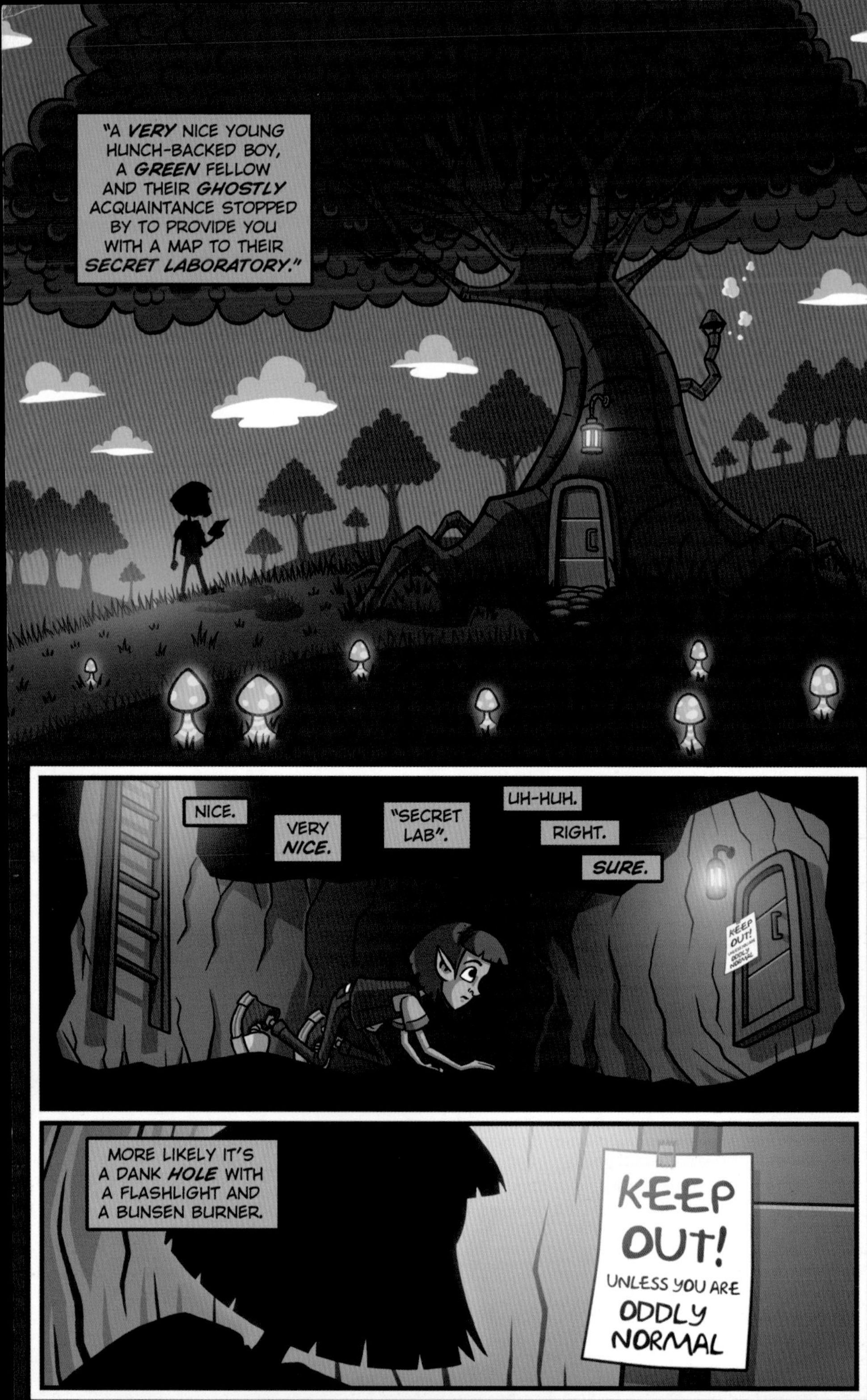
"A VERY NICE YOUNG HUNCH-BACKED BOY, A GREEN FELLOW AND THEIR GHOSTLY ACQUAINTANCE STOPPED BY TO PROVIDE YOU WITH A MAP TO THEIR SECRET LABORATORY."
NICE.
VERY NICE.
"SECRET LAB".
UH-HUH.
RIGHT.
SURE.
MORE LIKELY IT'S A DANK HOLE WITH A FLASHLIGHT AND A BUNSEN BURNER.
KEEP OUT!
UNLESS YOU ARE
ODDLY NORMAL

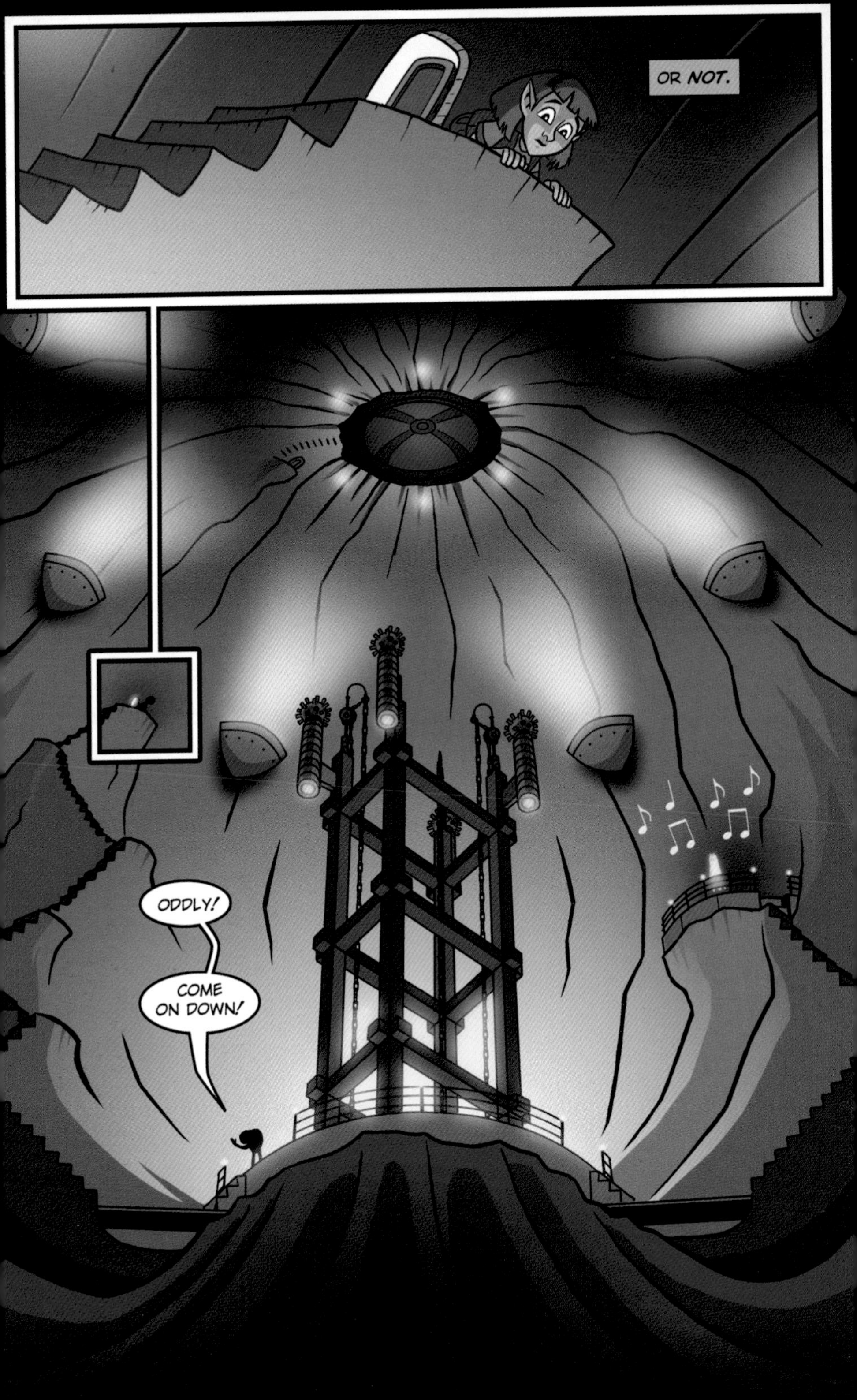
OR NOT.
ODDLY!
COME ON DOWN!

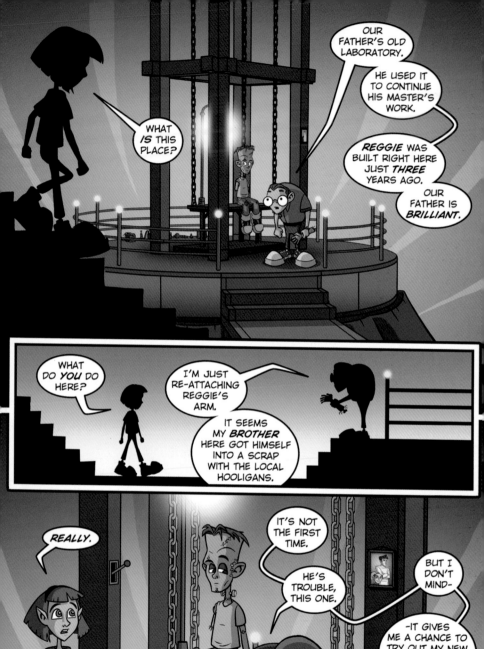

WHAT *IS* THIS PLACE?

OUR FATHER'S OLD LABORATORY.

HE USED IT TO CONTINUE HIS MASTER'S WORK.

REGGIE WAS BUILT RIGHT HERE JUST *THREE* YEARS AGO.

OUR FATHER IS *BRILLIANT*.

WHAT DO *YOU* DO HERE?

I'M JUST RE-ATTACHING REGGIE'S ARM.

IT SEEMS MY *BROTHER* HERE GOT HIMSELF INTO A SCRAP WITH THE LOCAL HOOLIGANS.

REALLY.

IT'S NOT THE FIRST TIME.

HE'S TROUBLE, THIS ONE.

BUT I DON'T MIND—

—IT GIVES ME A CHANCE TO TRY OUT MY NEW AND *IMPROVED* TRIPLE-POLYMER STITCHING.

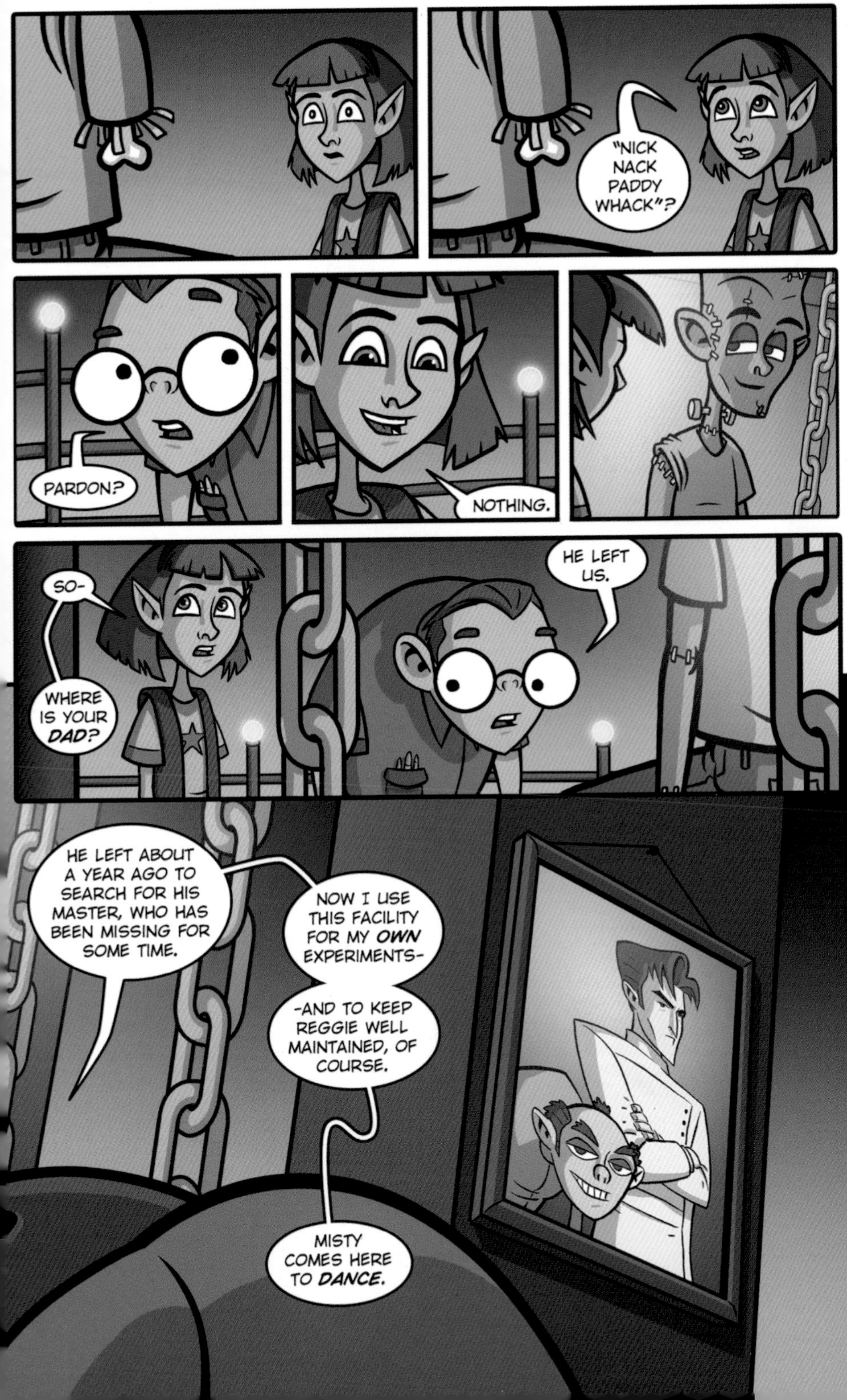
"NICK NACK PADDY WHACK"?
PARDON?
NOTHING.
SO-
WHERE IS YOUR *DAD?*
HE LEFT US.
HE LEFT ABOUT A YEAR AGO TO SEARCH FOR HIS MASTER, WHO HAS BEEN MISSING FOR SOME TIME.
NOW I USE THIS FACILITY FOR MY *OWN* EXPERIMENTS-
-AND TO KEEP REGGIE WELL MAINTAINED, OF COURSE.
MISTY COMES HERE TO *DANCE.*

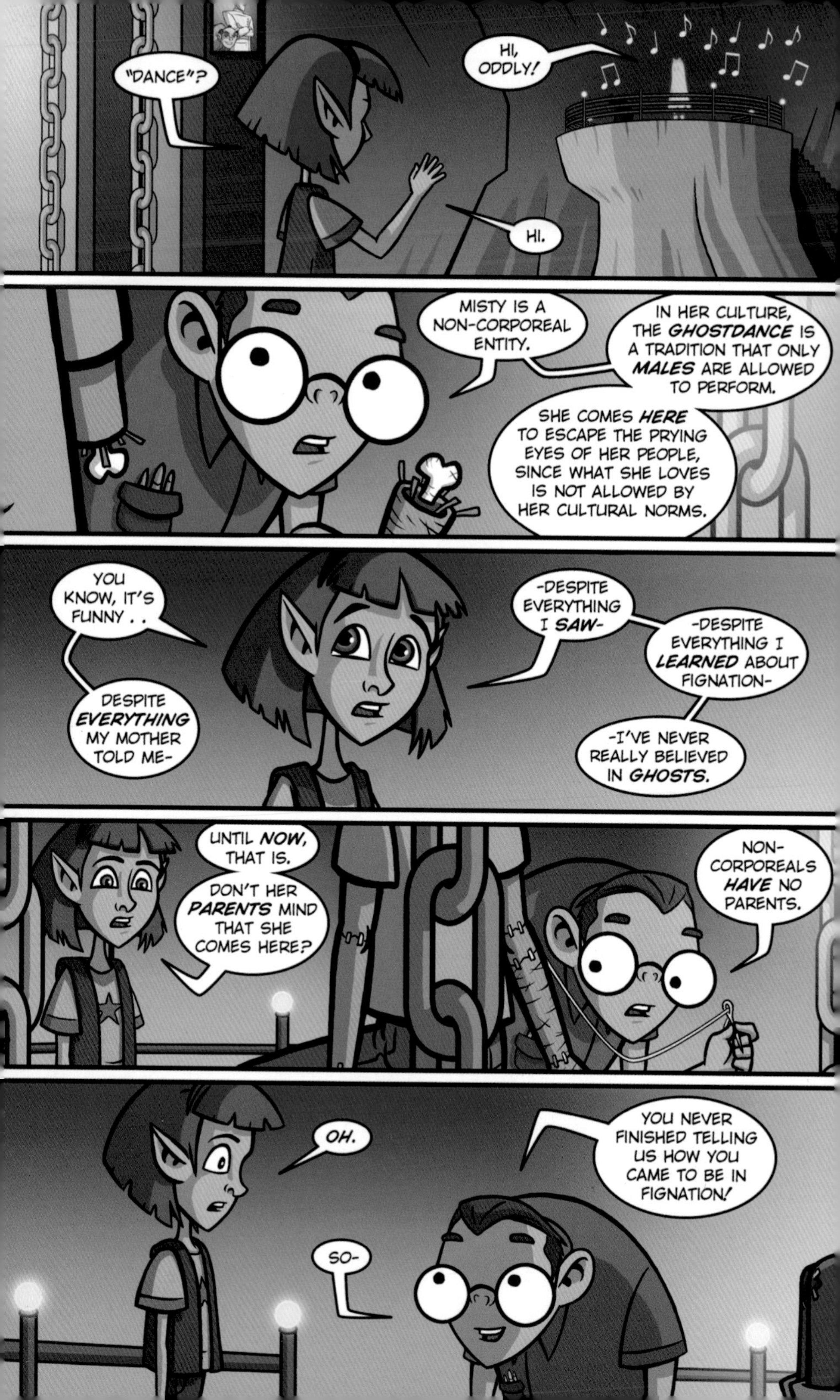
"DANCE"?
HI, ODDLY!
HI.
MISTY IS A NON-CORPOREAL ENTITY.
IN HER CULTURE, THE **GHOSTDANCE** IS A TRADITION THAT ONLY **MALES** ARE ALLOWED TO PERFORM.
SHE COMES **HERE** TO ESCAPE THE PRYING EYES OF HER PEOPLE, SINCE WHAT SHE LOVES IS NOT ALLOWED BY HER CULTURAL NORMS.
YOU KNOW, IT'S FUNNY . .
DESPITE **EVERYTHING** MY MOTHER TOLD ME-
-DESPITE EVERYTHING I **SAW**-
-DESPITE EVERYTHING I **LEARNED** ABOUT FIGNATION-
-I'VE NEVER REALLY BELIEVED IN **GHOSTS**.
UNTIL **NOW**, THAT IS.
DON'T HER **PARENTS** MIND THAT SHE COMES HERE?
NON-CORPOREALS **HAVE** NO PARENTS.
OH.
SO-
YOU NEVER FINISHED TELLING US HOW YOU CAME TO BE IN FIGNATION!

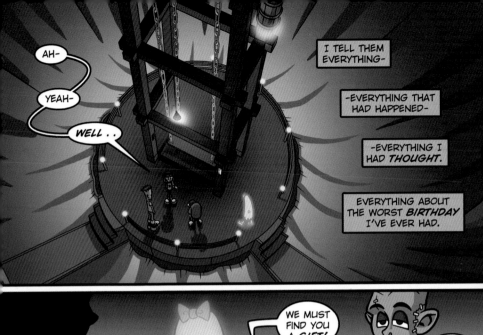

AH—

YEAH—

WELL . .

I TELL THEM EVERYTHING—

—EVERYTHING THAT HAD HAPPENED—

—EVERYTHING I HAD *THOUGHT*.

EVERYTHING ABOUT THE WORST *BIRTHDAY* I'VE EVER HAD.

IT WAS YOUR BIRTHDAY?

WHY DIDN'T YOU *TELL* US?

WE MUST FIND YOU A *GIFT!*

YEAH.

GIFT?

NO—

—YOU REALLY DON'T NEED TO—

LET'S SEE—

—I HAVE SO MANY INTERESTING ITEMS—

—CURIOUS TRINKETS . .

—OLD EXPERIMENTS—

WHAT IS *THAT?*

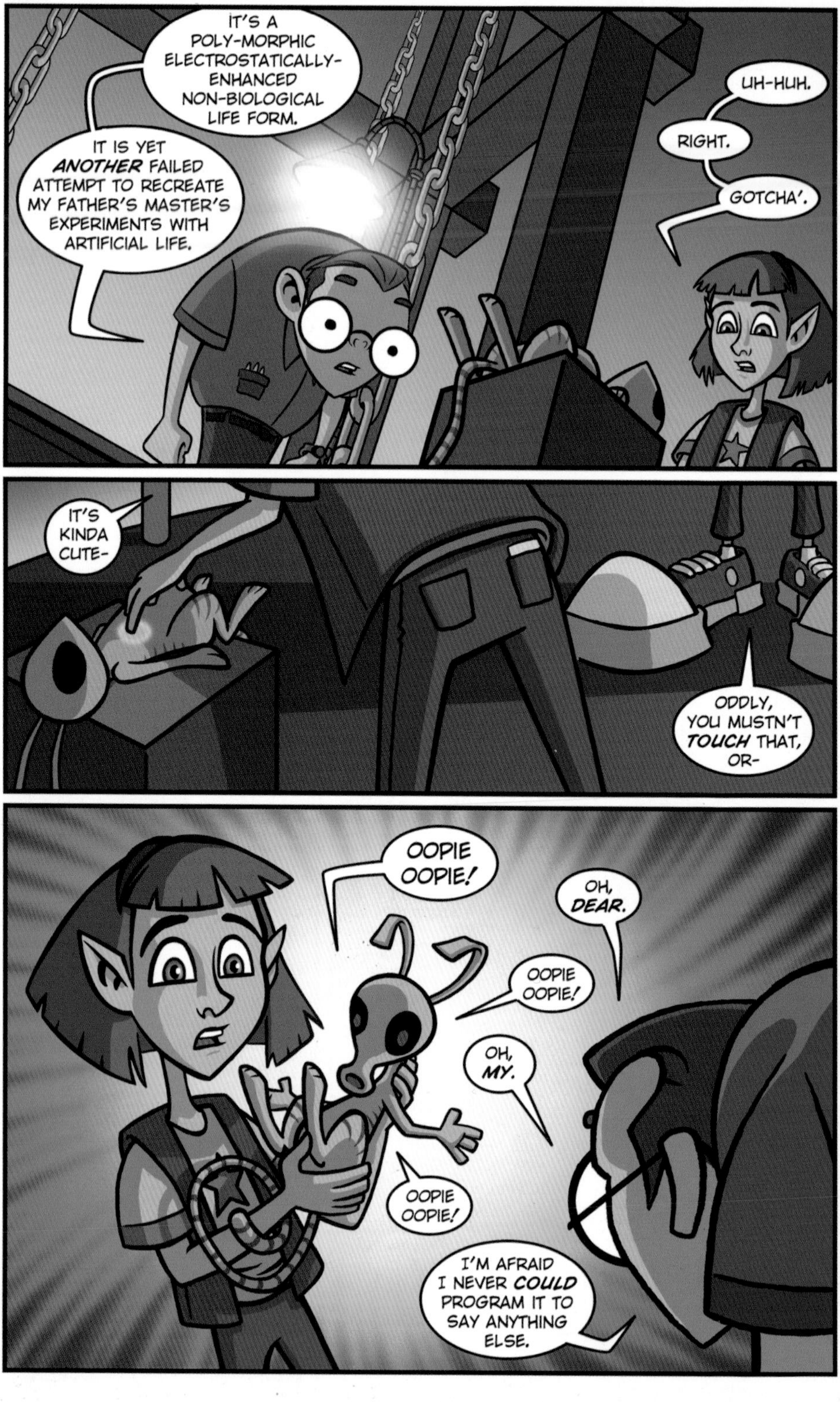
IT'S A POLY-MORPHIC ELECTROSTATICALLY-ENHANCED NON-BIOLOGICAL LIFE FORM.
IT IS YET ANOTHER FAILED ATTEMPT TO RECREATE MY FATHER'S MASTER'S EXPERIMENTS WITH ARTIFICIAL LIFE.
UH-HUH.
RIGHT.
GOTCHA'.
IT'S KINDA CUTE-
ODDLY, YOU MUSTN'T TOUCH THAT, OR-
OOPIE OOPIE!
OH, DEAR.
OOPIE OOPIE!
OH, MY.
OOPIE OOPIE!
I'M AFRAID I NEVER COULD PROGRAM IT TO SAY ANYTHING ELSE.

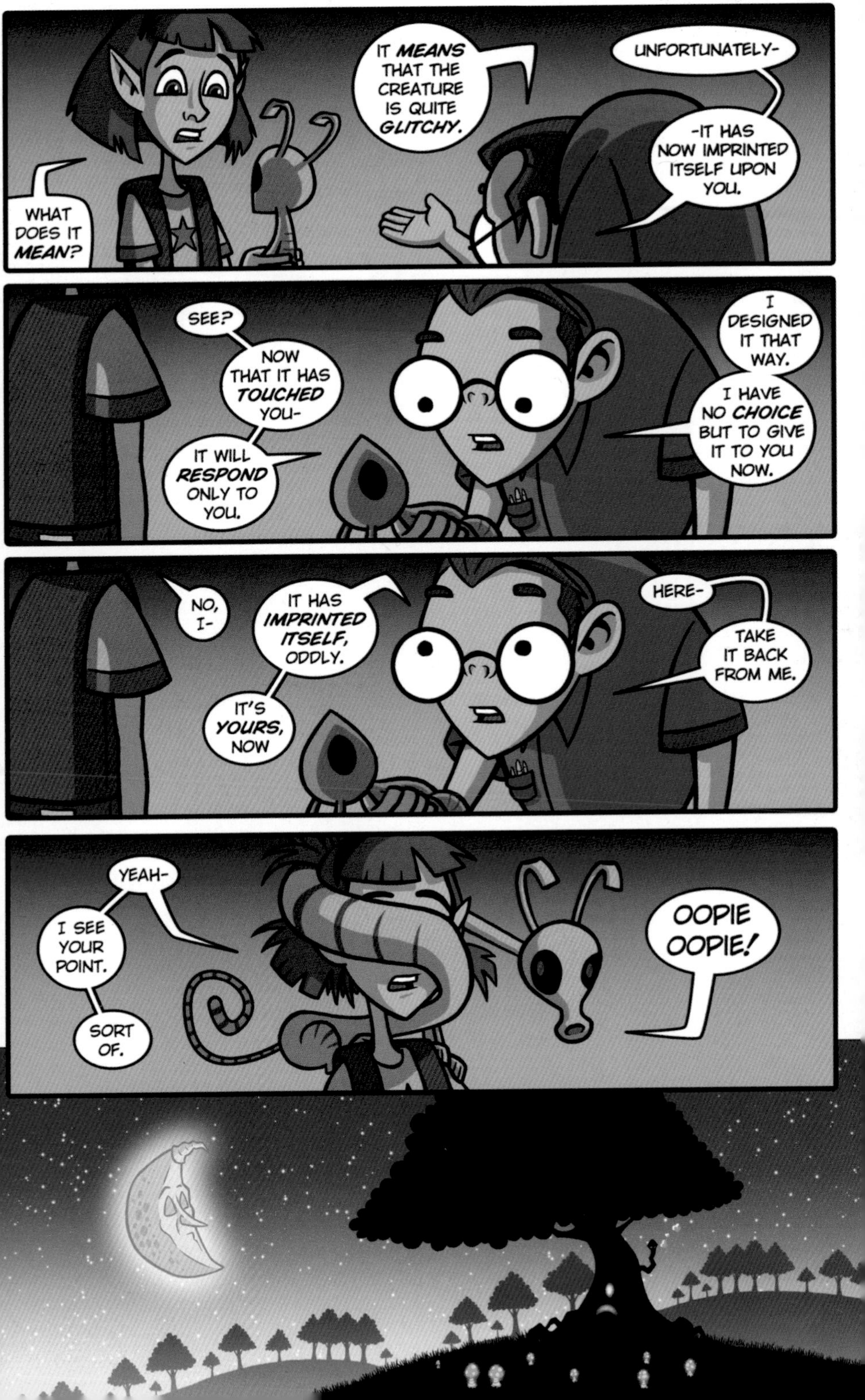
WHAT DOES IT MEAN?
IT MEANS THAT THE CREATURE IS QUITE GLITCHY.
UNFORTUNATELY-
-IT HAS NOW IMPRINTED ITSELF UPON YOU.
SEE?
NOW THAT IT HAS TOUCHED YOU-
IT WILL RESPOND ONLY TO YOU.
I DESIGNED IT THAT WAY.
I HAVE NO CHOICE BUT TO GIVE IT TO YOU NOW.
NO, I-
IT HAS IMPRINTED ITSELF, ODDLY.
IT'S YOURS, NOW
HERE-
TAKE IT BACK FROM ME.
YEAH-
I SEE YOUR POINT.
SORT OF.
OOPIE OOPIE!

Acro Avio & Hydro

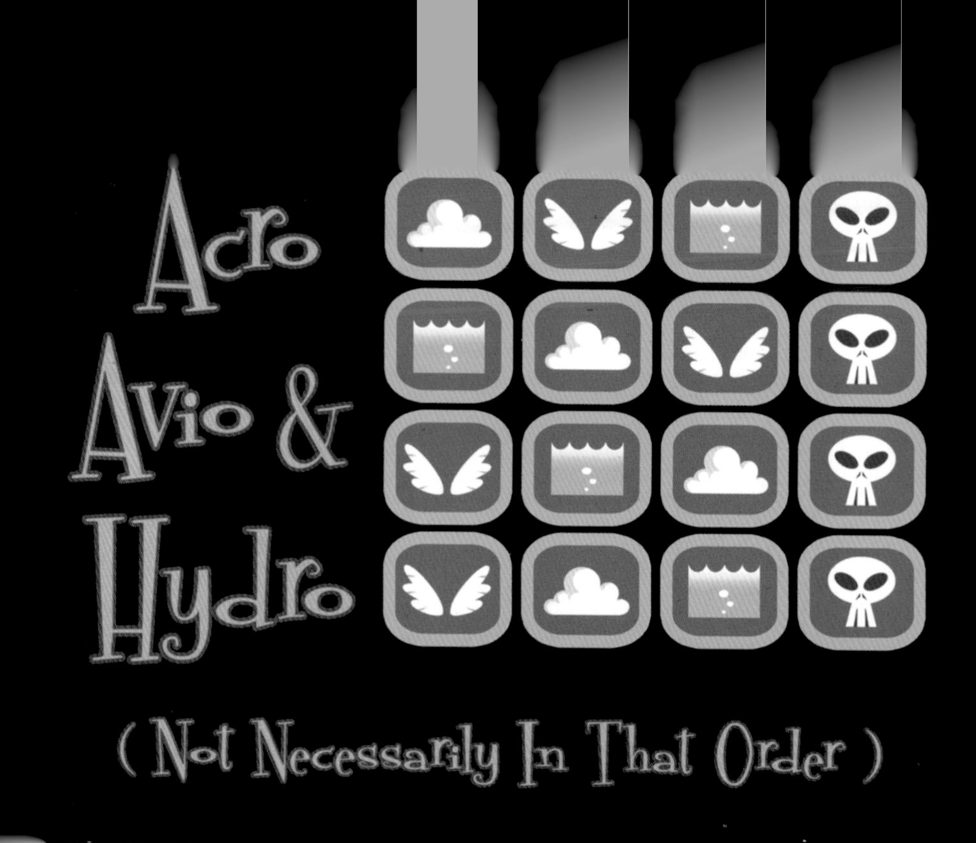

(Not Necessarily In That Order)

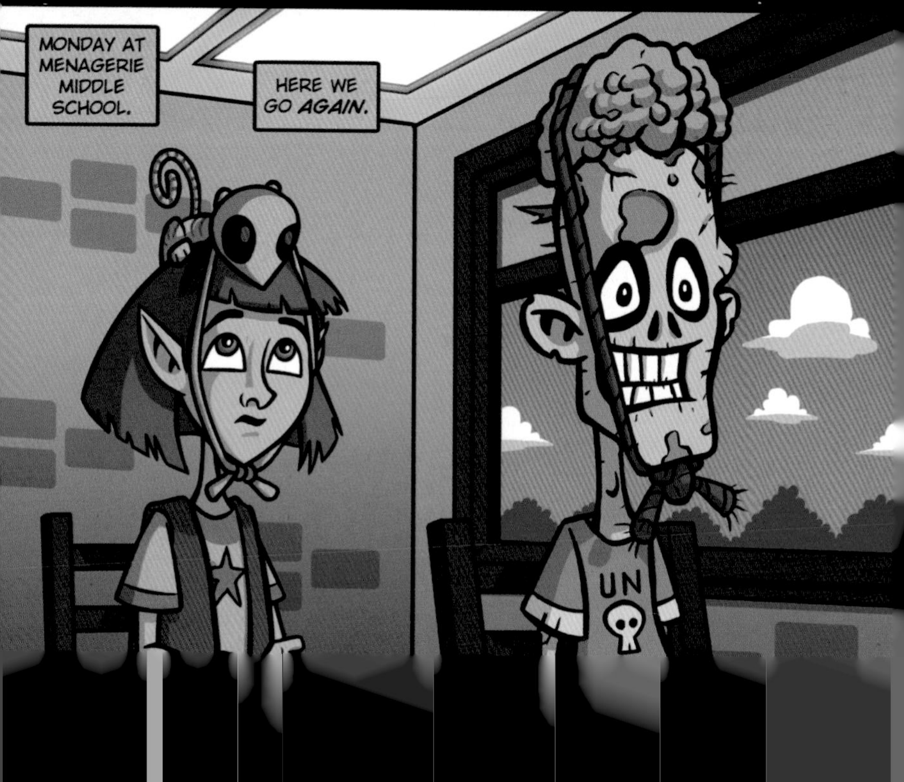
MONDAY AT MENAGERIE MIDDLE SCHOOL.
HERE WE GO AGAIN.
UN

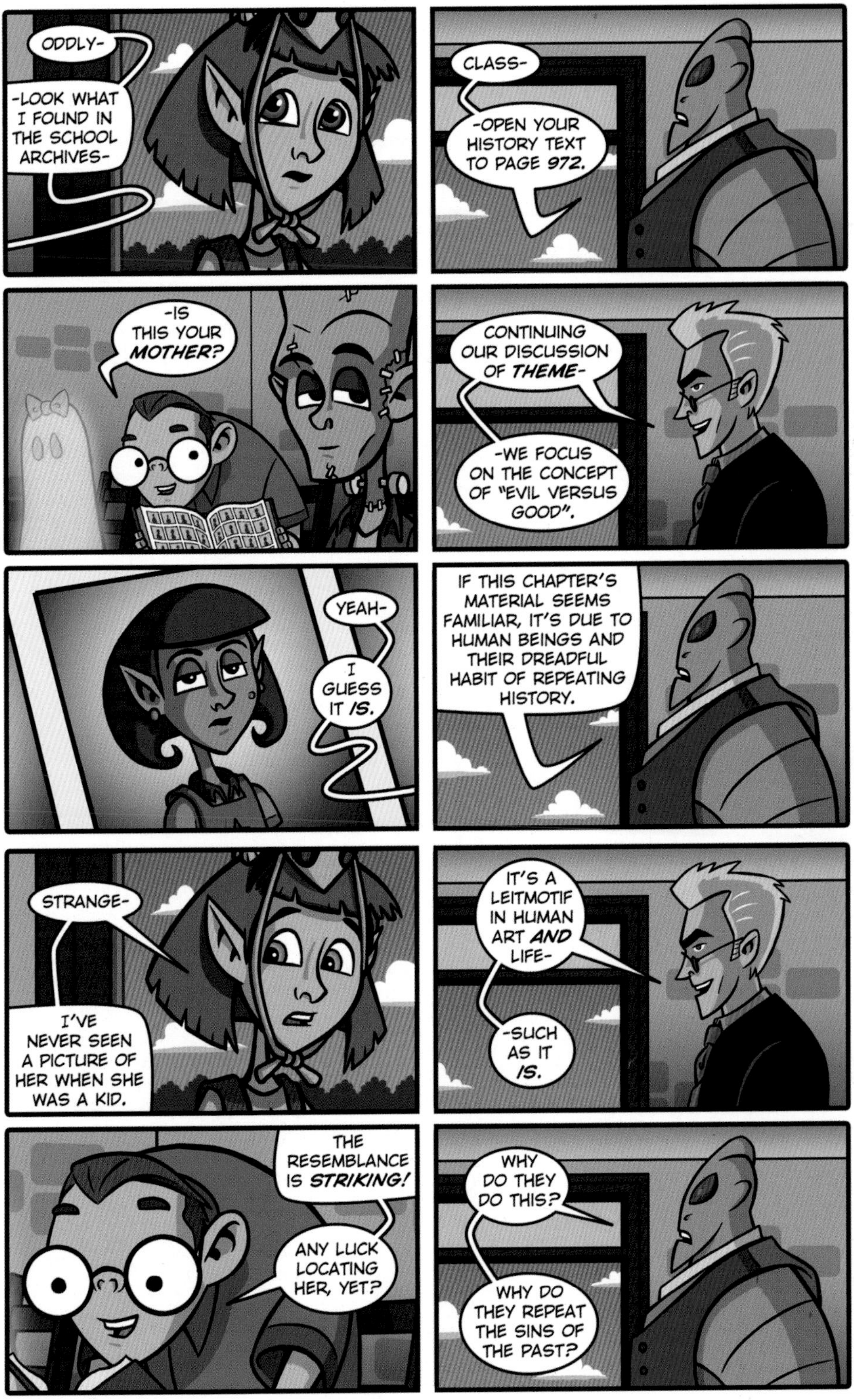
ODDLY-
-LOOK WHAT I FOUND IN THE SCHOOL ARCHIVES-
CLASS-
-OPEN YOUR HISTORY TEXT TO PAGE 972.
-IS THIS YOUR MOTHER?
CONTINUING OUR DISCUSSION OF THEME-
-WE FOCUS ON THE CONCEPT OF "EVIL VERSUS GOOD".
YEAH-
I GUESS IT IS.
IF THIS CHAPTER'S MATERIAL SEEMS FAMILIAR, IT'S DUE TO HUMAN BEINGS AND THEIR DREADFUL HABIT OF REPEATING HISTORY.
STRANGE-
I'VE NEVER SEEN A PICTURE OF HER WHEN SHE WAS A KID.
IT'S A LEITMOTIF IN HUMAN ART AND LIFE-
-SUCH AS IT IS.
THE RESEMBLANCE IS STRIKING!
ANY LUCK LOCATING HER, YET?
WHY DO THEY DO THIS?
WHY DO THEY REPEAT THE SINS OF THE PAST?

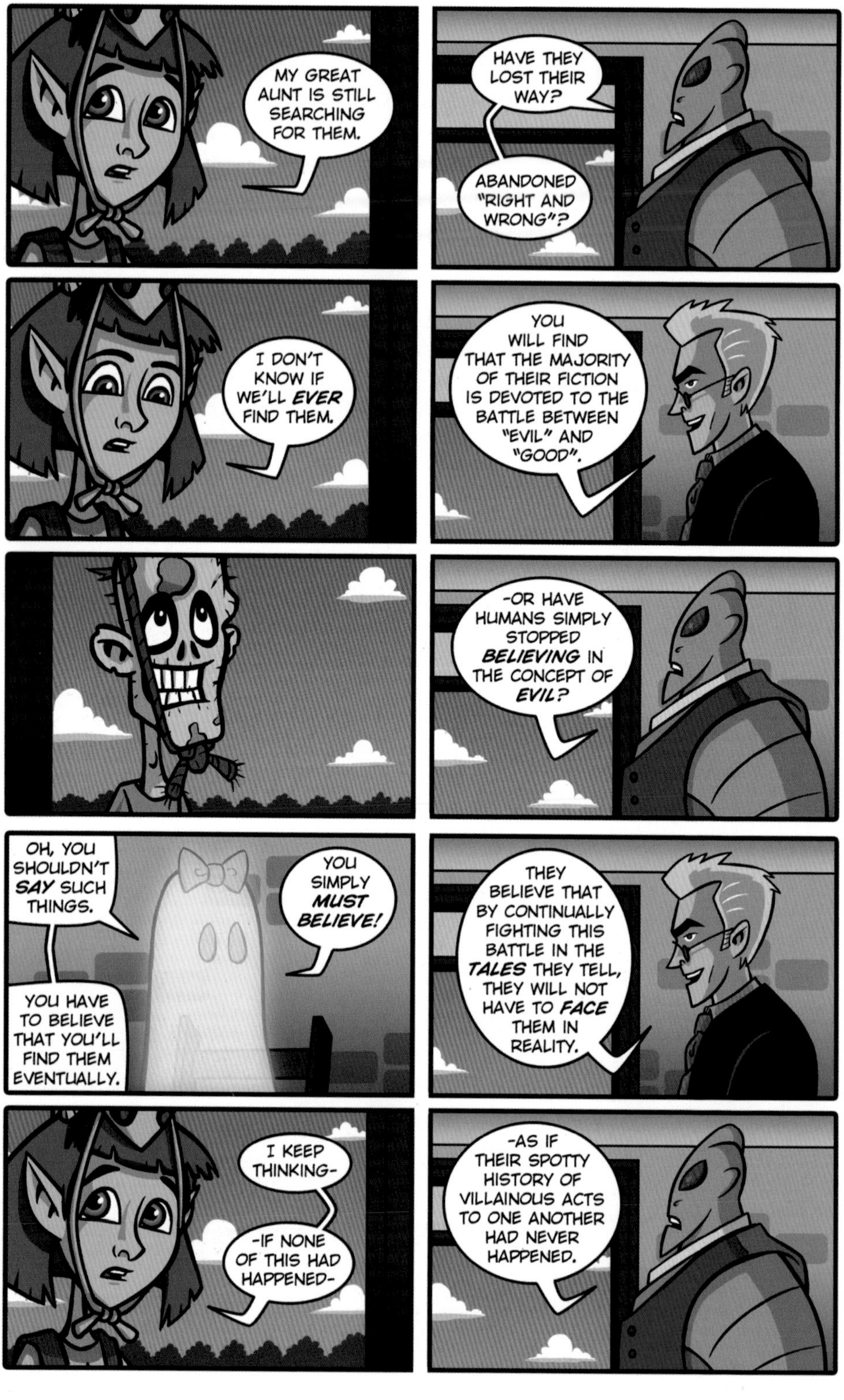
MY GREAT AUNT IS STILL SEARCHING FOR THEM.
HAVE THEY LOST THEIR WAY?
ABANDONED "RIGHT AND WRONG"?
I DON'T KNOW IF WE'LL ***EVER*** FIND THEM.
YOU WILL FIND THAT THE MAJORITY OF THEIR FICTION IS DEVOTED TO THE BATTLE BETWEEN "EVIL" AND "GOOD".
-OR HAVE HUMANS SIMPLY STOPPED ***BELIEVING*** IN THE CONCEPT OF ***EVIL***?
OH, YOU SHOULDN'T ***SAY*** SUCH THINGS.
YOU HAVE TO BELIEVE THAT YOU'LL FIND THEM EVENTUALLY.
YOU SIMPLY ***MUST BELIEVE!***
THEY BELIEVE THAT BY CONTINUALLY FIGHTING THIS BATTLE IN THE ***TALES*** THEY TELL, THEY WILL NOT HAVE TO ***FACE*** THEM IN REALITY.
I KEEP THINKING-
-IF NONE OF THIS HAD HAPPENED-
-AS IF THEIR SPOTTY HISTORY OF VILLAINOUS ACTS TO ONE ANOTHER HAD NEVER HAPPENED.

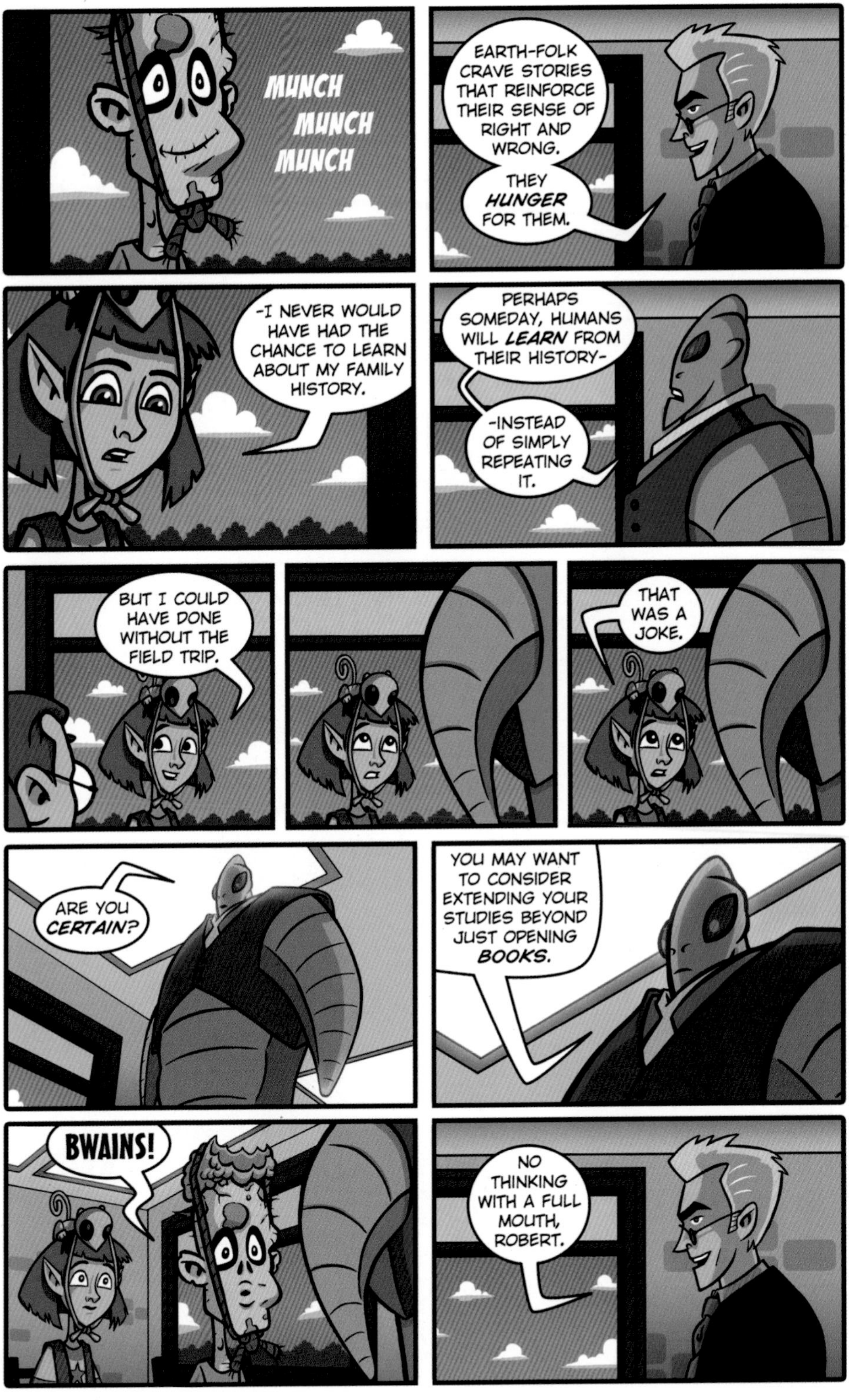
MUNCH MUNCH MUNCH
EARTH-FOLK CRAVE STORIES THAT REINFORCE THEIR SENSE OF RIGHT AND WRONG.
THEY HUNGER FOR THEM.
-I NEVER WOULD HAVE HAD THE CHANCE TO LEARN ABOUT MY FAMILY HISTORY.
PERHAPS SOMEDAY, HUMANS WILL LEARN FROM THEIR HISTORY-
-INSTEAD OF SIMPLY REPEATING IT.
BUT I COULD HAVE DONE WITHOUT THE FIELD TRIP.
THAT WAS A JOKE.
ARE YOU CERTAIN?
YOU MAY WANT TO CONSIDER EXTENDING YOUR STUDIES BEYOND JUST OPENING BOOKS.
BWAINS!
NO THINKING WITH A FULL MOUTH, ROBERT.

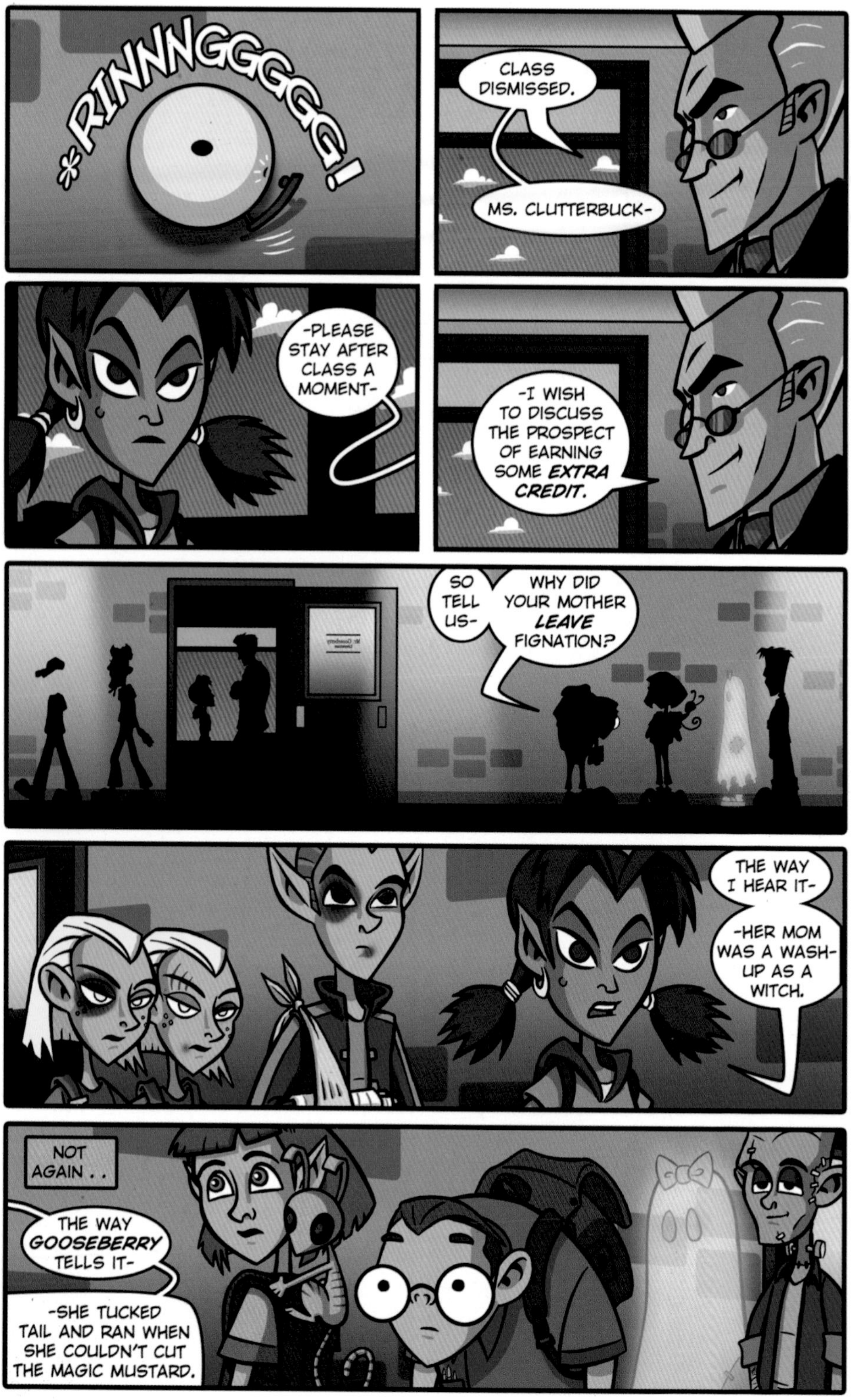
*RINNNGGGGG!
CLASS DISMISSED.
MS. CLUTTERBUCK-
-PLEASE STAY AFTER CLASS A MOMENT-
-I WISH TO DISCUSS THE PROSPECT OF EARNING SOME EXTRA CREDIT.
SO TELL US-
WHY DID YOUR MOTHER LEAVE FIGNATION?
THE WAY I HEAR IT-
-HER MOM WAS A WASH-UP AS A WITCH.
NOT AGAIN . .
THE WAY GOOSEBERRY TELLS IT-
-SHE TUCKED TAIL AND RAN WHEN SHE COULDN'T CUT THE MAGIC MUSTARD.

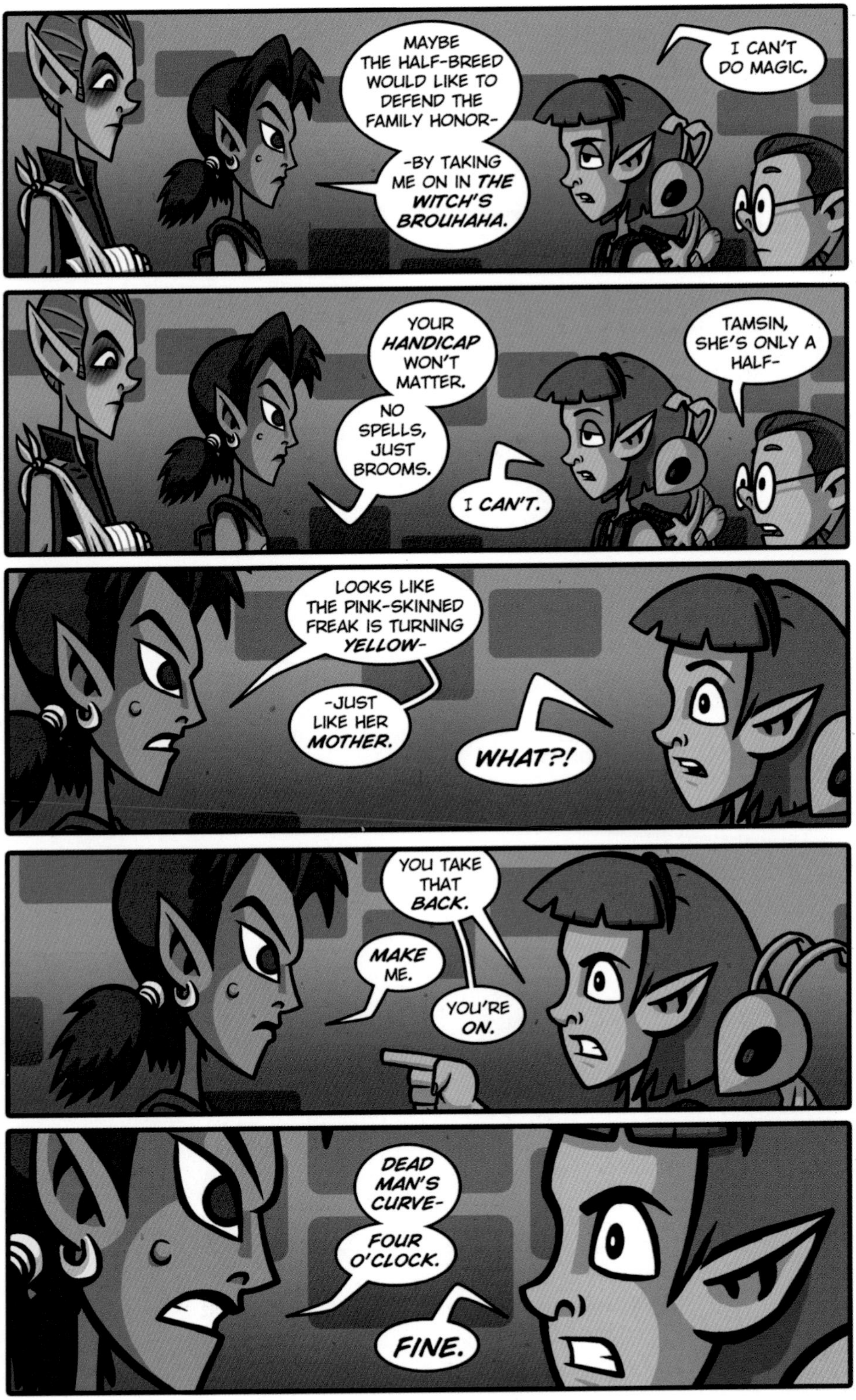
MAYBE THE HALF-BREED WOULD LIKE TO DEFEND THE FAMILY HONOR-
-BY TAKING ME ON IN THE WITCH'S BROUHAHA.
I CAN'T DO MAGIC.
YOUR HANDICAP WON'T MATTER.
NO SPELLS, JUST BROOMS.
TAMSIN, SHE'S ONLY A HALF-
I CAN'T.
LOOKS LIKE THE PINK-SKINNED FREAK IS TURNING YELLOW-
-JUST LIKE HER MOTHER.
WHAT?!
YOU TAKE THAT BACK.
MAKE ME.
YOU'RE ON.
DEAD MAN'S CURVE-
FOUR O'CLOCK.
FINE.

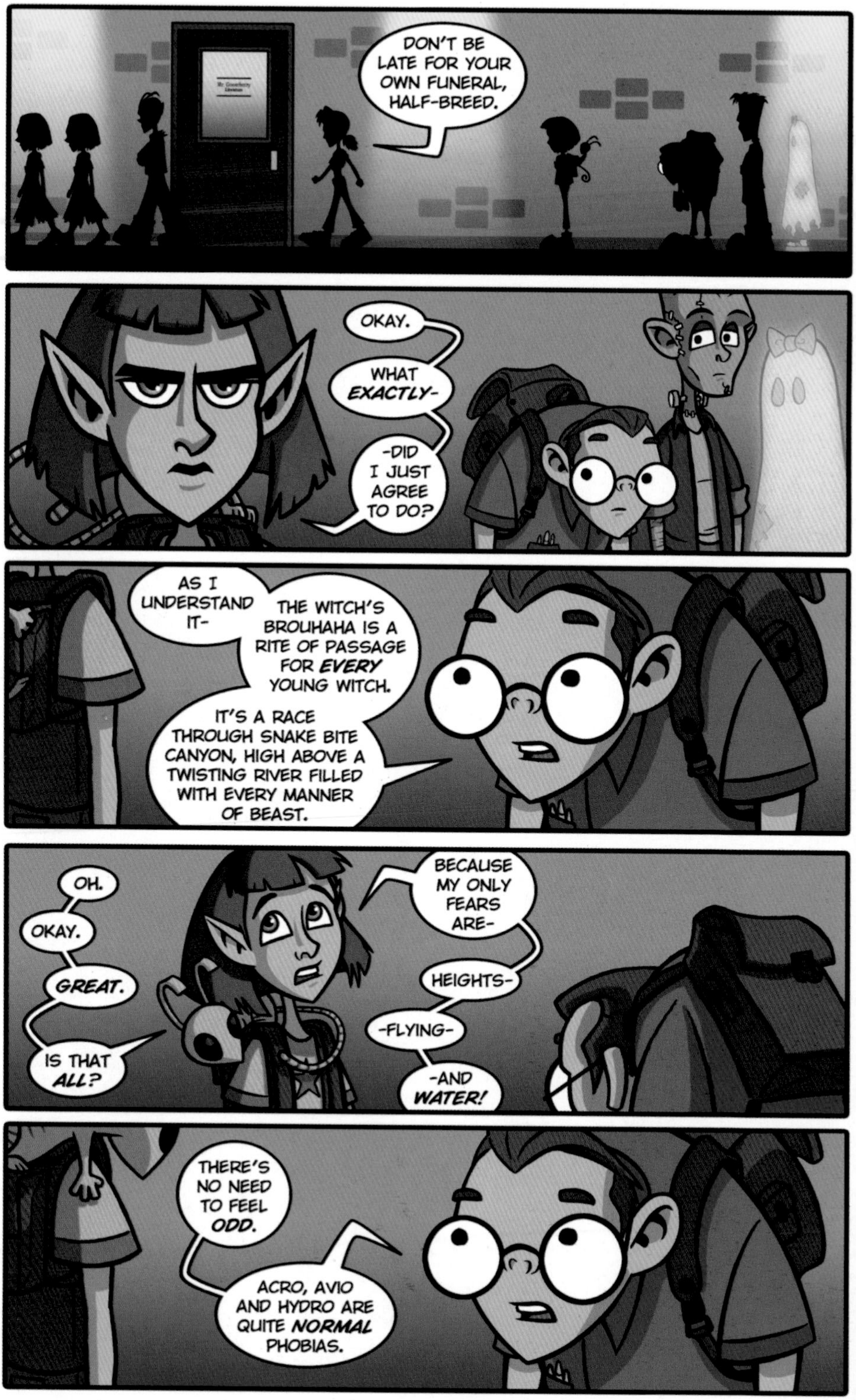
DON'T BE LATE FOR YOUR OWN FUNERAL, HALF-BREED.
OKAY.
WHAT *EXACTLY*-
-DID I JUST AGREE TO DO?
AS I UNDERSTAND IT-
THE WITCH'S BROUHAHA IS A RITE OF PASSAGE FOR *EVERY* YOUNG WITCH.
IT'S A RACE THROUGH SNAKE BITE CANYON, HIGH ABOVE A TWISTING RIVER FILLED WITH EVERY MANNER OF BEAST.
OH.
OKAY.
GREAT.
IS THAT *ALL?*
BECAUSE MY ONLY FEARS ARE-
HEIGHTS-
-FLYING-
-AND *WATER!*
THERE'S NO NEED TO FEEL *ODD.*
ACRO, AVIO AND HYDRO ARE QUITE *NORMAL* PHOBIAS.

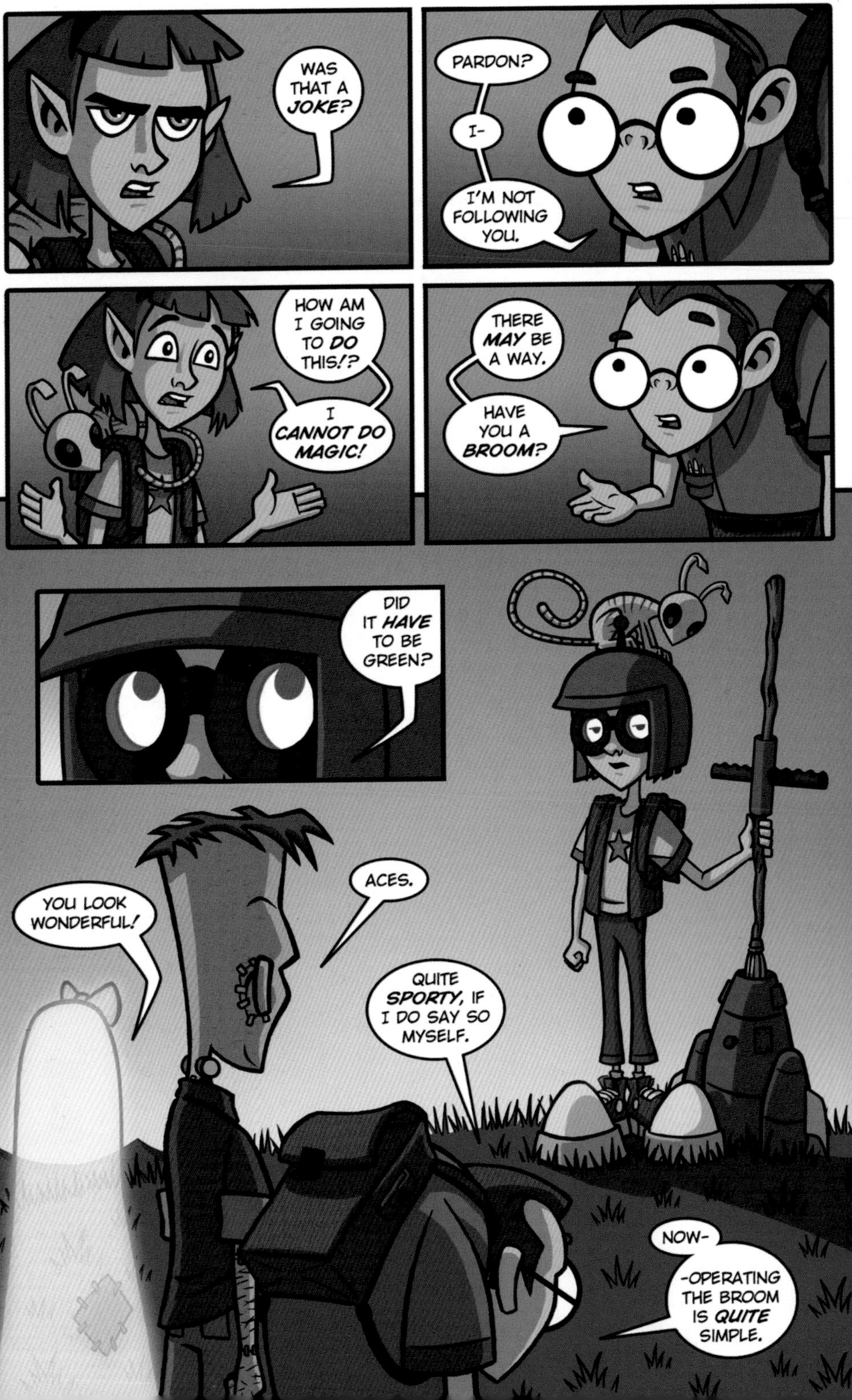
WAS THAT A JOKE?
PARDON?
I-
I'M NOT FOLLOWING YOU.
HOW AM I GOING TO DO THIS!?
I CANNOT DO MAGIC!
THERE MAY BE A WAY.
HAVE YOU A BROOM?
DID IT HAVE TO BE GREEN?
YOU LOOK WONDERFUL!
ACES.
QUITE SPORTY, IF I DO SAY SO MYSELF.
NOW-
-OPERATING THE BROOM IS QUITE SIMPLE.

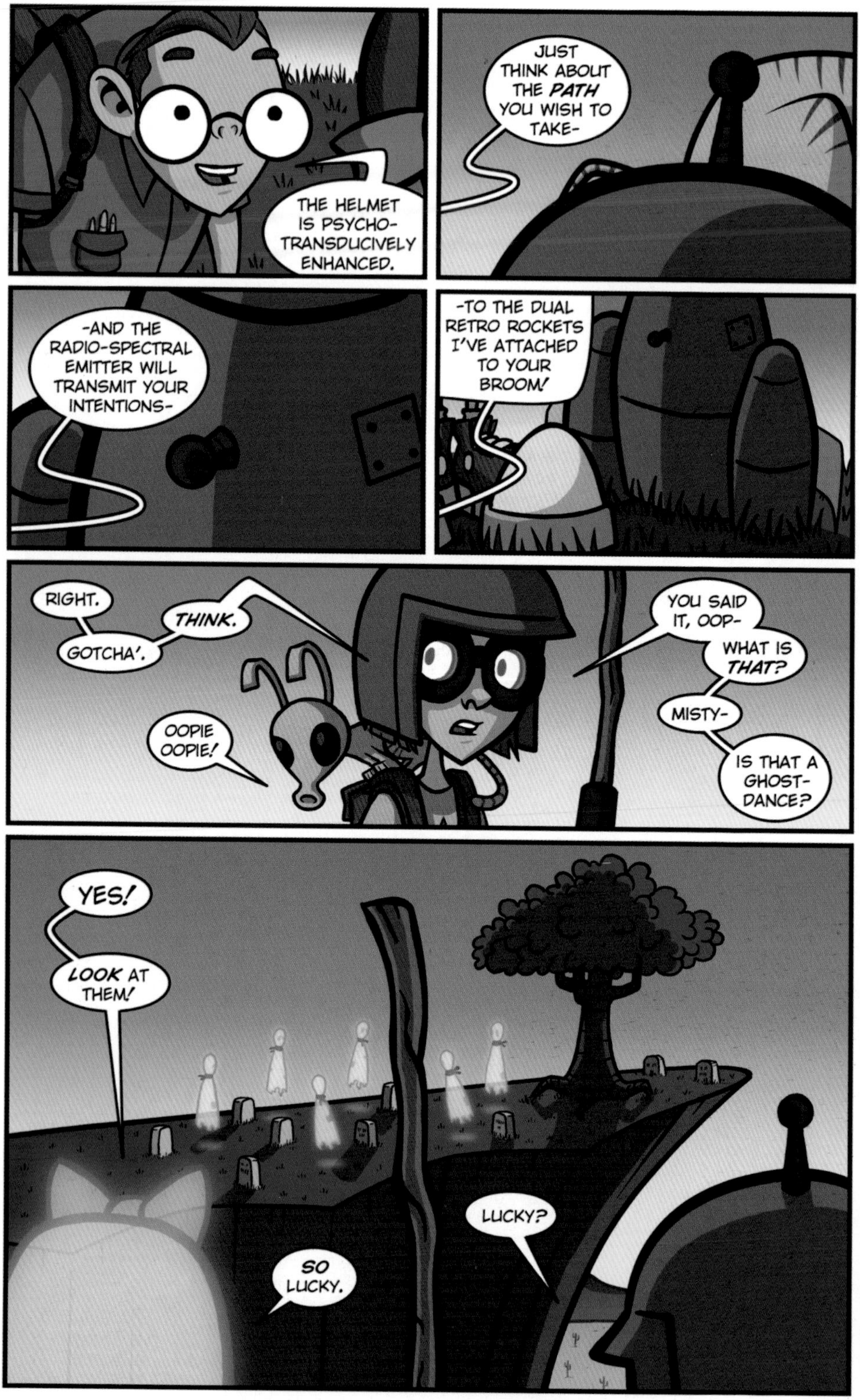
THE HELMET IS PSYCHO-TRANSDUCIVELY ENHANCED.
JUST THINK ABOUT THE *PATH* YOU WISH TO TAKE-
-AND THE RADIO-SPECTRAL EMITTER WILL TRANSMIT YOUR INTENTIONS-
-TO THE DUAL RETRO ROCKETS I'VE ATTACHED TO YOUR BROOM!
RIGHT.
GOTCHA'.
THINK.
OOPIE OOPIE!
YOU SAID IT, OOP-
WHAT IS *THAT?*
MISTY-
IS THAT A GHOST-DANCE?
YES!
LOOK AT THEM!
LUCKY?
SO LUCKY.

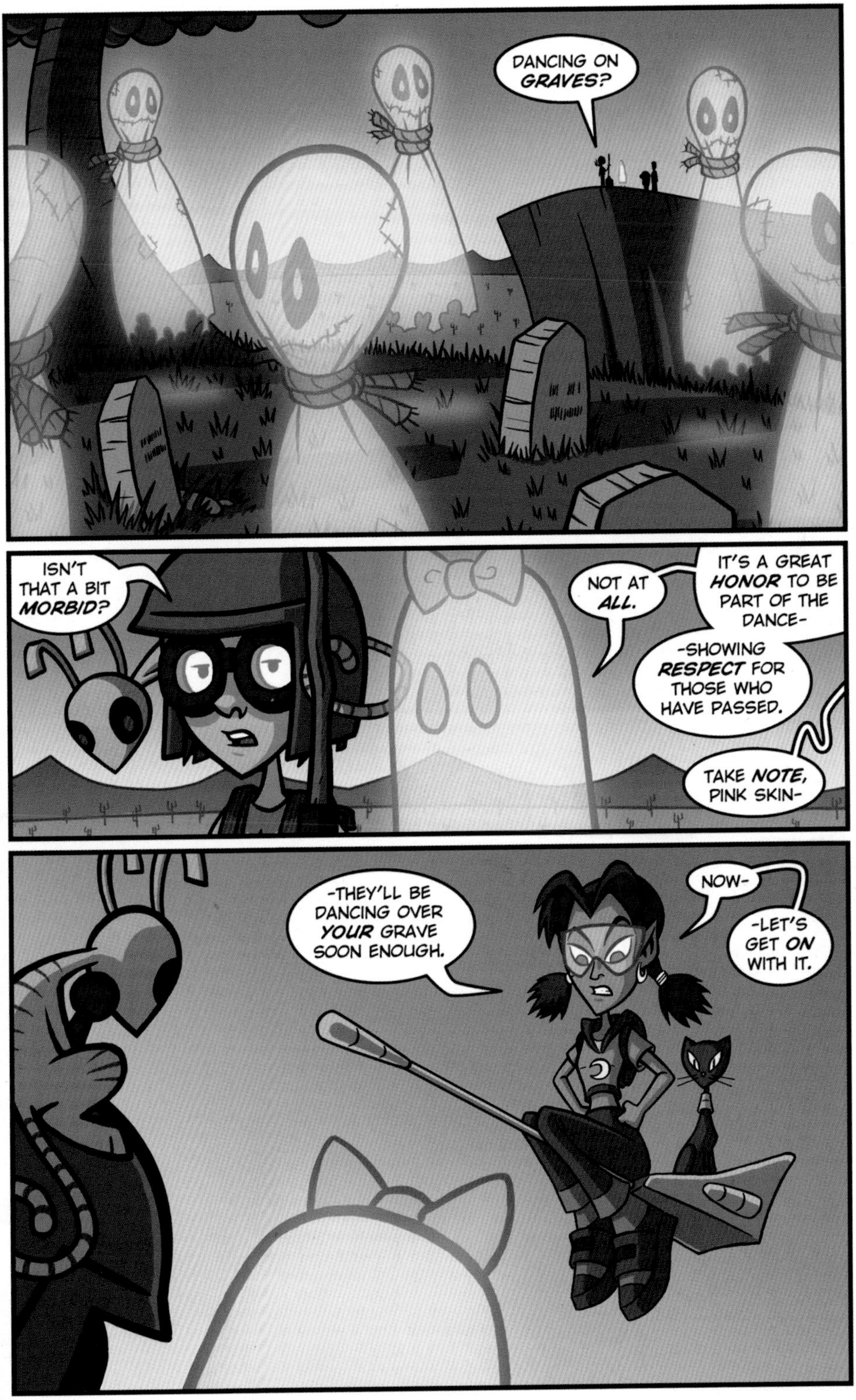

DANCING ON *GRAVES?*
ISN'T THAT A BIT *MORBID?*
NOT AT *ALL.*
IT'S A GREAT *HONOR* TO BE PART OF THE DANCE-
-SHOWING *RESPECT* FOR THOSE WHO HAVE PASSED.
TAKE *NOTE,* PINK SKIN-
-THEY'LL BE DANCING OVER *YOUR* GRAVE SOON ENOUGH.
NOW-
-LET'S GET *ON* WITH IT.

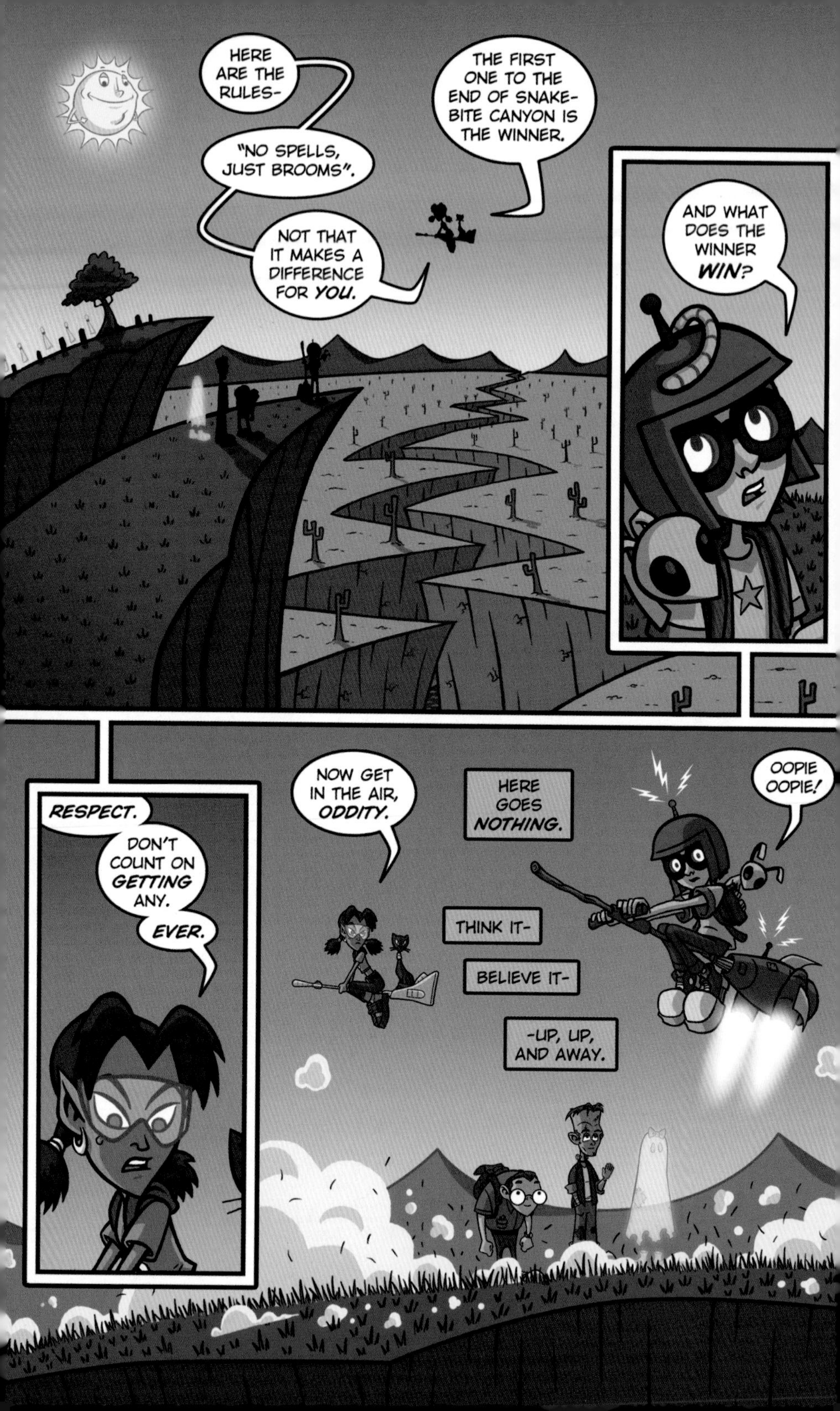
HERE ARE THE RULES-
"NO SPELLS, JUST BROOMS".
NOT THAT IT MAKES A DIFFERENCE FOR YOU.
THE FIRST ONE TO THE END OF SNAKE-BITE CANYON IS THE WINNER.
AND WHAT DOES THE WINNER WIN?
RESPECT.
DON'T COUNT ON GETTING ANY.
EVER.
NOW GET IN THE AIR, ODDITY.
HERE GOES NOTHING.
OOPIE OOPIE!
THINK IT-
BELIEVE IT-
-UP, UP, AND AWAY.

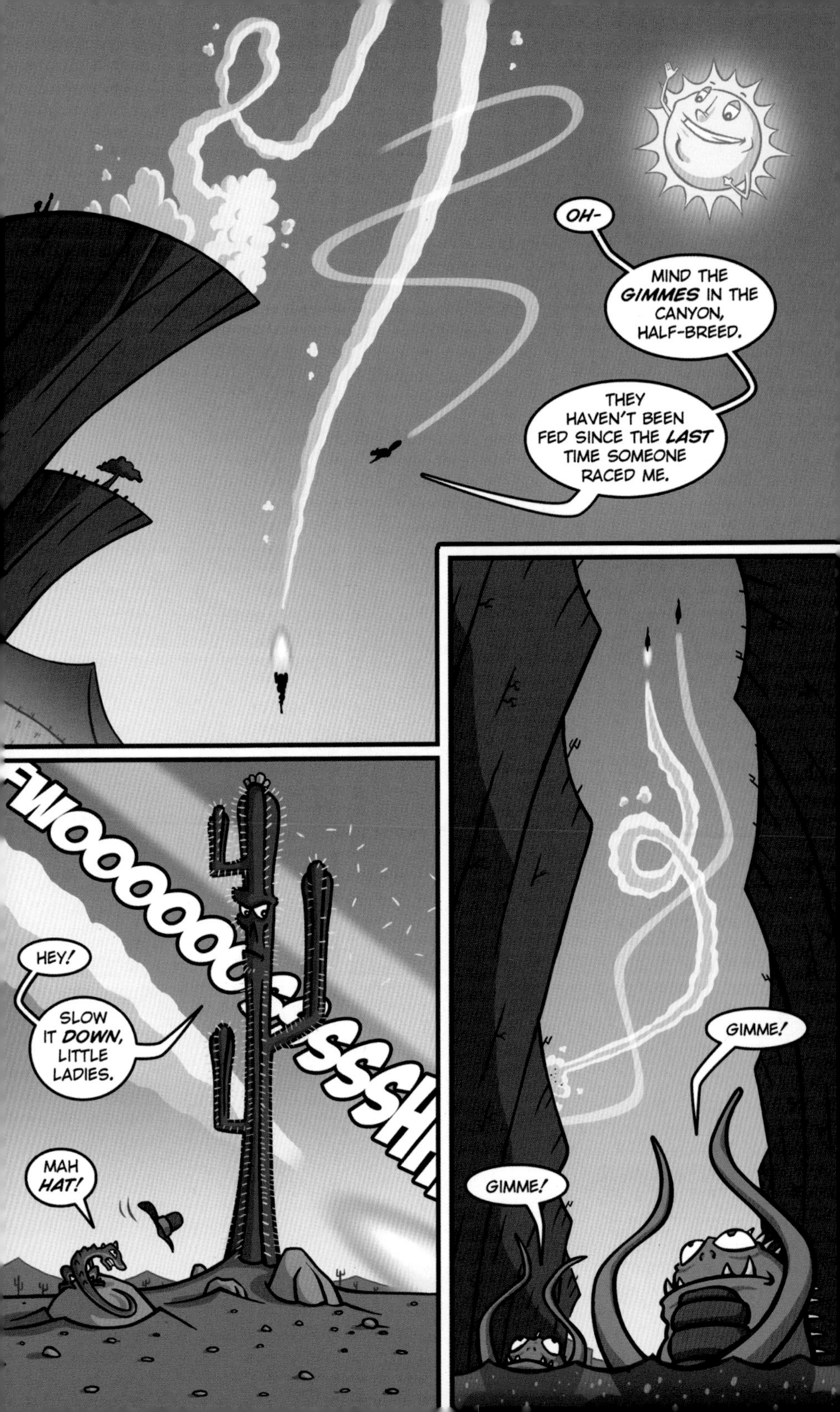
OH-
MIND THE GIMMES IN THE CANYON, HALF-BREED.
THEY HAVEN'T BEEN FED SINCE THE LAST TIME SOMEONE RACED ME.
FWOOOOOOOSSSHH
HEY!
SLOW IT DOWN, LITTLE LADIES.
MAH HAT!
GIMME!
GIMME!

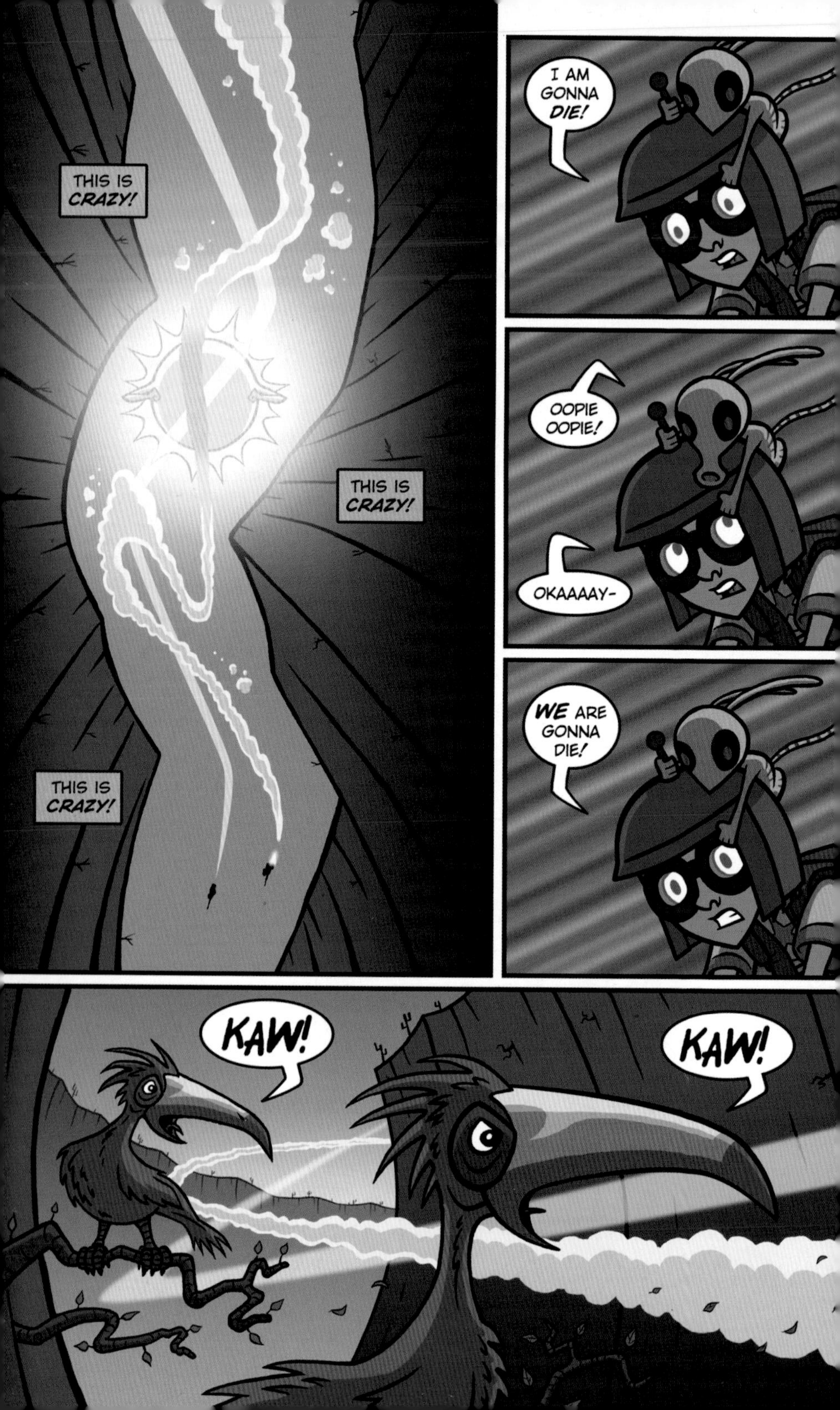
THIS IS CRAZY!
THIS IS CRAZY!
THIS IS CRAZY!
I AM GONNA DIE!
OOPIE OOPIE!
OKAAAAY-
WE ARE GONNA DIE!
KAW!
KAW!

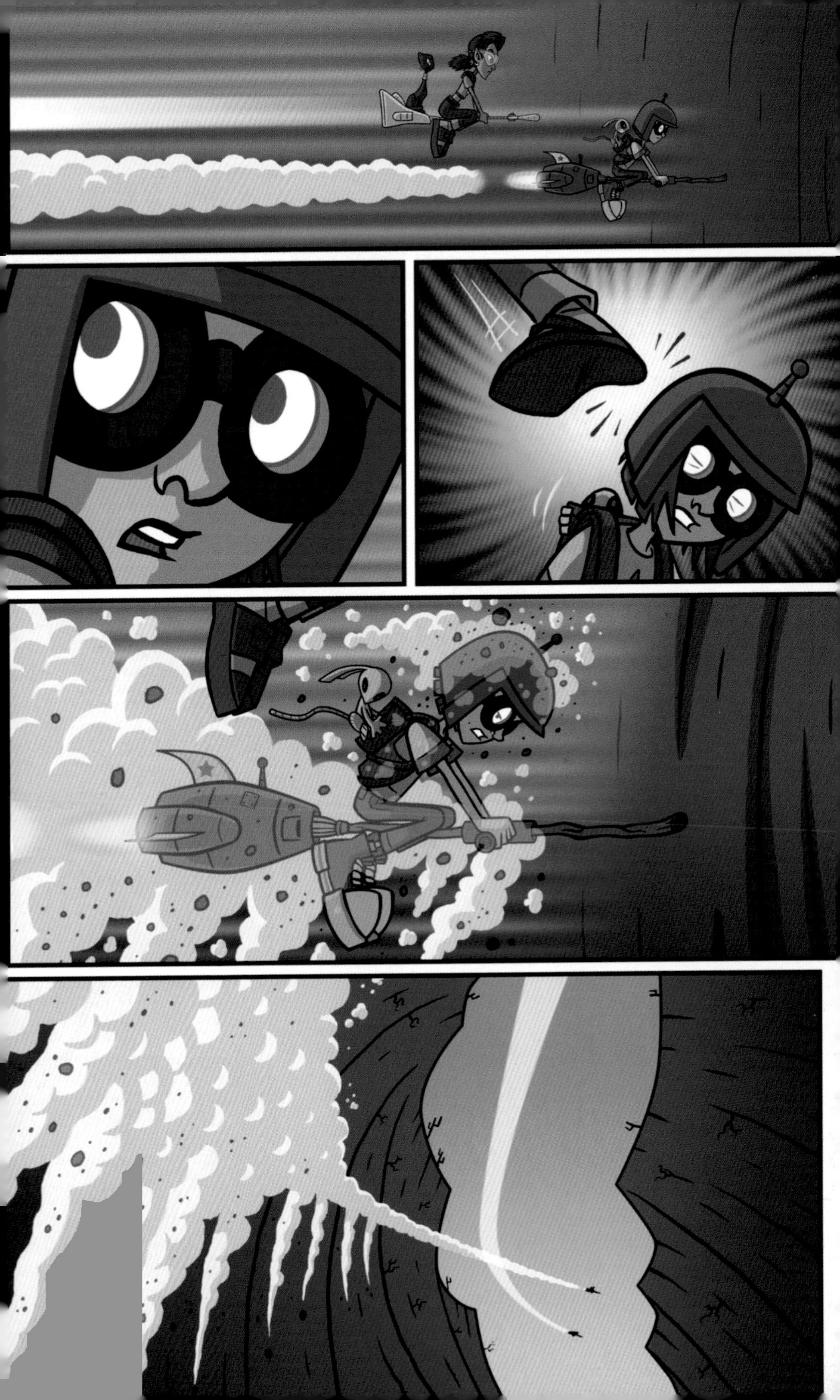

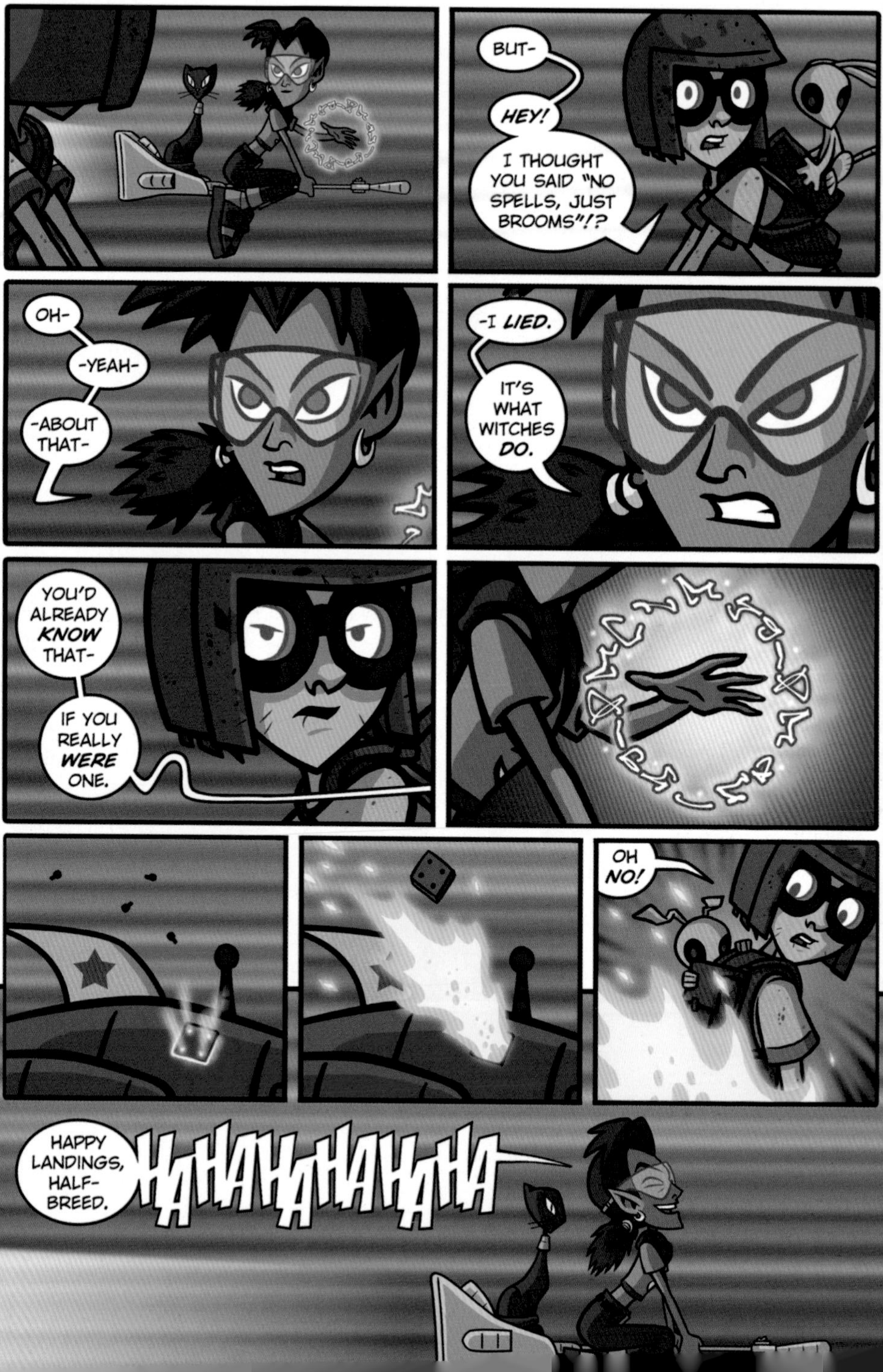
BUT-
HEY!
I THOUGHT YOU SAID "NO SPELLS, JUST BROOMS"!?
OH-
-YEAH-
-ABOUT THAT-
-I LIED.
IT'S WHAT WITCHES DO.
YOU'D ALREADY KNOW THAT-
IF YOU REALLY WERE ONE.
OH NO!
HAPPY LANDINGS, HALF-BREED.
HAHAHAHAHAHAHA

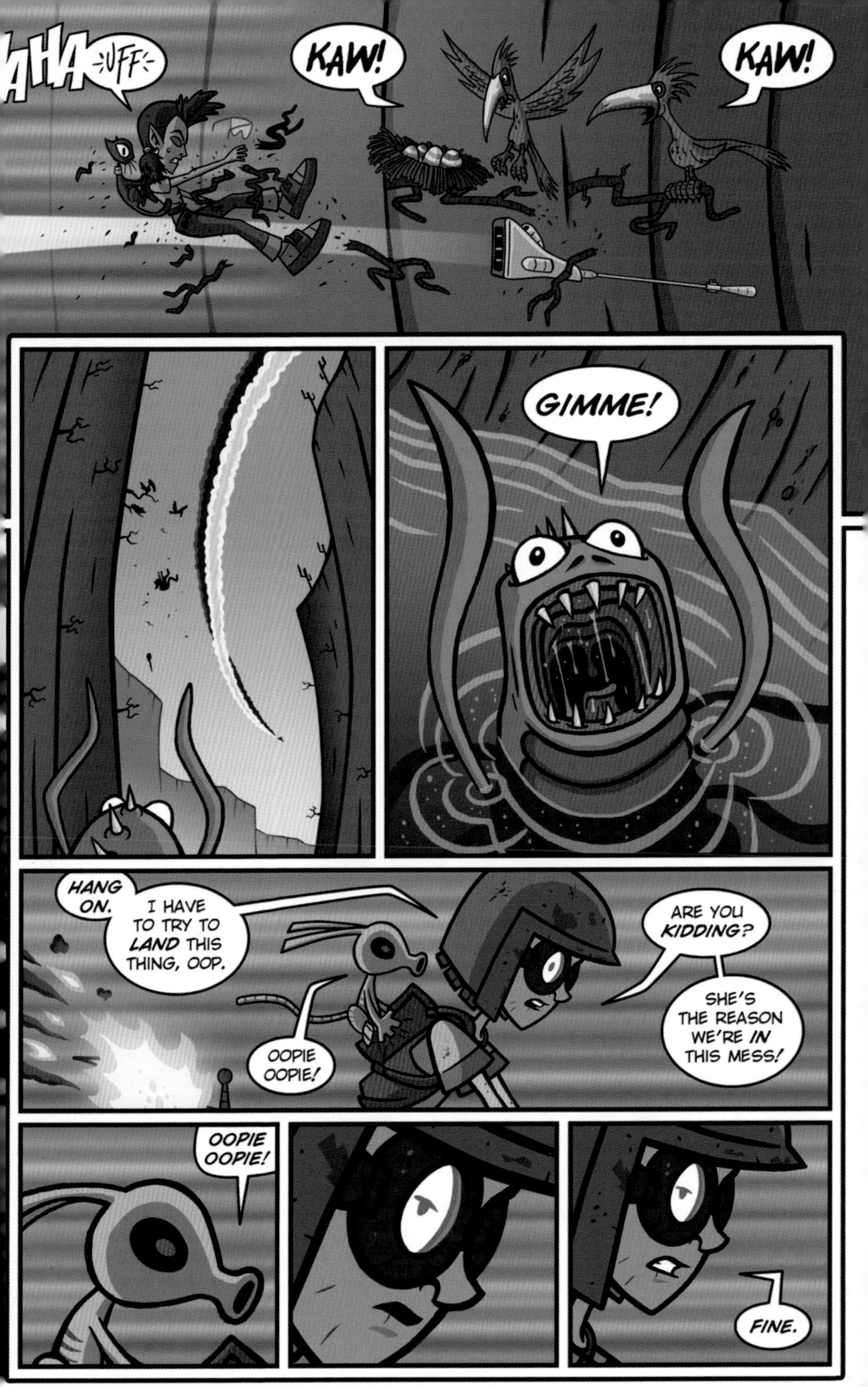
AHA
UFF
KAW!
KAW!
GIMME!
HANG ON.
I HAVE TO TRY TO LAND THIS THING, OOP.
ARE YOU KIDDING?
SHE'S THE REASON WE'RE IN THIS MESS!
OOPIE OOPIE!
OOPIE OOPIE!
FINE.

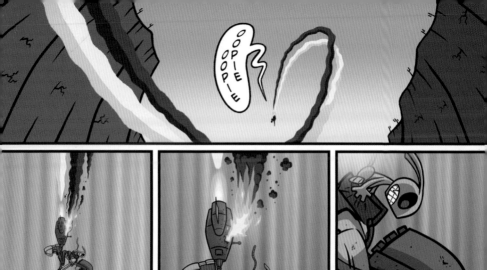

JUST A
LITTLE
FASTER-

JUST A
LITTLE FARTHER-

REACH
OUT-

TAKE
HOLD-

BEFORE
THIS BROOM
GOES KA-

Oddly ★ Normal

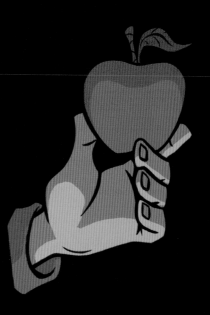

Chapter 7

The Angel of the Bottomless Pit

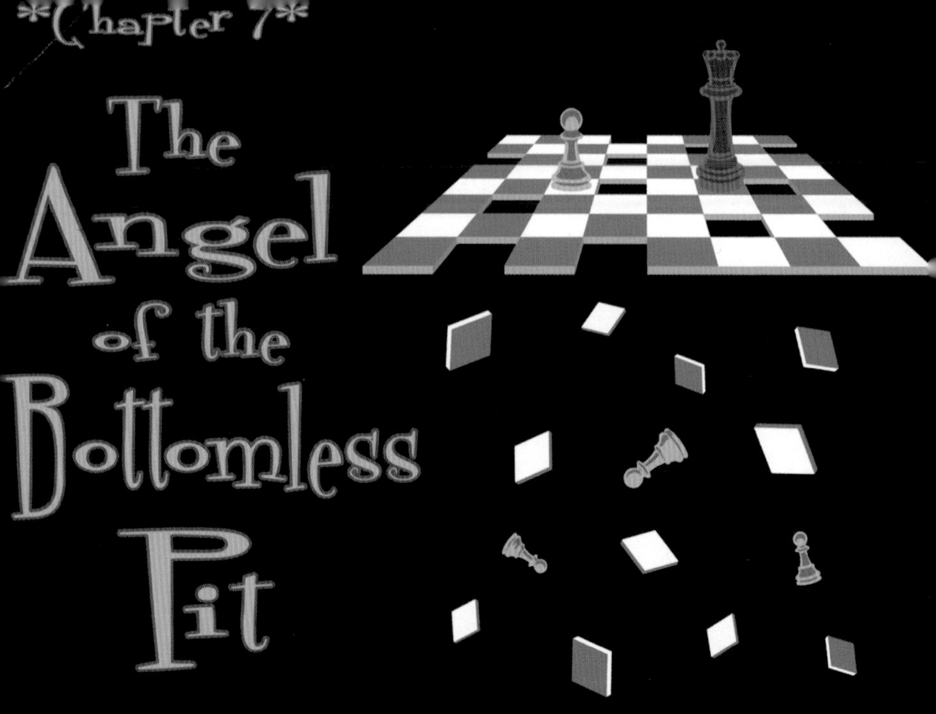

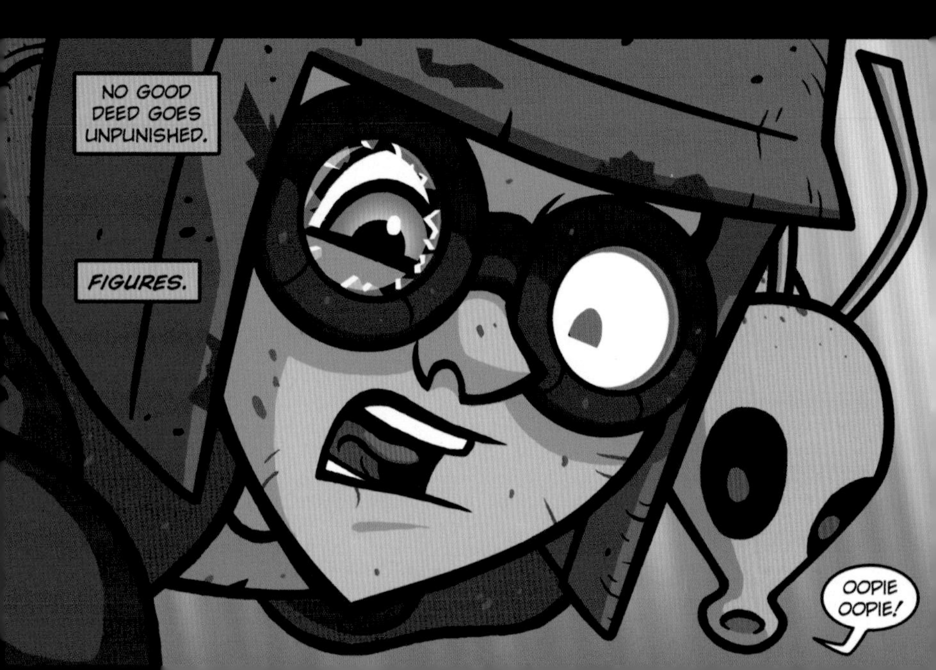
NO GOOD DEED GOES UNPUNISHED.
FIGURES.
OOPIE OOPIE!

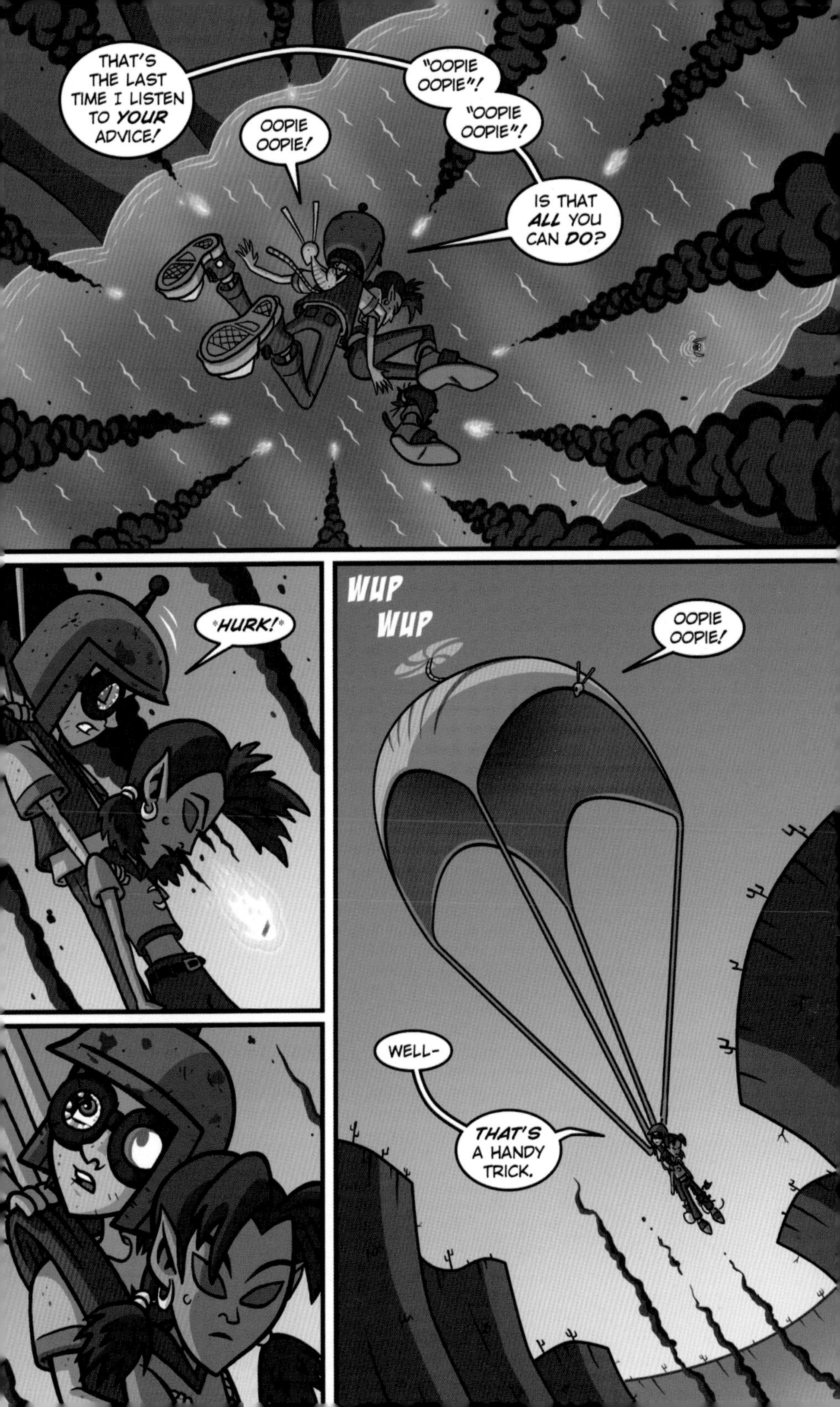
THAT'S THE LAST TIME I LISTEN TO YOUR ADVICE!
OOPIE OOPIE!
"OOPIE OOPIE"!
"OOPIE OOPIE"!
IS THAT ALL YOU CAN DO?
HURK!
WUP WUP
OOPIE OOPIE!
WELL-
THAT'S A HANDY TRICK.

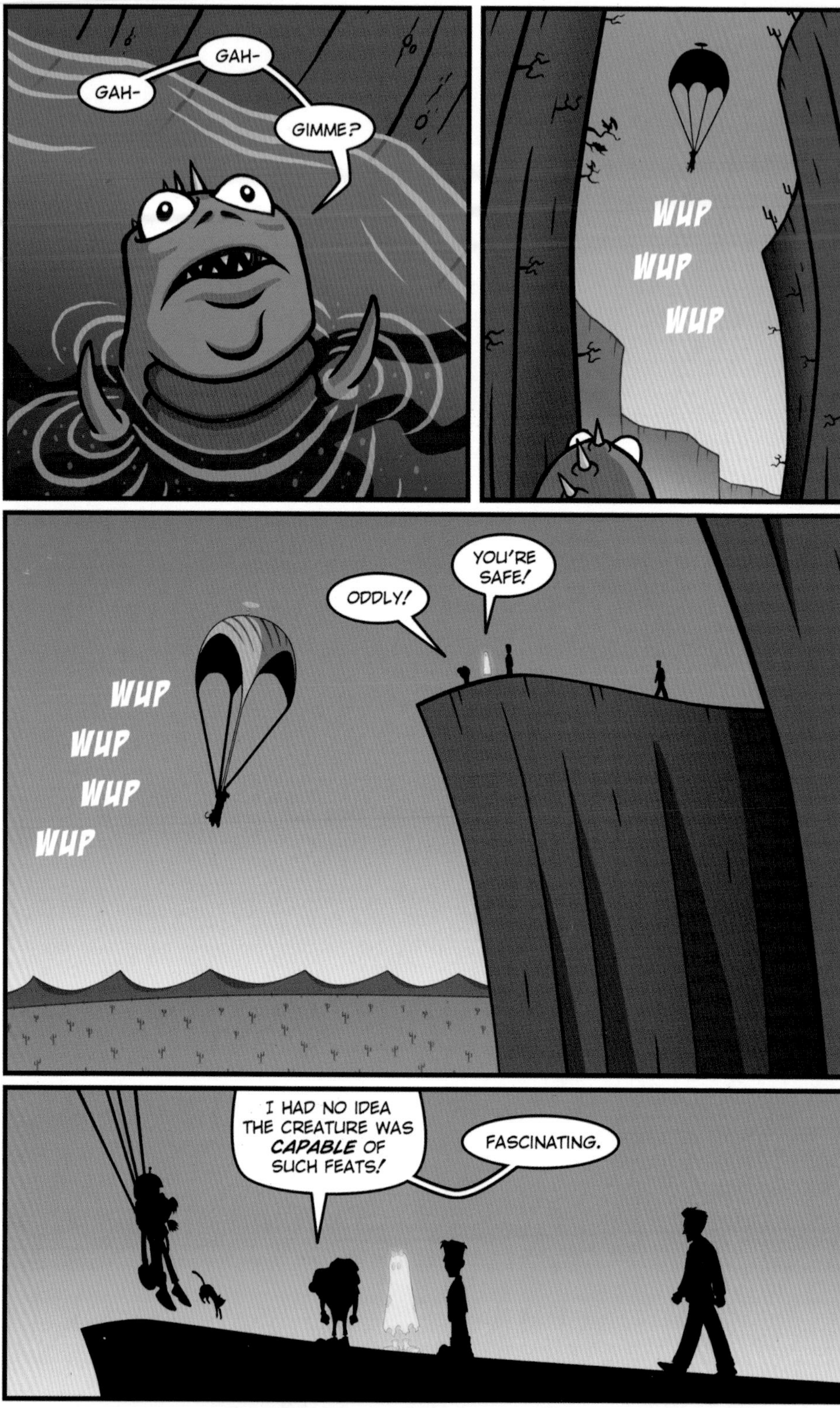
GAH-
GAH-
GIMME?
WUP
WUP
WUP
YOU'RE SAFE!
ODDLY!
WUP
WUP
WUP
WUP
I HAD NO IDEA THE CREATURE WAS *CAPABLE* OF SUCH FEATS!
FASCINATING.

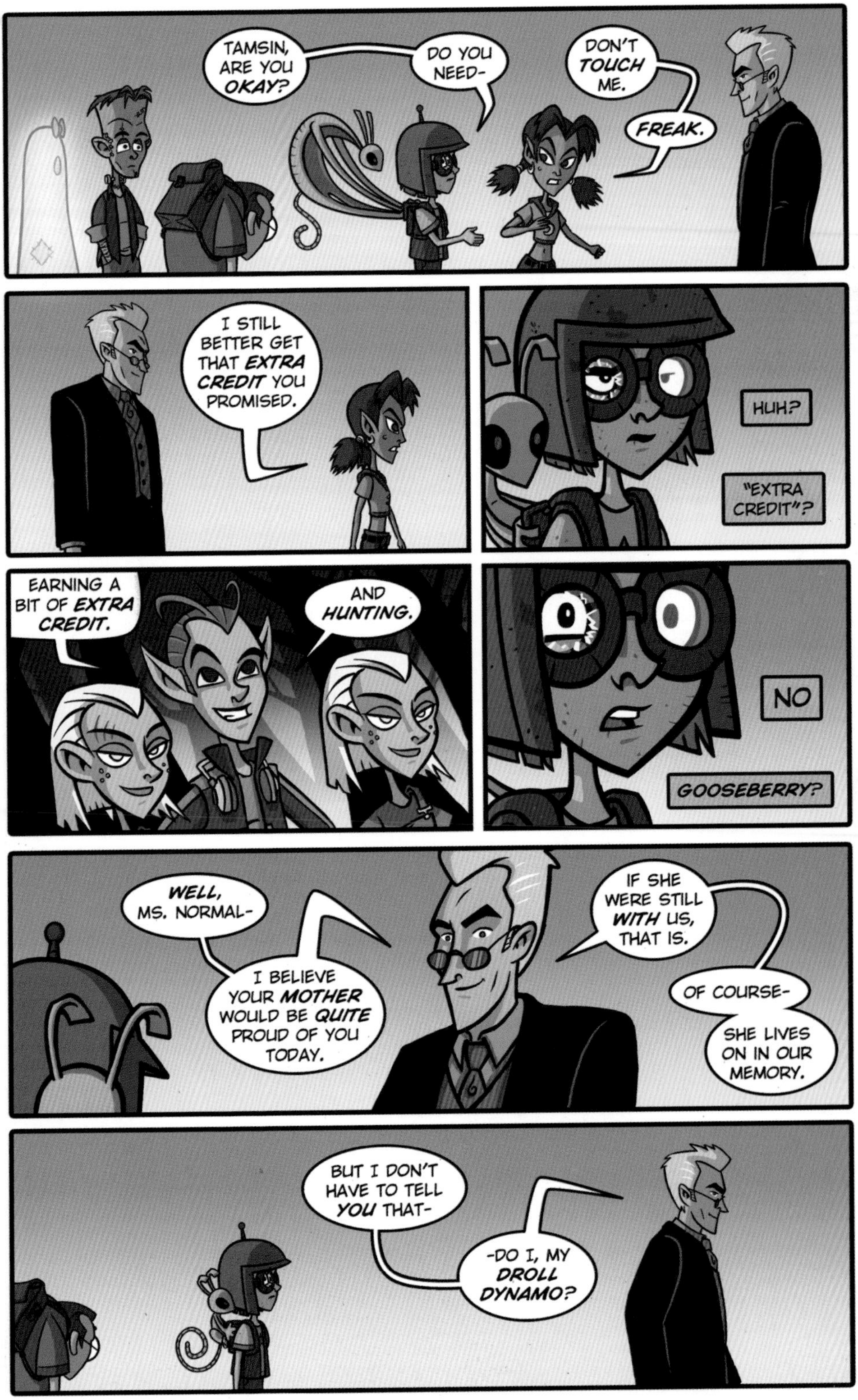
TAMSIN, ARE YOU OKAY?
DO YOU NEED-
DON'T TOUCH ME.
FREAK.
I STILL BETTER GET THAT EXTRA CREDIT YOU PROMISED.
HUH?
"EXTRA CREDIT"?
EARNING A BIT OF EXTRA CREDIT.
AND HUNTING.
NO
GOOSEBERRY?
WELL, MS. NORMAL-
I BELIEVE YOUR MOTHER WOULD BE QUITE PROUD OF YOU TODAY.
IF SHE WERE STILL WITH US, THAT IS.
OF COURSE-
SHE LIVES ON IN OUR MEMORY.
BUT I DON'T HAVE TO TELL YOU THAT-
-DO I, MY DROLL DYNAMO?

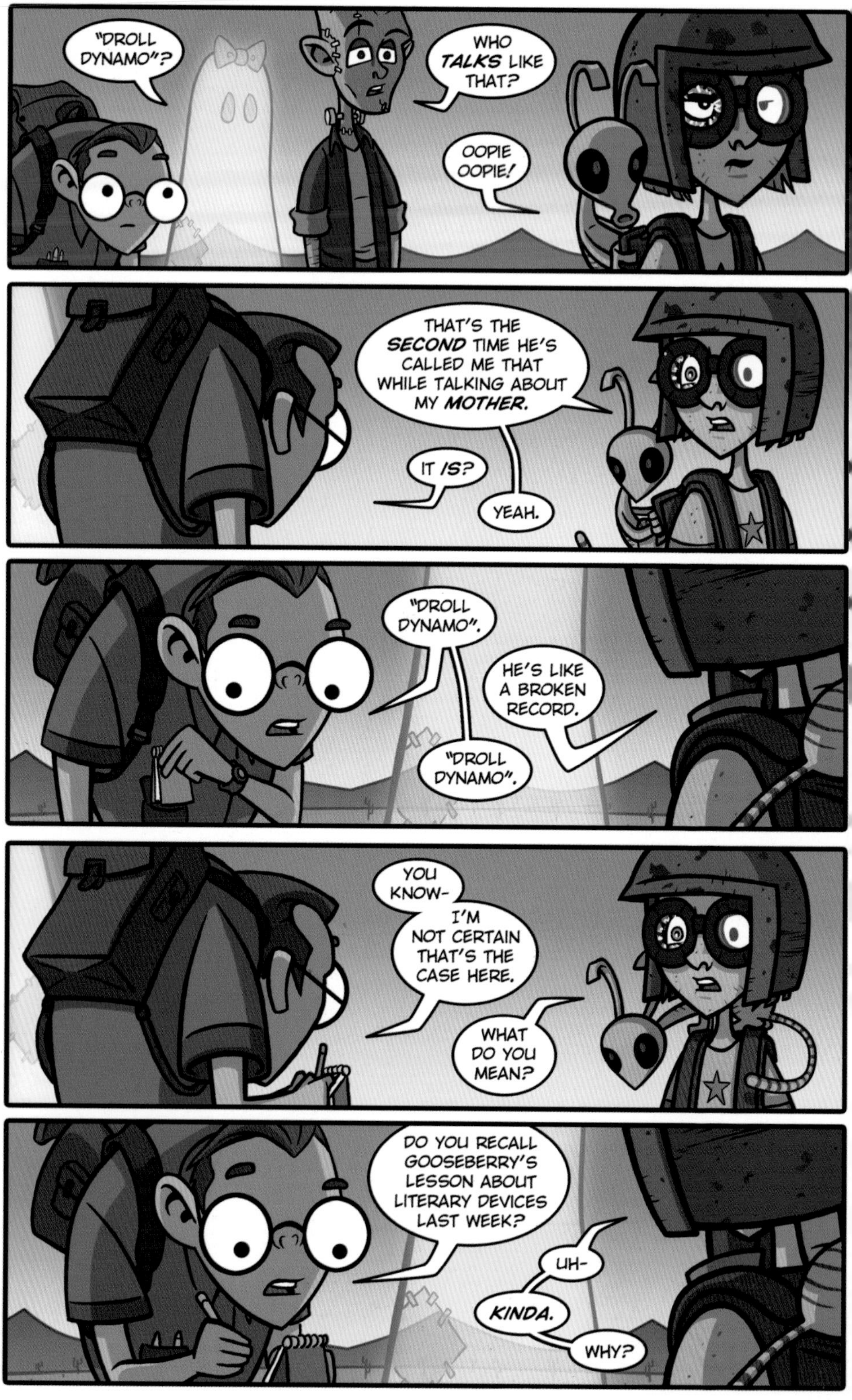
"DROLL DYNAMO"?
WHO *TALKS* LIKE THAT?
OOPIE OOPIE!
THAT'S THE *SECOND* TIME HE'S CALLED ME THAT WHILE TALKING ABOUT MY *MOTHER*.
IT *IS*?
YEAH.
"DROLL DYNAMO".
"DROLL DYNAMO".
HE'S LIKE A BROKEN RECORD.
YOU KNOW-
I'M NOT CERTAIN THAT'S THE CASE HERE.
WHAT DO YOU MEAN?
DO YOU RECALL GOOSEBERRY'S LESSON ABOUT LITERARY DEVICES LAST WEEK?
UH-
KINDA.
WHY?

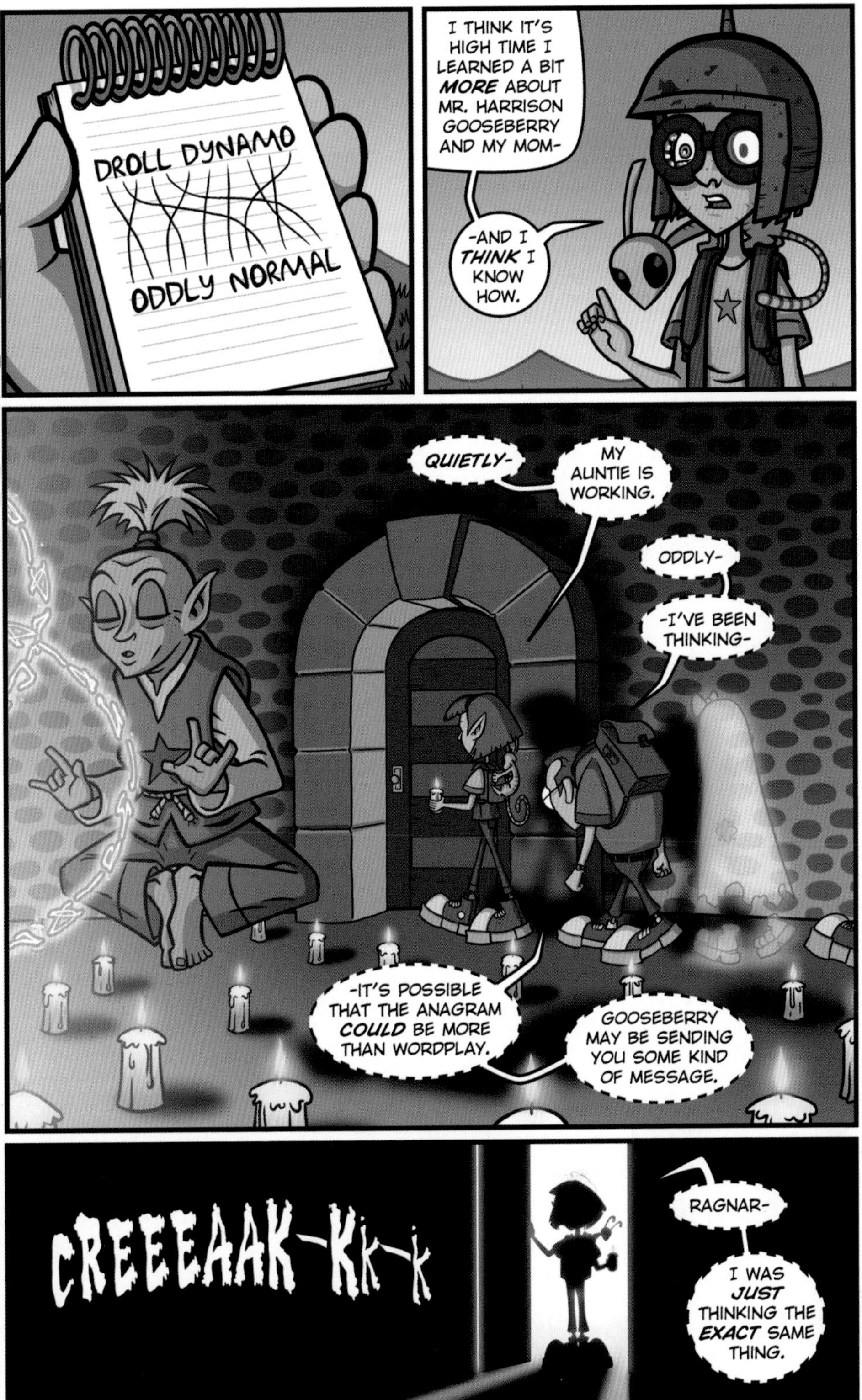
DROLL DYNAMO
ODDLY NORMAL
I THINK IT'S HIGH TIME I LEARNED A BIT *MORE* ABOUT MR. HARRISON GOOSEBERRY AND MY MOM-
-AND I *THINK* I KNOW HOW.
QUIETLY-
MY AUNTIE IS WORKING.
ODDLY-
-I'VE BEEN THINKING-
-IT'S POSSIBLE THAT THE ANAGRAM *COULD* BE MORE THAN WORDPLAY.
GOOSEBERRY MAY BE SENDING YOU SOME KIND OF MESSAGE.
CREEEAAK-Kk-k
RAGNAR-
I WAS *JUST* THINKING THE *EXACT* SAME THING.

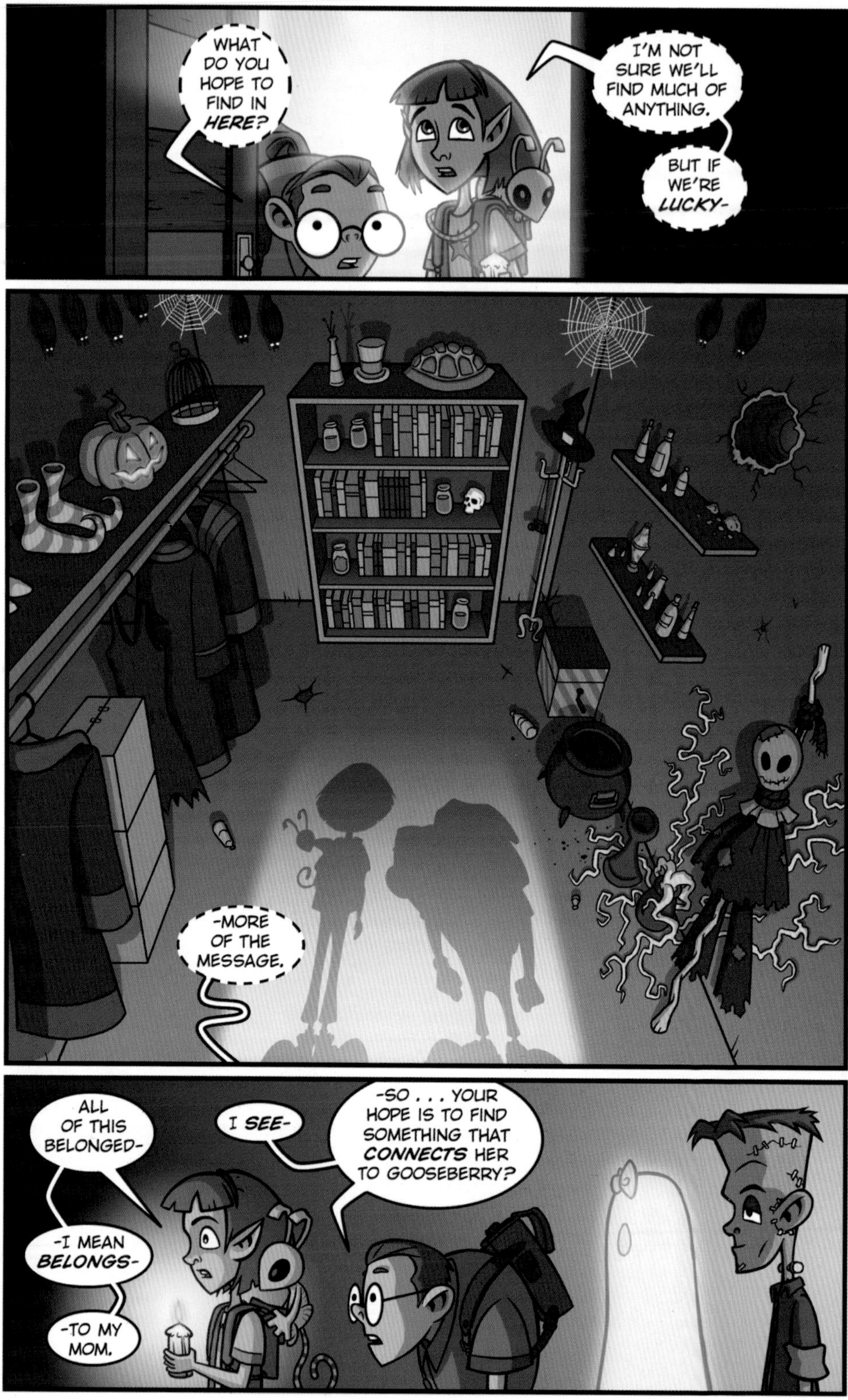
WHAT DO YOU HOPE TO FIND IN *HERE?*
I'M NOT SURE WE'LL FIND MUCH OF ANYTHING.
BUT IF WE'RE *LUCKY*-
-MORE OF THE MESSAGE.
ALL OF THIS BELONGED-
I *SEE*-
-SO . . . YOUR HOPE IS TO FIND SOMETHING THAT *CONNECTS* HER TO GOOSEBERRY?
-I MEAN *BELONGS*-
-TO MY MOM.

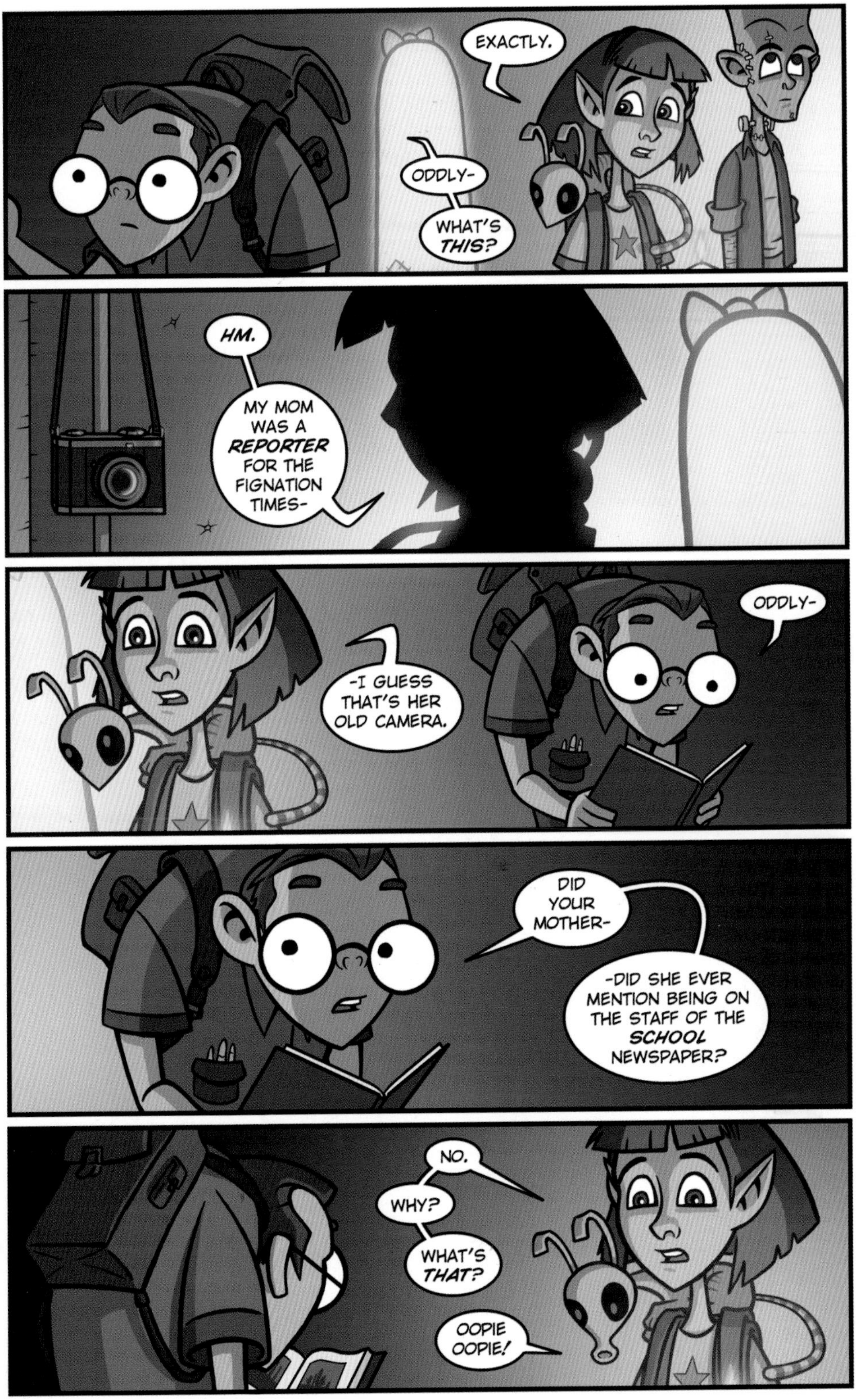
EXACTLY.
ODDLY-
WHAT'S *THIS?*
HM.
MY MOM WAS A *REPORTER* FOR THE FIGNATION TIMES-
-I GUESS THAT'S HER OLD CAMERA.
ODDLY-
DID YOUR MOTHER-
-DID SHE EVER MENTION BEING ON THE STAFF OF THE *SCHOOL* NEWSPAPER?
NO.
WHY?
WHAT'S *THAT?*
OOPIE OOPIE!

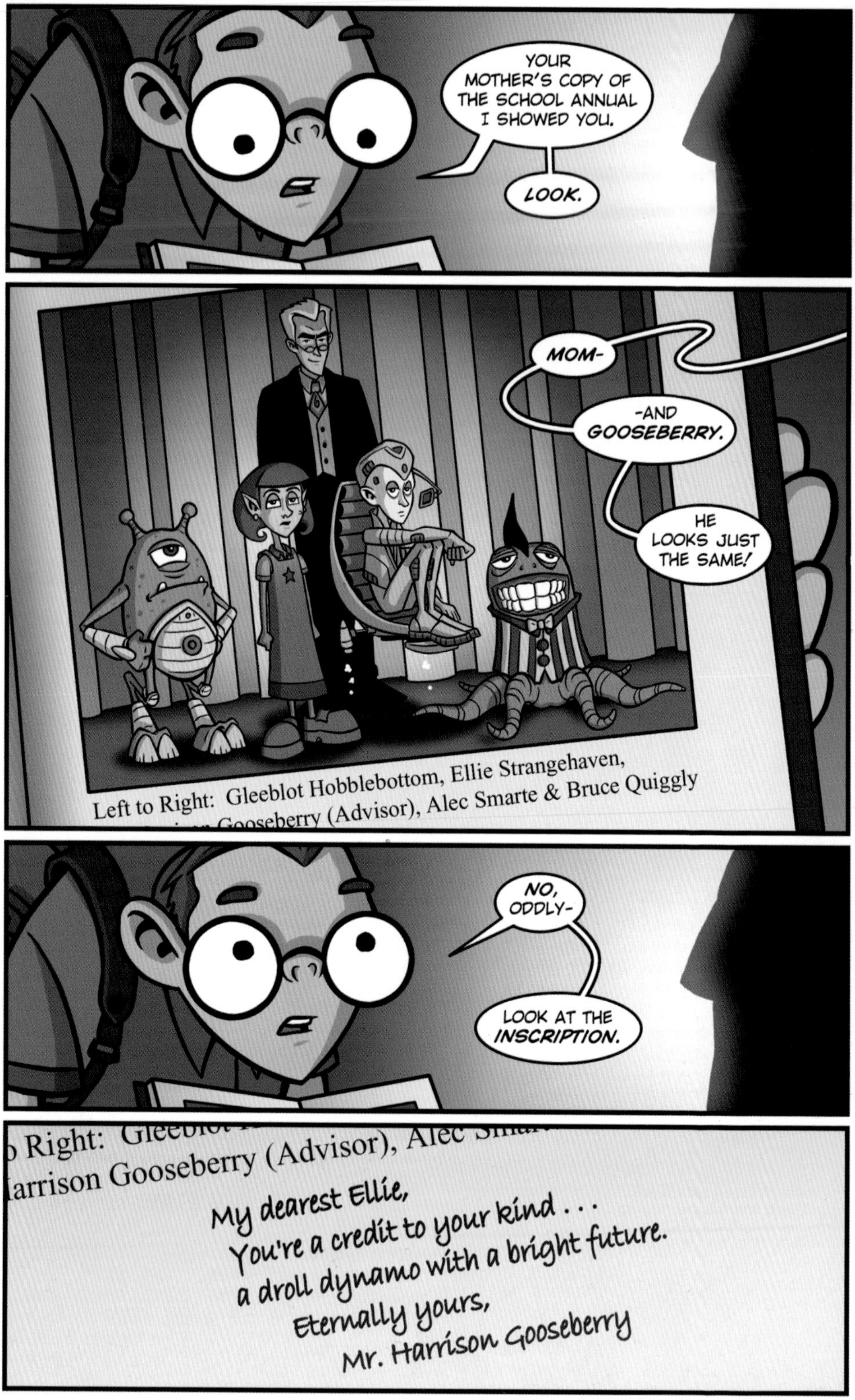
YOUR MOTHER'S COPY OF THE SCHOOL ANNUAL I SHOWED YOU.
LOOK.
MOM-
-AND GOOSEBERRY.
HE LOOKS JUST THE SAME!
Left to Right: Gleeblot Hobblebottom, Ellie Strangehaven,
Gooseberry (Advisor), Alec Smarte & Bruce Quiggly
NO, ODDLY-
LOOK AT THE INSCRIPTION.
Right: Gleeblot
Harrison Gooseberry (Advisor), Alec
My dearest Ellie,
You're a credit to your kind . . .
a droll dynamo with a bright future.
Eternally yours,
Mr. Harrison Gooseberry

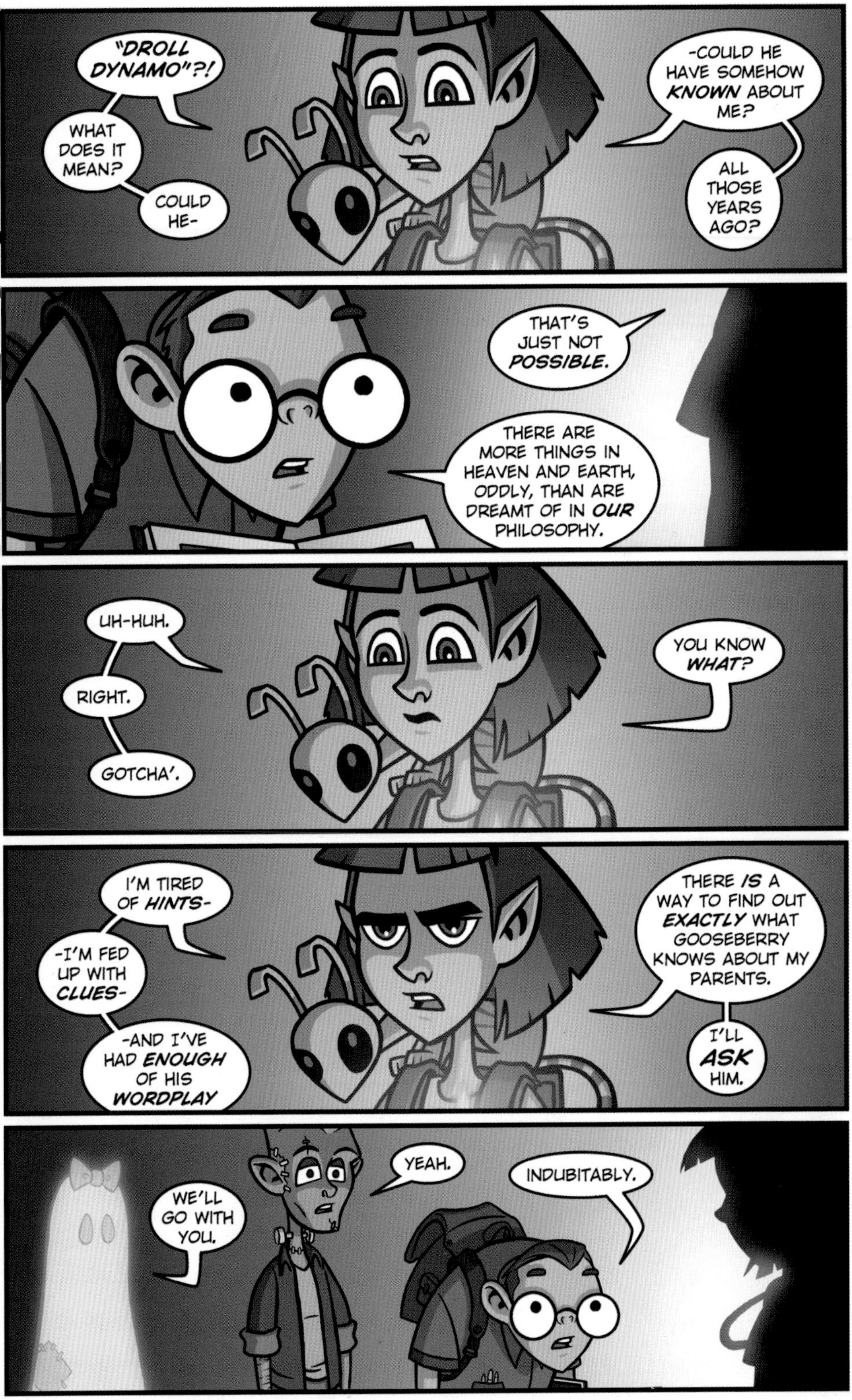
"DROLL DYNAMO"?!
WHAT DOES IT MEAN?
COULD HE-
-COULD HE HAVE SOMEHOW KNOWN ABOUT ME?
ALL THOSE YEARS AGO?
THAT'S JUST NOT POSSIBLE.
THERE ARE MORE THINGS IN HEAVEN AND EARTH, ODDLY, THAN ARE DREAMT OF IN OUR PHILOSOPHY.
UH-HUH.
RIGHT.
GOTCHA'.
YOU KNOW WHAT?
I'M TIRED OF HINTS-
-I'M FED UP WITH CLUES-
-AND I'VE HAD ENOUGH OF HIS WORDPLAY
THERE IS A WAY TO FIND OUT EXACTLY WHAT GOOSEBERRY KNOWS ABOUT MY PARENTS.
I'LL ASK HIM.
WE'LL GO WITH YOU.
YEAH.
INDUBITABLY.

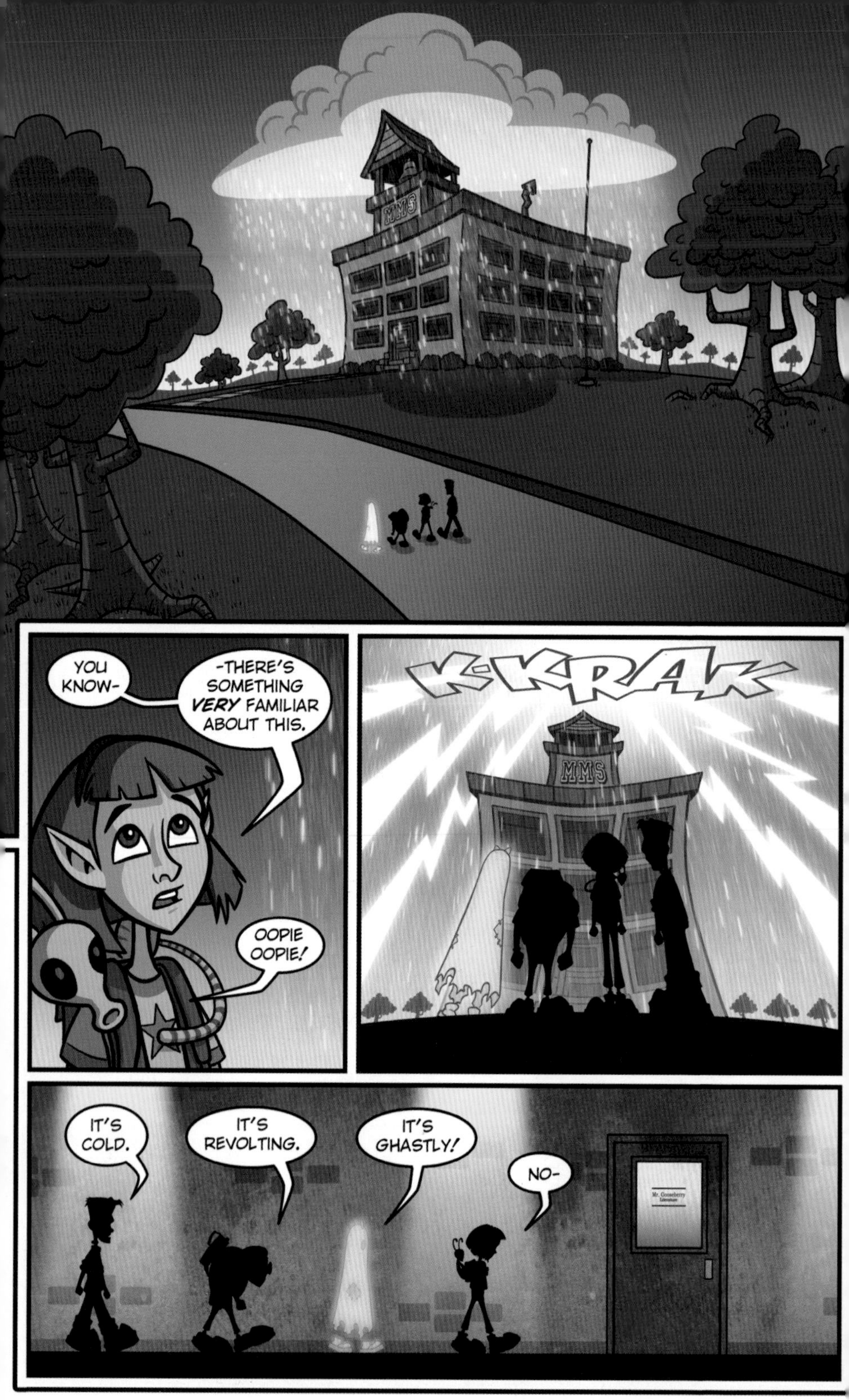
MMS
YOU KNOW-
-THERE'S SOMETHING *VERY* FAMILIAR ABOUT THIS.
OOPIE OOPIE!
K-KRAK
MMS
IT'S COLD.
IT'S REVOLTING.
IT'S GHASTLY!
NO-
Mr. Gooseberry
Literature

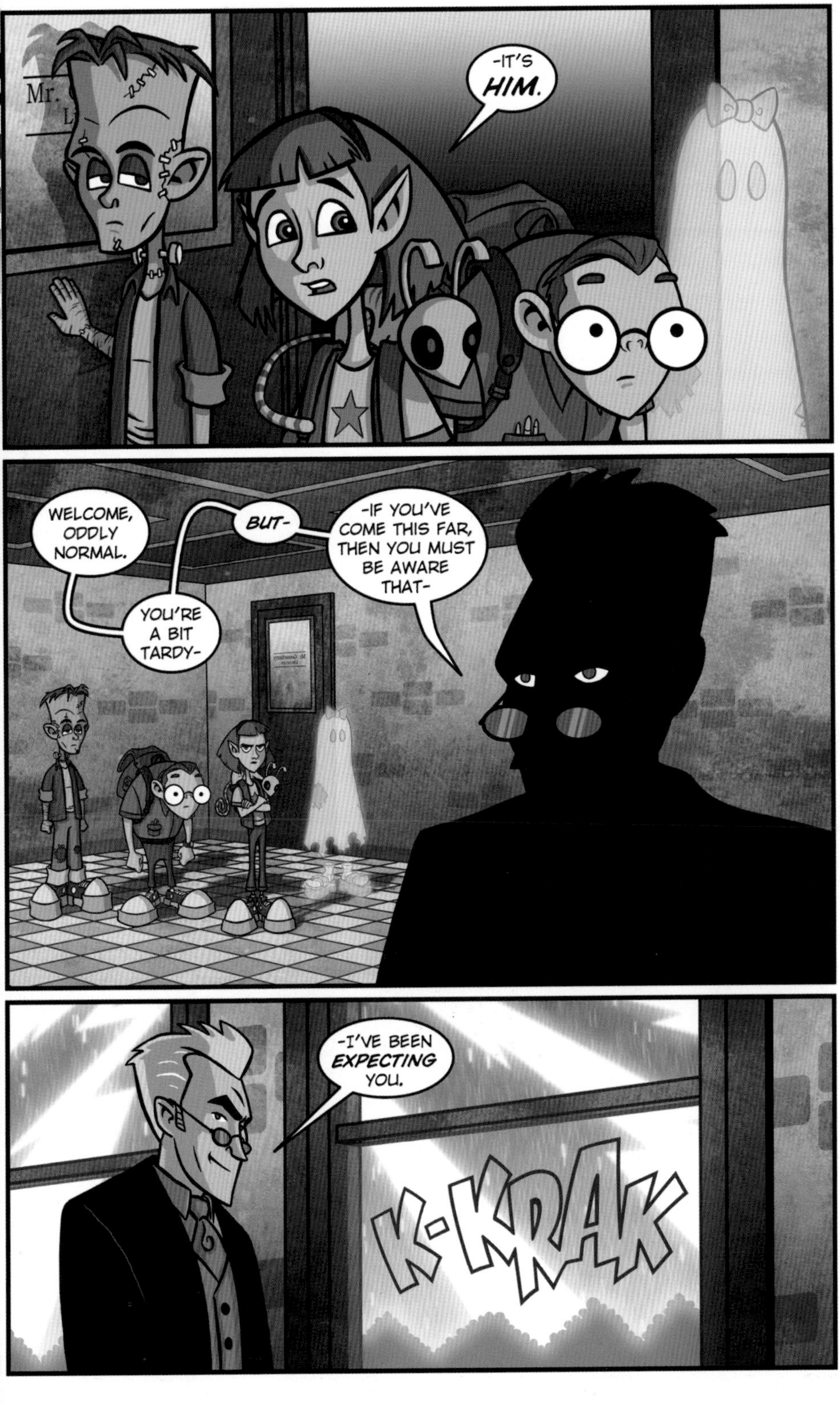

-IT'S HIM.
WELCOME, ODDLY NORMAL.
YOU'RE A BIT TARDY-
BUT-
-IF YOU'VE COME THIS FAR, THEN YOU MUST BE AWARE THAT-
-I'VE BEEN EXPECTING YOU.
K-KRAK

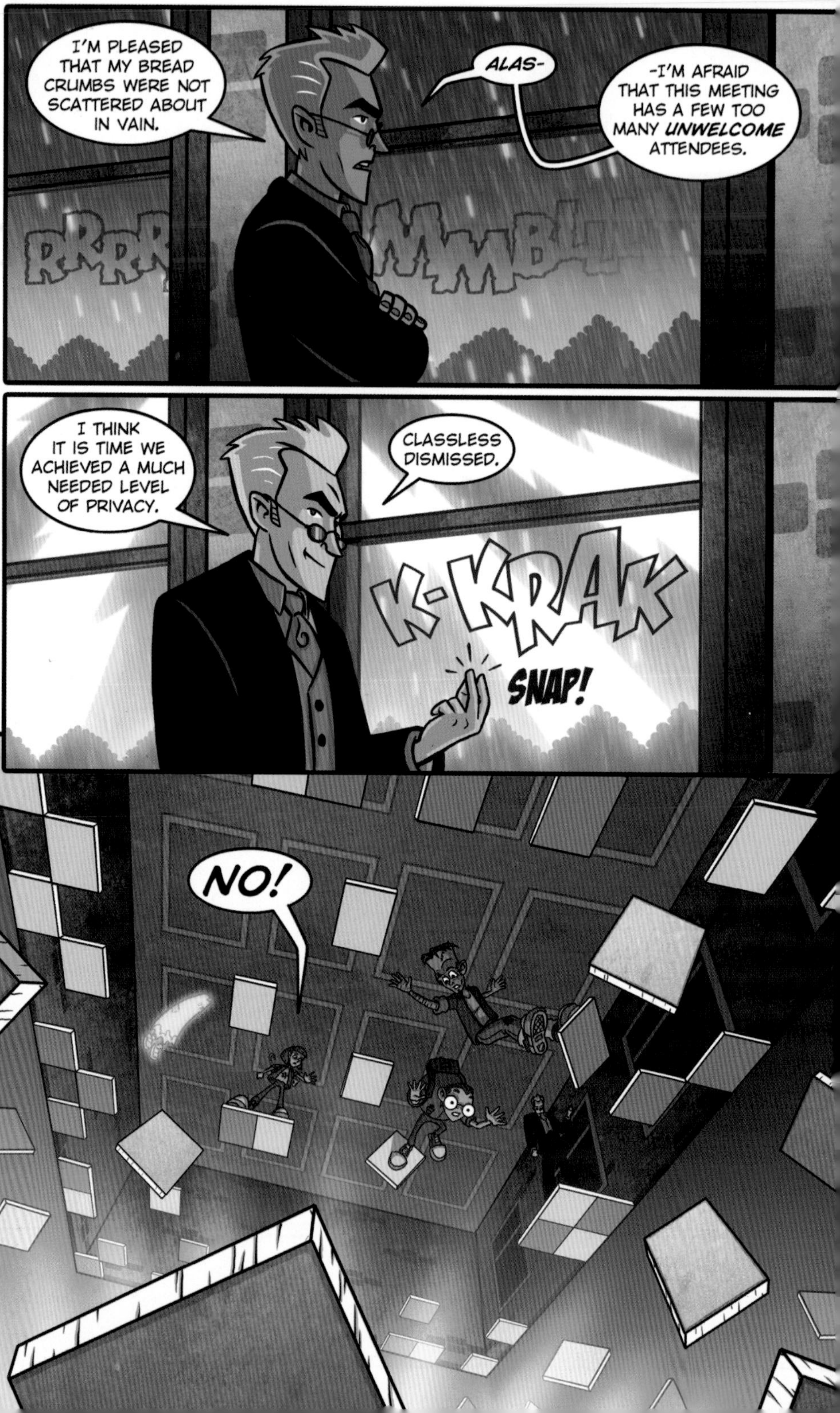
I'M PLEASED THAT MY BREAD CRUMBS WERE NOT SCATTERED ABOUT IN VAIN.
ALAS-
-I'M AFRAID THAT THIS MEETING HAS A FEW TOO MANY *UNWELCOME* ATTENDEES.
RRRRUMMBLE
I THINK IT IS TIME WE ACHIEVED A MUCH NEEDED LEVEL OF PRIVACY.
CLASSLESS DISMISSED.
K-KRAK
SNAP!
NO!

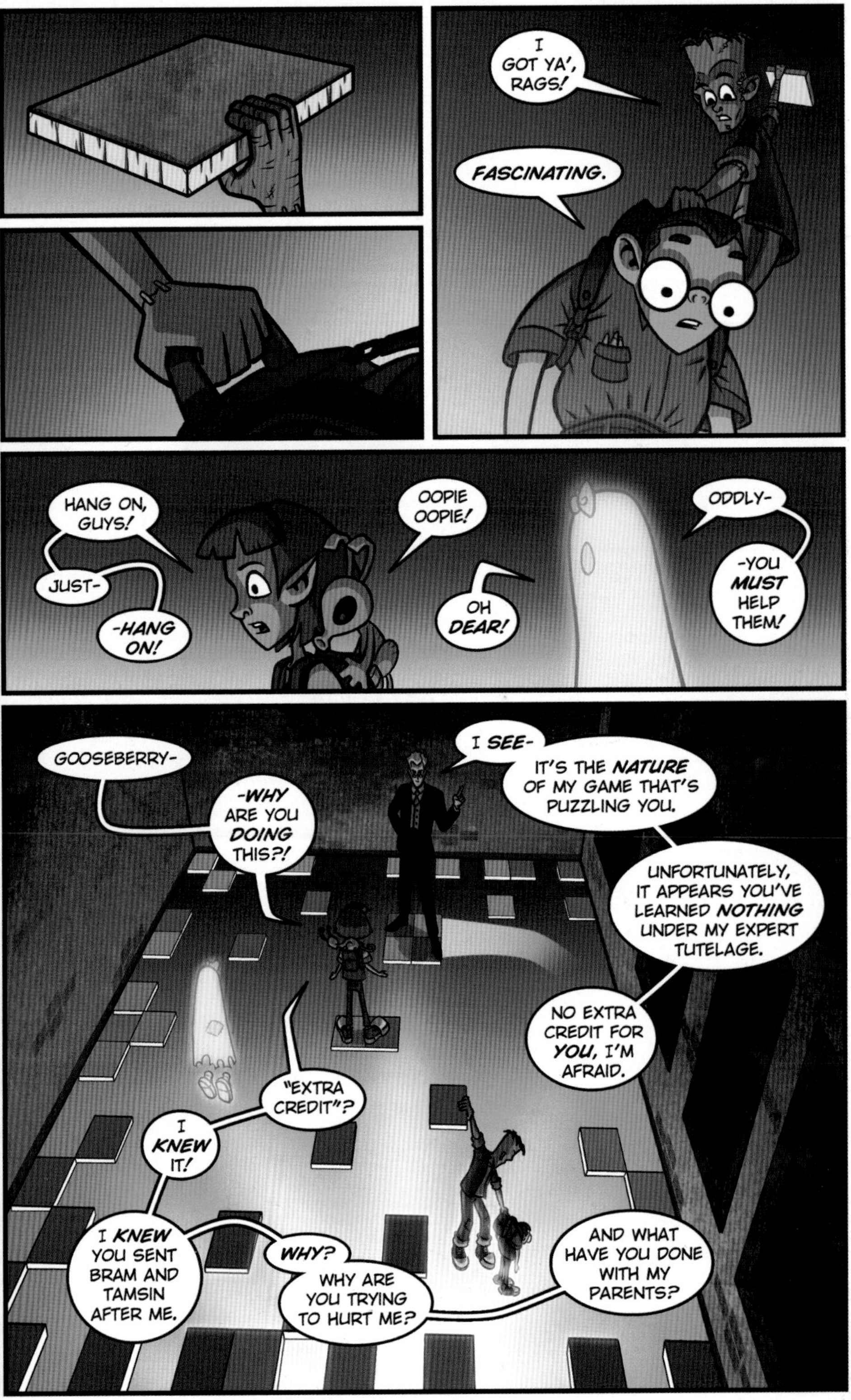
I GOT YA', RAGS!
FASCINATING.
HANG ON, GUYS!
JUST-
-HANG ON!
OOPIE OOPIE!
OH DEAR!
ODDLY-
-YOU MUST HELP THEM!
GOOSEBERRY-
-WHY ARE YOU DOING THIS?!
I SEE-
IT'S THE NATURE OF MY GAME THAT'S PUZZLING YOU.
UNFORTUNATELY, IT APPEARS YOU'VE LEARNED NOTHING UNDER MY EXPERT TUTELAGE.
NO EXTRA CREDIT FOR YOU, I'M AFRAID.
"EXTRA CREDIT"?
I KNEW IT!
I KNEW YOU SENT BRAM AND TAMSIN AFTER ME.
WHY?
WHY ARE YOU TRYING TO HURT ME?
AND WHAT HAVE YOU DONE WITH MY PARENTS?

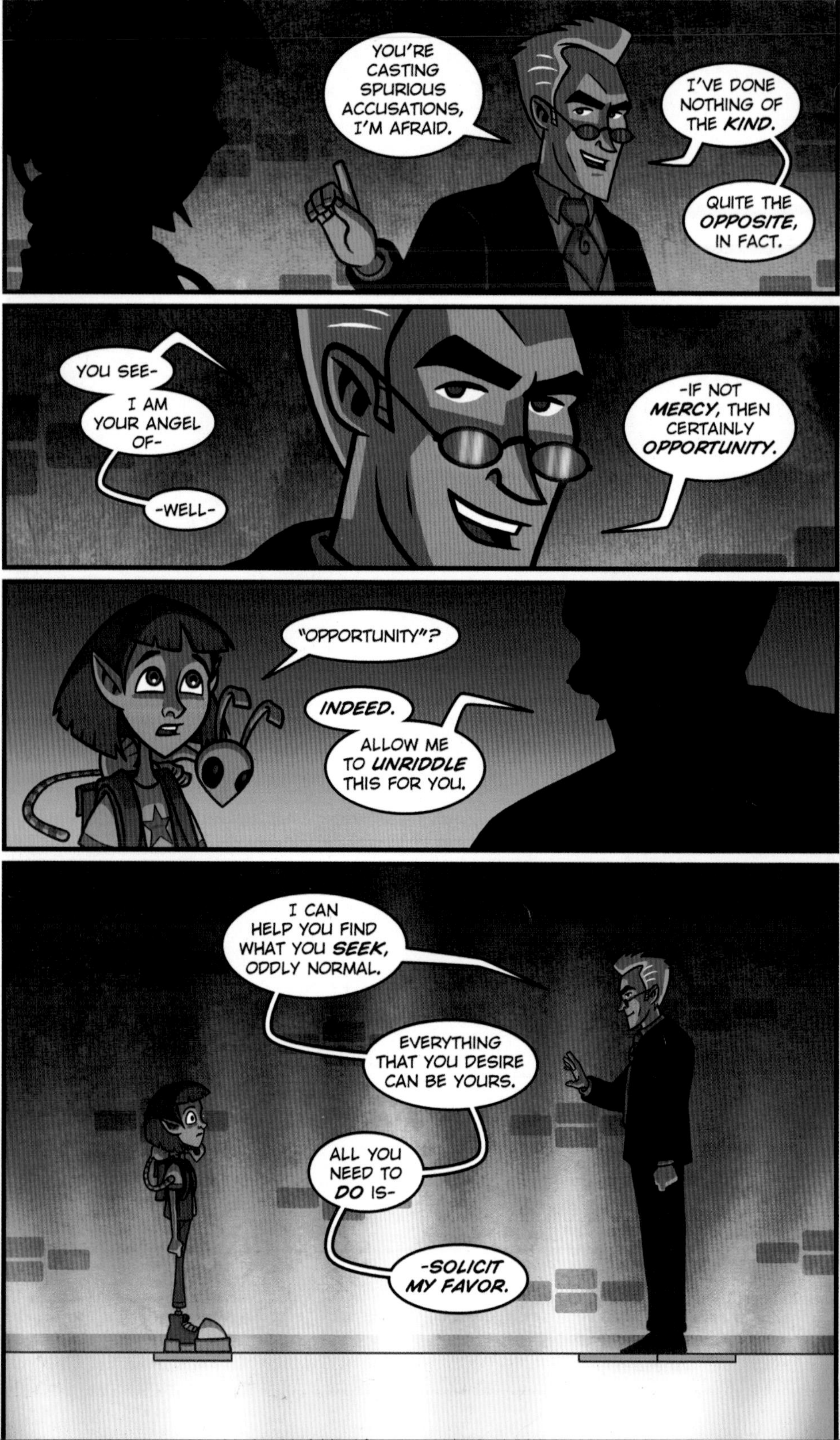

YOU'RE CASTING SPURIOUS ACCUSATIONS, I'M AFRAID.
I'VE DONE NOTHING OF THE KIND.
QUITE THE OPPOSITE, IN FACT.
YOU SEE-
I AM YOUR ANGEL OF-
-WELL-
-IF NOT MERCY, THEN CERTAINLY OPPORTUNITY.
"OPPORTUNITY"?
INDEED.
ALLOW ME TO UNRIDDLE THIS FOR YOU.
I CAN HELP YOU FIND WHAT YOU SEEK, ODDLY NORMAL.
EVERYTHING THAT YOU DESIRE CAN BE YOURS.
ALL YOU NEED TO DO IS-
-SOLICIT MY FAVOR.

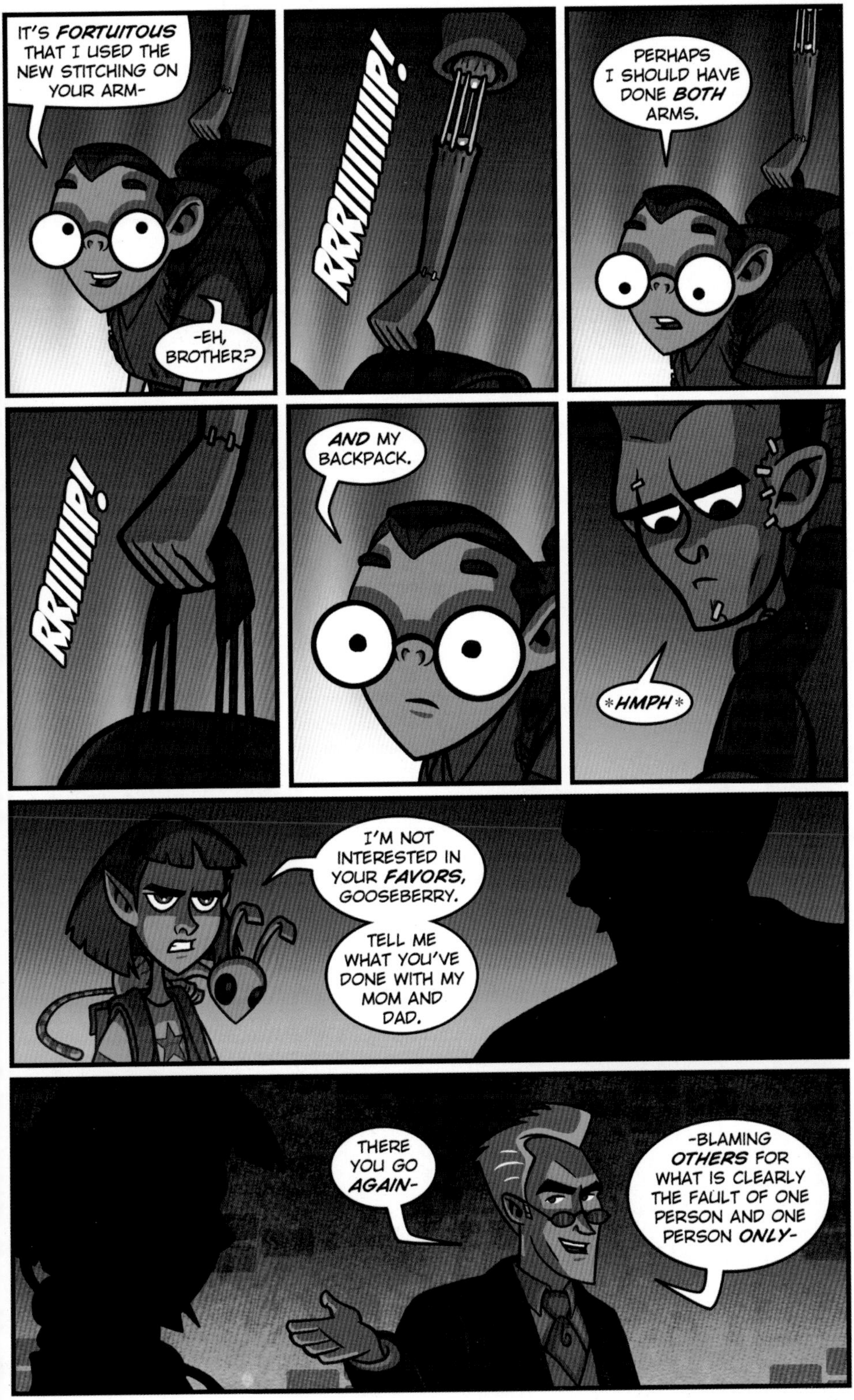
IT'S FORTUITOUS THAT I USED THE NEW STITCHING ON YOUR ARM-
-EH, BROTHER?
RRRIIIIIP!
PERHAPS I SHOULD HAVE DONE BOTH ARMS.
RRIIIIIP!
AND MY BACKPACK.
HMPH
I'M NOT INTERESTED IN YOUR FAVORS, GOOSEBERRY.
TELL ME WHAT YOU'VE DONE WITH MY MOM AND DAD.
THERE YOU GO AGAIN-
-BLAMING OTHERS FOR WHAT IS CLEARLY THE FAULT OF ONE PERSON AND ONE PERSON ONLY-

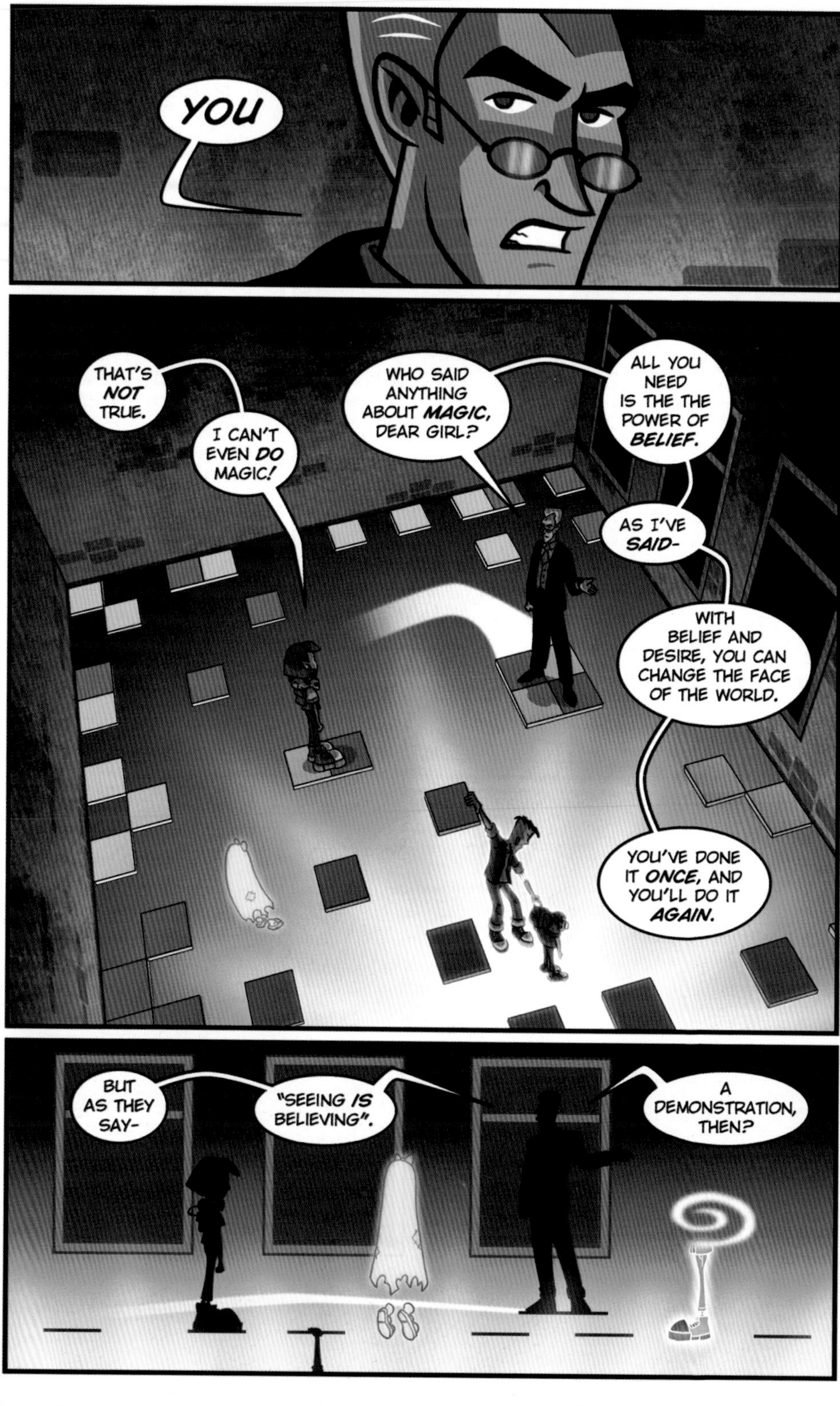
YOU
THAT'S NOT TRUE.
I CAN'T EVEN DO MAGIC!
WHO SAID ANYTHING ABOUT MAGIC, DEAR GIRL?
ALL YOU NEED IS THE THE POWER OF BELIEF.
AS I'VE SAID-
WITH BELIEF AND DESIRE, YOU CAN CHANGE THE FACE OF THE WORLD.
YOU'VE DONE IT ONCE, AND YOU'LL DO IT AGAIN.
BUT AS THEY SAY-
"SEEING IS BELIEVING".
A DEMONSTRATION, THEN?

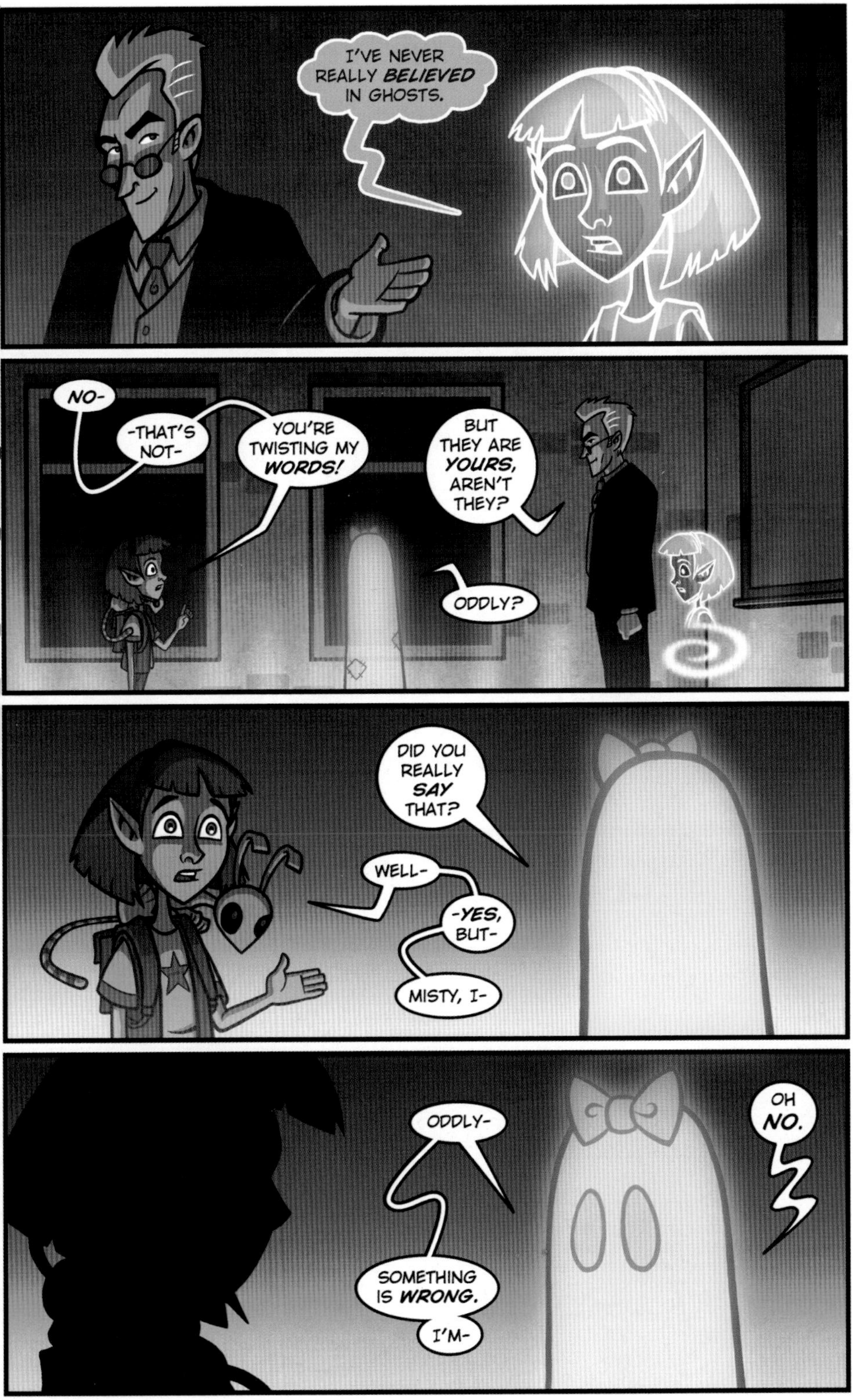
I'VE NEVER REALLY BELIEVED IN GHOSTS.
NO-
-THAT'S NOT-
YOU'RE TWISTING MY WORDS!
BUT THEY ARE YOURS, AREN'T THEY?
ODDLY?
DID YOU REALLY SAY THAT?
WELL-
-YES, BUT-
MISTY, I-
ODDLY-
SOMETHING IS WRONG.
I'M-
OH NO.

"MISTY", *INDEED.*

WHOA.

NO.

WHERE *IS* SHE?

IT SHOULD BE CLEAR AS CRYSTAL, EVEN FOR SOMEONE AS OBTUSE AS YOURSELF.

SHE'S *GONE.*

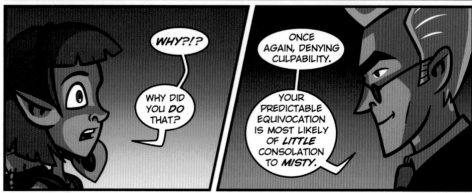

WHY?!?

WHY DID YOU *DO* THAT?

ONCE AGAIN, DENYING CULPABILITY.

YOUR PREDICTABLE EQUIVOCATION IS MOST LIKELY OF *LITTLE* CONSOLATION TO *MISTY.*

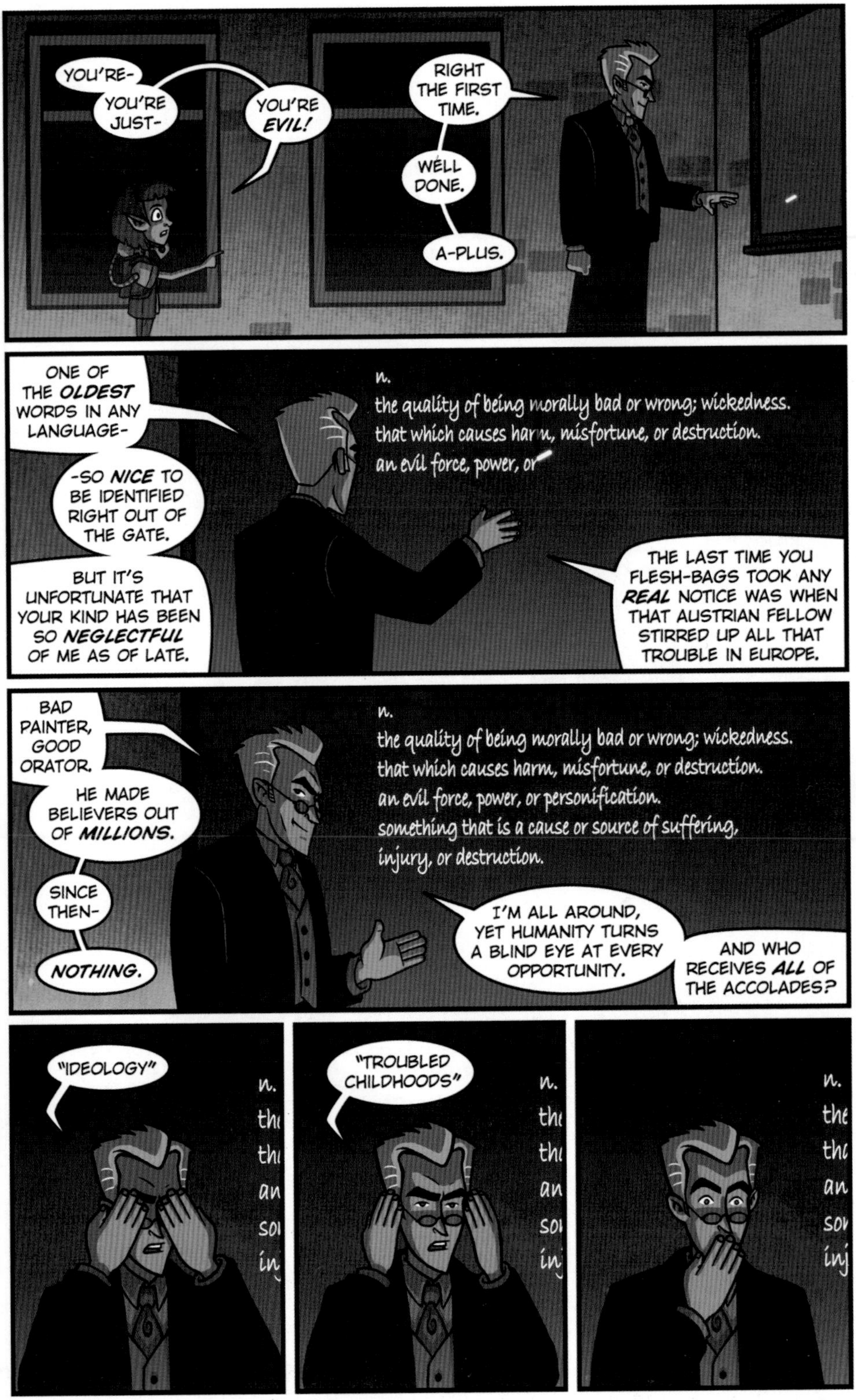

YOU'RE-
YOU'RE JUST-
YOU'RE EVIL!
RIGHT THE FIRST TIME.
WELL DONE.
A-PLUS.
ONE OF THE OLDEST WORDS IN ANY LANGUAGE-
-SO NICE TO BE IDENTIFIED RIGHT OUT OF THE GATE.
n.
the quality of being morally bad or wrong; wickedness.
that which causes harm, misfortune, or destruction.
an evil force, power, or
BUT IT'S UNFORTUNATE THAT YOUR KIND HAS BEEN SO NEGLECTFUL OF ME AS OF LATE.
THE LAST TIME YOU FLESH-BAGS TOOK ANY REAL NOTICE WAS WHEN THAT AUSTRIAN FELLOW STIRRED UP ALL THAT TROUBLE IN EUROPE.
BAD PAINTER, GOOD ORATOR.
HE MADE BELIEVERS OUT OF MILLIONS.
n.
the quality of being morally bad or wrong; wickedness.
that which causes harm, misfortune, or destruction.
an evil force, power, or personification.
something that is a cause or source of suffering, injury, or destruction.
SINCE THEN-
NOTHING.
I'M ALL AROUND, YET HUMANITY TURNS A BLIND EYE AT EVERY OPPORTUNITY.
AND WHO RECEIVES ALL OF THE ACCOLADES?
"IDEOLOGY"
"TROUBLED CHILDHOODS"

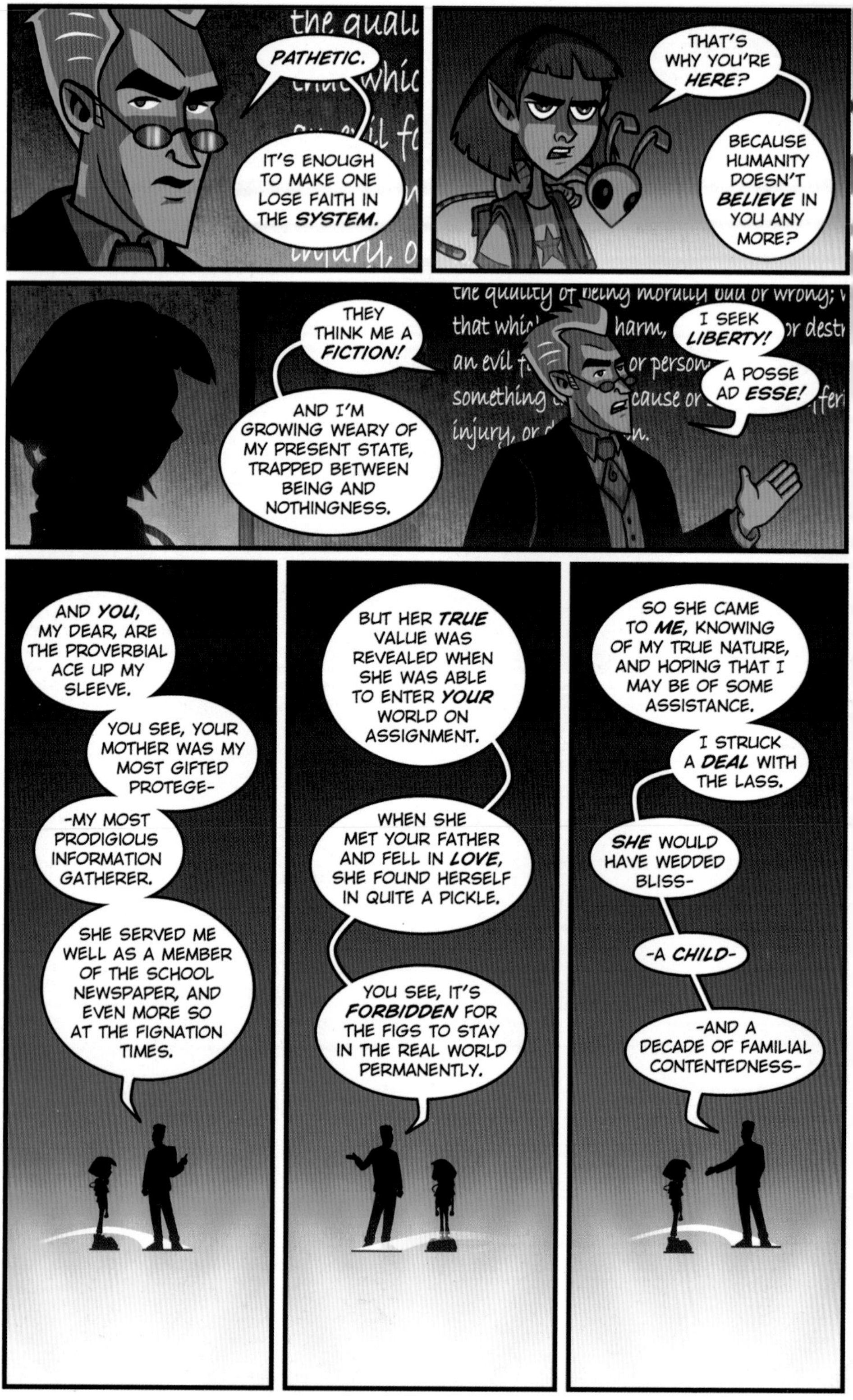
PATHETIC.
IT'S ENOUGH TO MAKE ONE LOSE FAITH IN THE SYSTEM.
THAT'S WHY YOU'RE HERE?
BECAUSE HUMANITY DOESN'T BELIEVE IN YOU ANY MORE?
THEY THINK ME A FICTION!
AND I'M GROWING WEARY OF MY PRESENT STATE, TRAPPED BETWEEN BEING AND NOTHINGNESS.
I SEEK LIBERTY!
A POSSE AD ESSE!
AND YOU, MY DEAR, ARE THE PROVERBIAL ACE UP MY SLEEVE.
YOU SEE, YOUR MOTHER WAS MY MOST GIFTED PROTEGE-
-MY MOST PRODIGIOUS INFORMATION GATHERER.
SHE SERVED ME WELL AS A MEMBER OF THE SCHOOL NEWSPAPER, AND EVEN MORE SO AT THE FIGNATION TIMES.
BUT HER TRUE VALUE WAS REVEALED WHEN SHE WAS ABLE TO ENTER YOUR WORLD ON ASSIGNMENT.
WHEN SHE MET YOUR FATHER AND FELL IN LOVE, SHE FOUND HERSELF IN QUITE A PICKLE.
YOU SEE, IT'S FORBIDDEN FOR THE FIGS TO STAY IN THE REAL WORLD PERMANENTLY.
SO SHE CAME TO ME, KNOWING OF MY TRUE NATURE, AND HOPING THAT I MAY BE OF SOME ASSISTANCE.
I STRUCK A DEAL WITH THE LASS.
SHE WOULD HAVE WEDDED BLISS-
-A CHILD-
-AND A DECADE OF FAMILIAL CONTENTEDNESS-

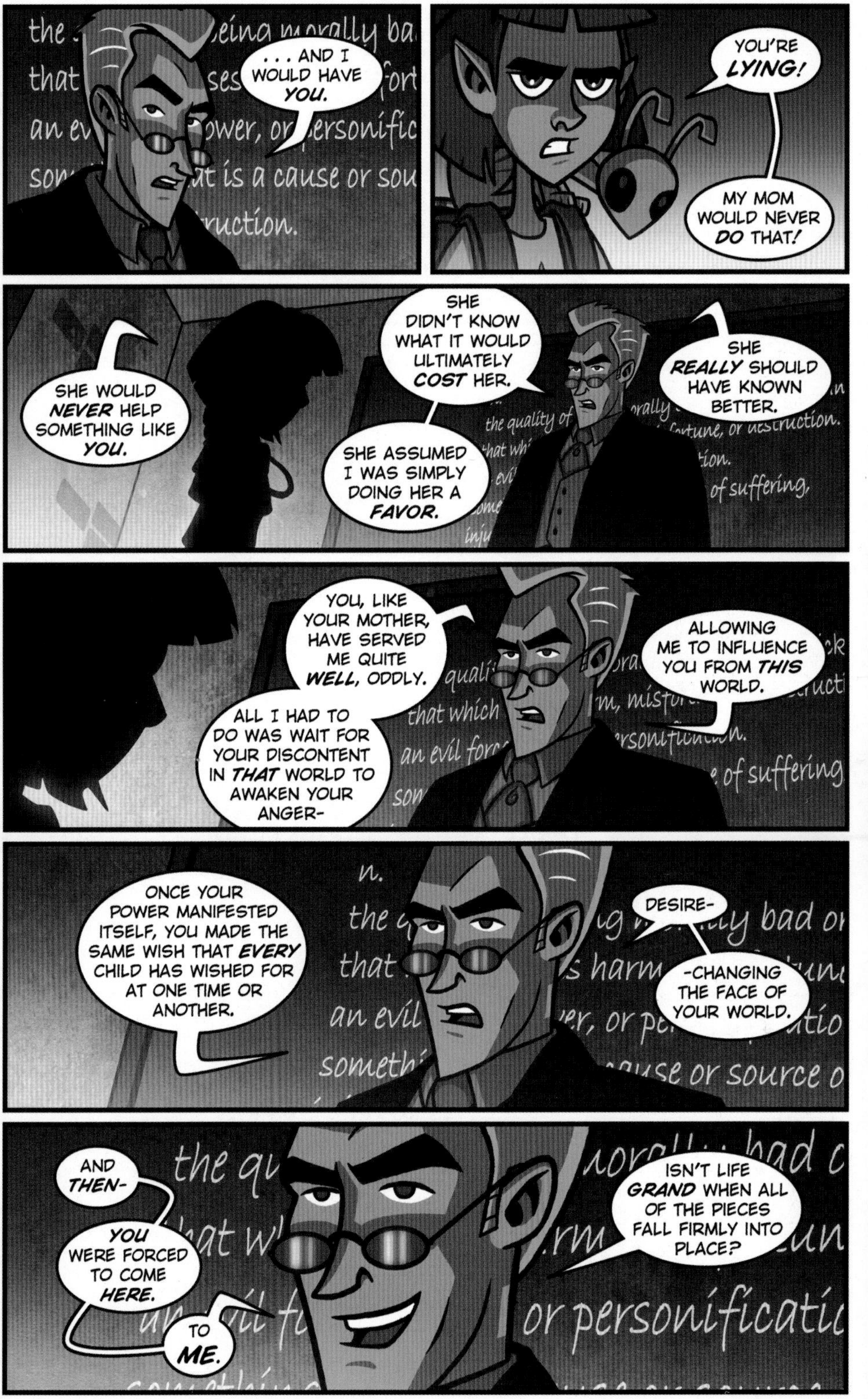
. . . AND I WOULD HAVE YOU.
YOU'RE LYING!
MY MOM WOULD NEVER DO THAT!
SHE WOULD NEVER HELP SOMETHING LIKE YOU.
SHE DIDN'T KNOW WHAT IT WOULD ULTIMATELY COST HER.
SHE ASSUMED I WAS SIMPLY DOING HER A FAVOR.
SHE REALLY SHOULD HAVE KNOWN BETTER.
YOU, LIKE YOUR MOTHER, HAVE SERVED ME QUITE WELL, ODDLY.
ALL I HAD TO DO WAS WAIT FOR YOUR DISCONTENT IN THAT WORLD TO AWAKEN YOUR ANGER-
ALLOWING ME TO INFLUENCE YOU FROM THIS WORLD.
ONCE YOUR POWER MANIFESTED ITSELF, YOU MADE THE SAME WISH THAT EVERY CHILD HAS WISHED FOR AT ONE TIME OR ANOTHER.
DESIRE-
-CHANGING THE FACE OF YOUR WORLD.
AND THEN-
YOU WERE FORCED TO COME HERE.
TO ME.
ISN'T LIFE GRAND WHEN ALL OF THE PIECES FALL FIRMLY INTO PLACE?

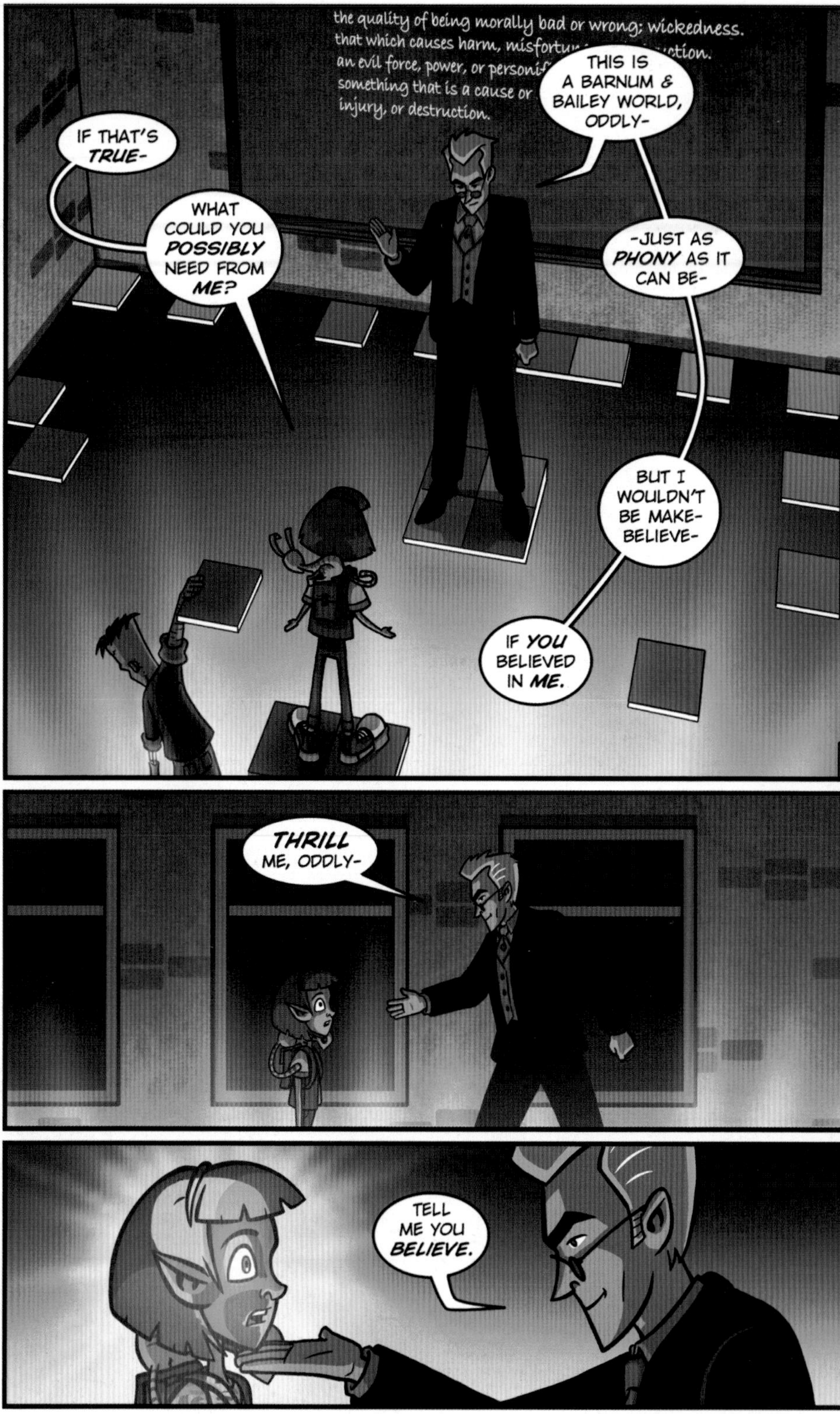
the quality of being morally bad or wrong; wickedness.
that which causes harm, misfortu
an evil force, power, or personi
something that is a cause or
injury, or destruction.
IF THAT'S TRUE-
WHAT COULD YOU POSSIBLY NEED FROM ME?
THIS IS A BARNUM & BAILEY WORLD, ODDLY-
-JUST AS PHONY AS IT CAN BE-
BUT I WOULDN'T BE MAKE-BELIEVE-
IF YOU BELIEVED IN ME.
THRILL ME, ODDLY-
TELL ME YOU BELIEVE.

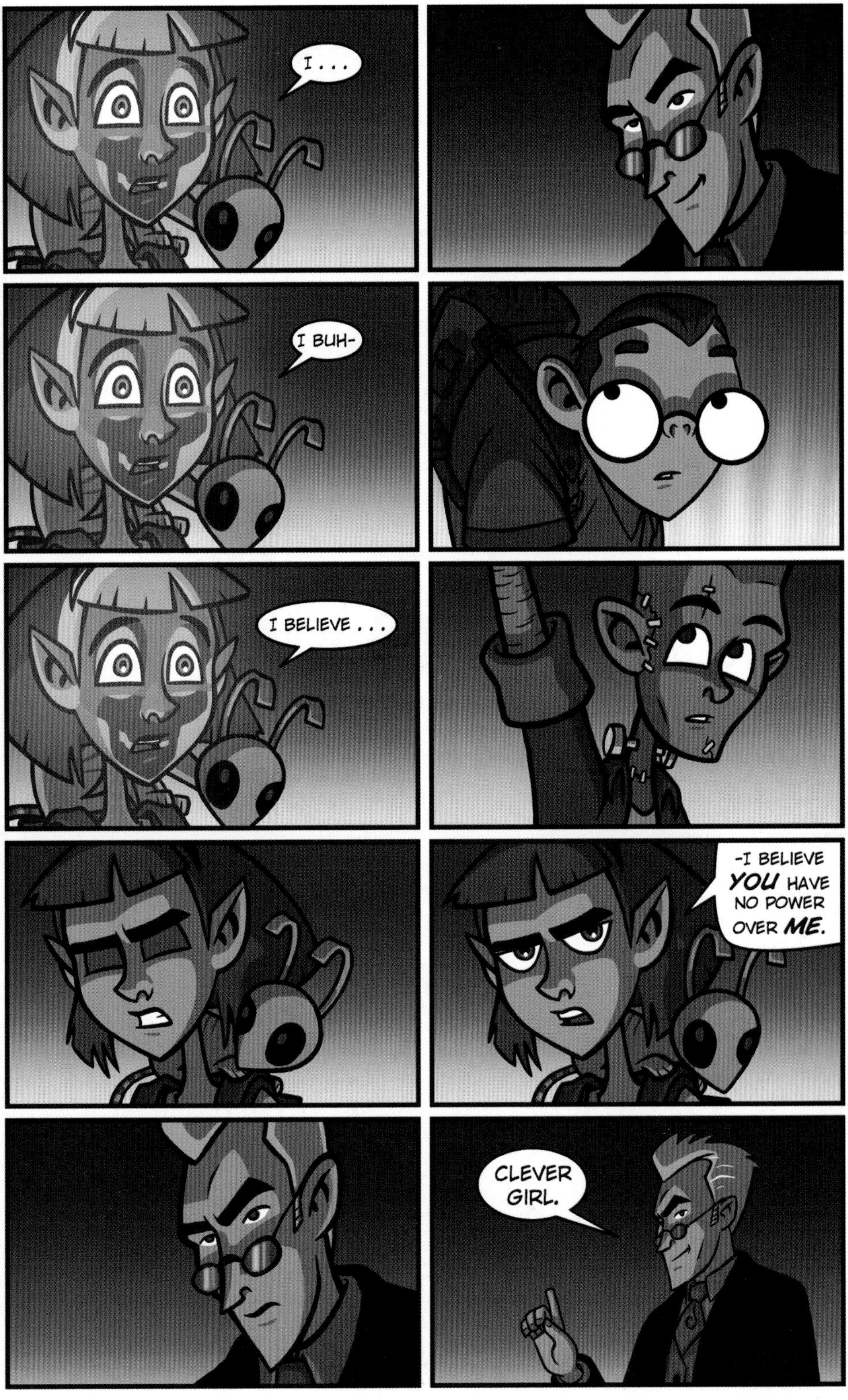
I...
I BUH-
I BELIEVE...
-I BELIEVE YOU HAVE NO POWER OVER ME.
CLEVER GIRL.

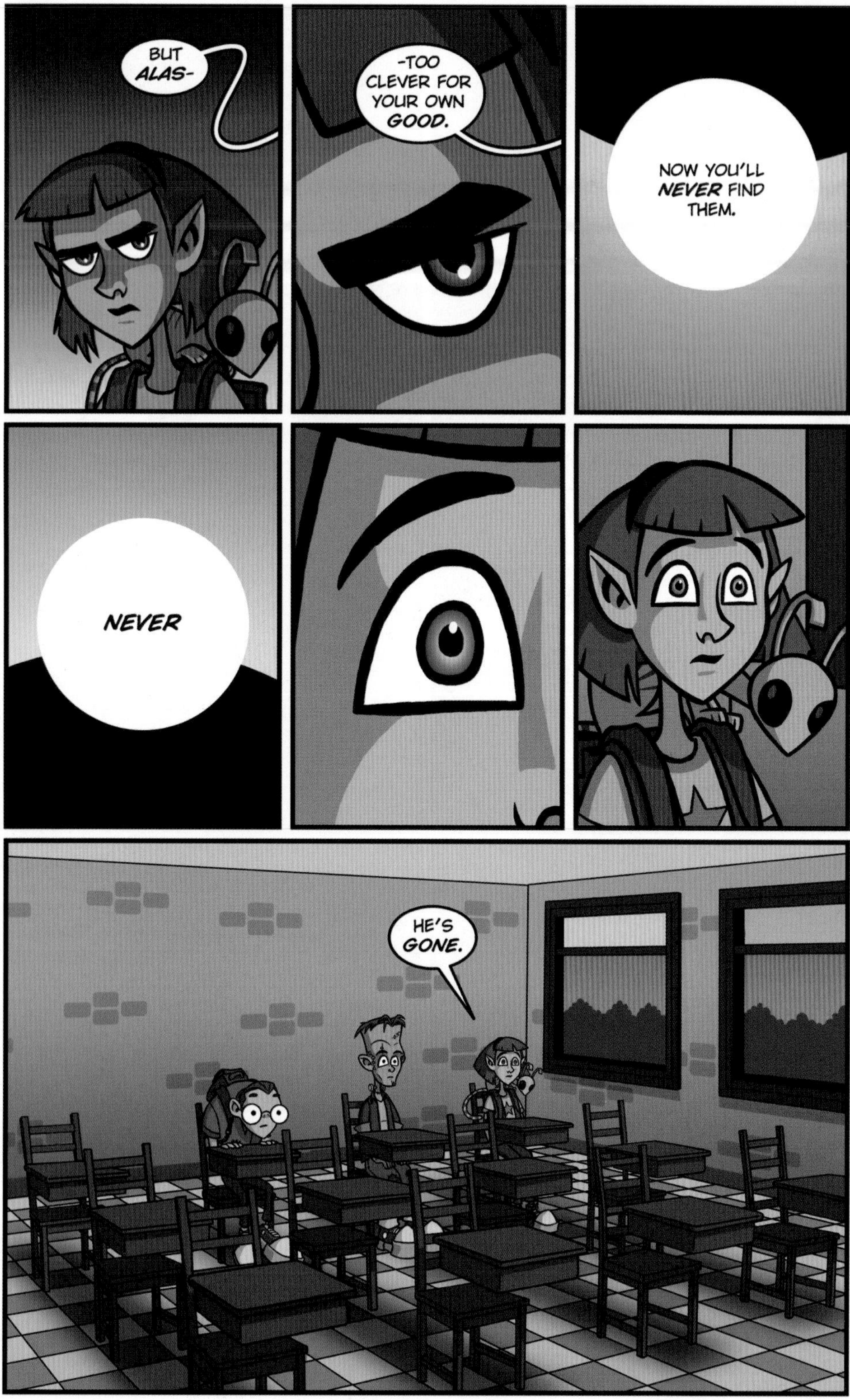
BUT ALAS-
-TOO CLEVER FOR YOUR OWN GOOD.
NOW YOU'LL NEVER FIND THEM.
NEVER
HE'S GONE.

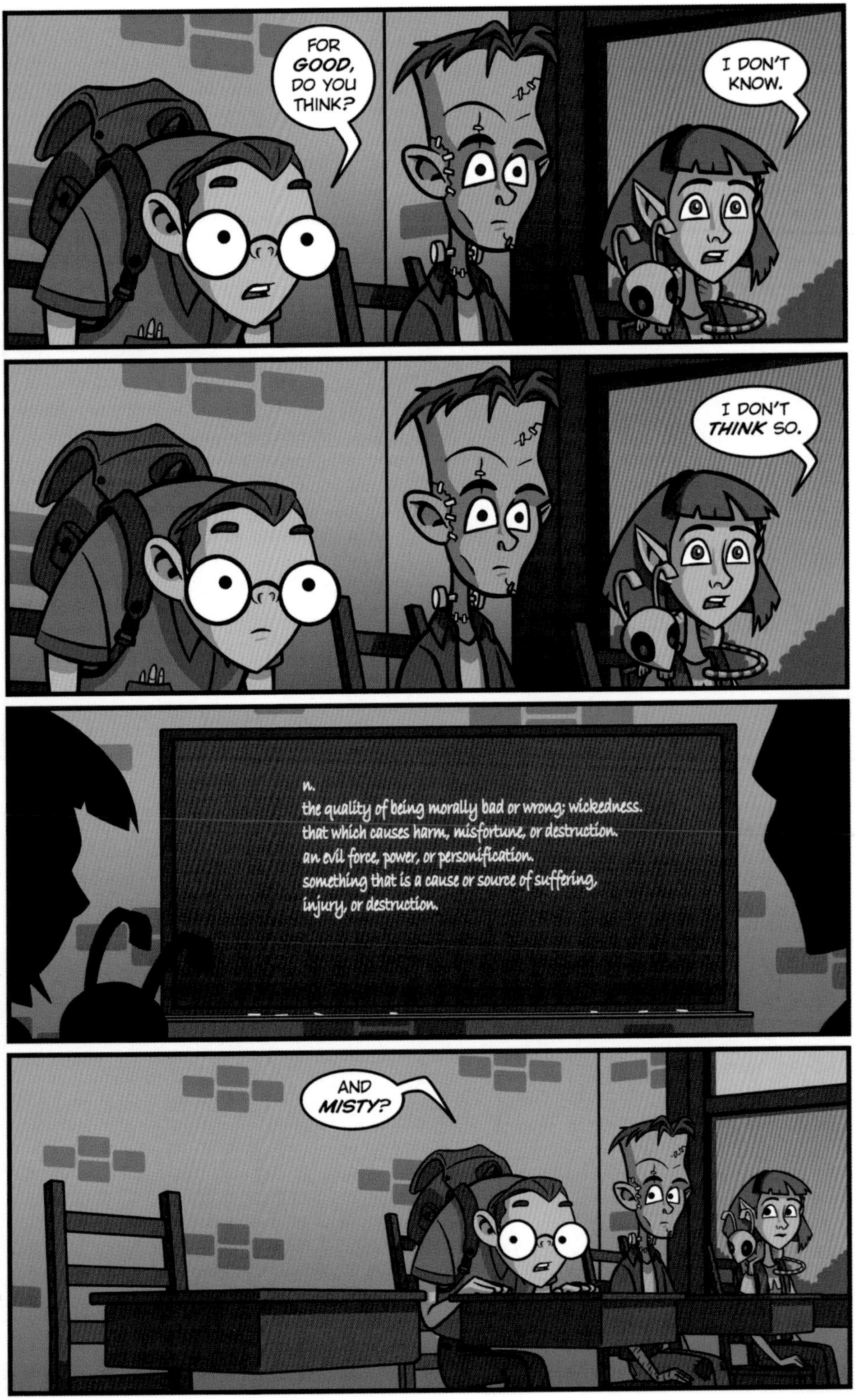
FOR GOOD, DO YOU THINK?
I DON'T KNOW.
I DON'T THINK SO.
n.
the quality of being morally bad or wrong; wickedness.
that which causes harm, misfortune, or destruction.
an evil force, power, or personification.
something that is a cause or source of suffering, injury, or destruction.
AND MISTY?

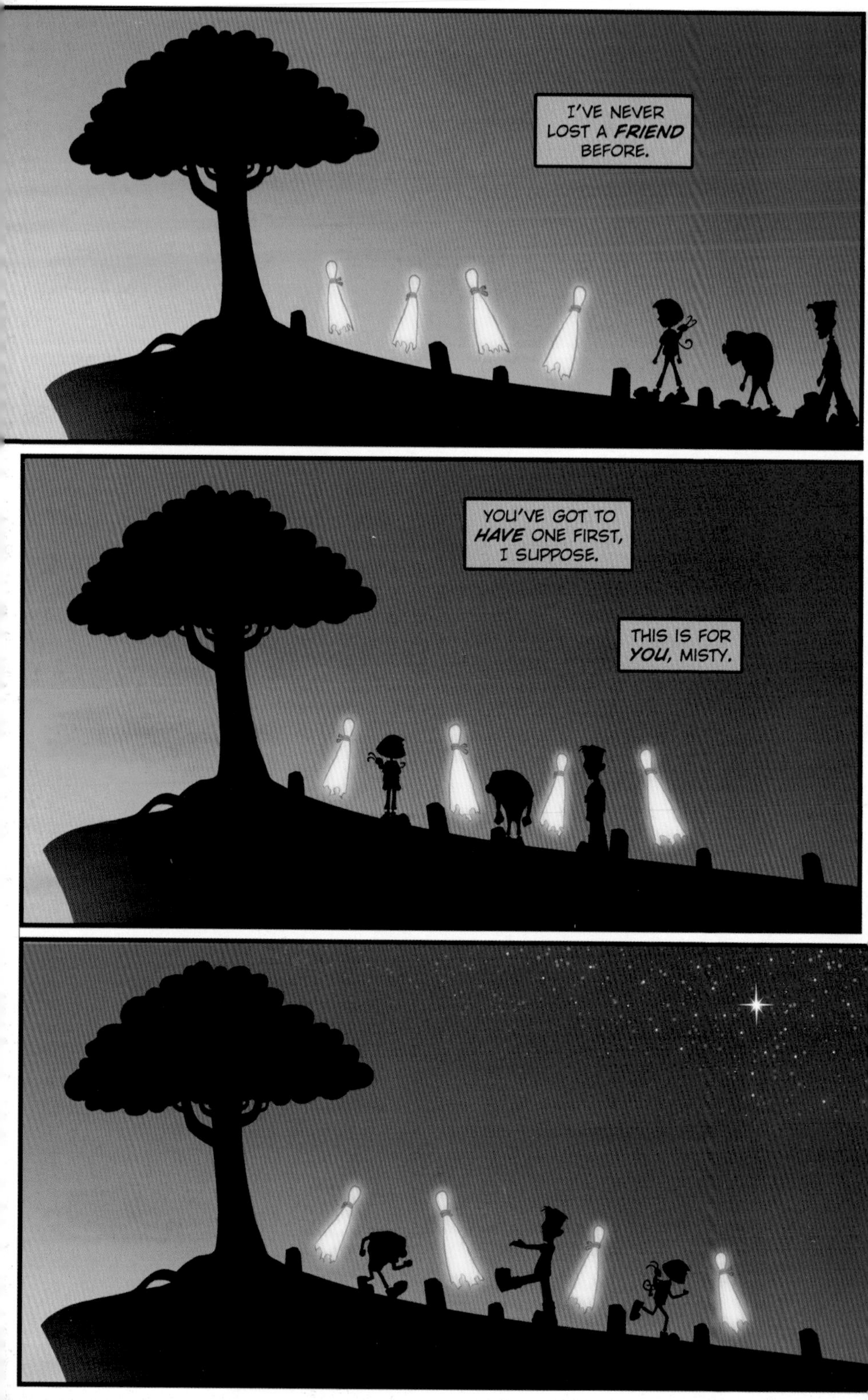
I'VE NEVER LOST A FRIEND BEFORE.
YOU'VE GOT TO HAVE ONE FIRST, I SUPPOSE.
THIS IS FOR YOU, MISTY.

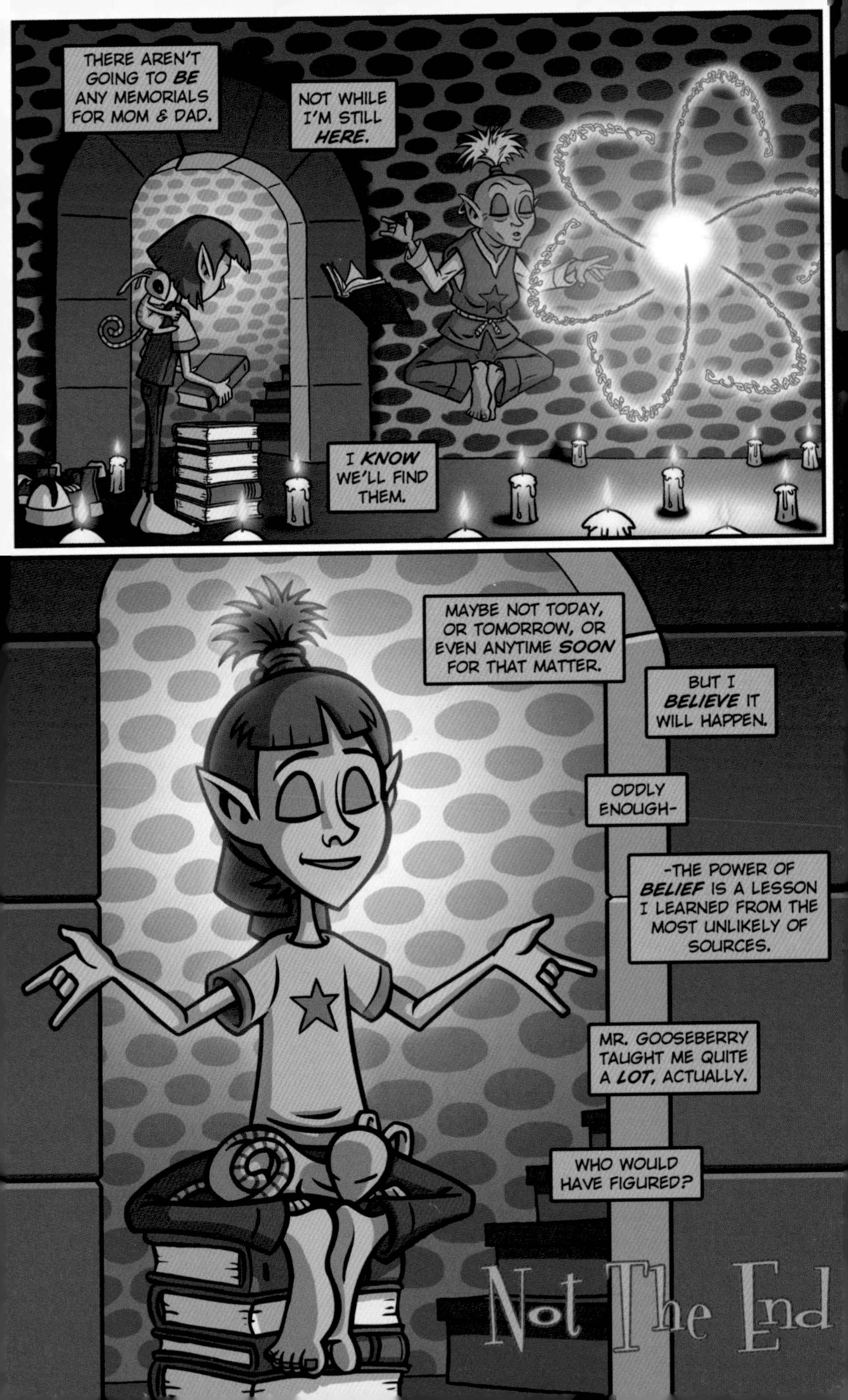
THERE AREN'T GOING TO BE ANY MEMORIALS FOR MOM & DAD.
NOT WHILE I'M STILL HERE.
I KNOW WE'LL FIND THEM.
MAYBE NOT TODAY, OR TOMORROW, OR EVEN ANYTIME SOON FOR THAT MATTER.
BUT I BELIEVE IT WILL HAPPEN.
ODDLY ENOUGH-
-THE POWER OF BELIEF IS A LESSON I LEARNED FROM THE MOST UNLIKELY OF SOURCES.
MR. GOOSEBERRY TAUGHT ME QUITE A LOT, ACTUALLY.
WHO WOULD HAVE FIGURED?
Not The End

ACKNOWLEDGEMENTS

First and foremost, I want to thank the people to whom this series was dedicated . . my mom and dad, Mary and Otis. I was lucky enough to have parents who did not, in any way, attempt to dissuade me from my dream of being a professional writer and artist. They always encouraged my creative ventures and for that, I thank them.

Thanks also go out to . . .

Tracey for supporting her big brother, Gisela for believing in me through thick and thin (and also for "Oopie Oopie"!), James Powell for editing issue 1 and 2 and David Hopkins for editing issue 3 and 4 (everyone needs a second set of eyes to catch those pesky mistakes), Josh Howard for a gracious welcome to the Viper's nest, Lea Hernandez & Joey Manley for being early Oddly fans, Crystal for her "babysitting" duties, the guys and gals of the 30th for their support and for putting up with me, Sandy at Amazing Fantasy Comics for her amazing support for local creators, Maryn Roos for letting me use "Bumble Betty", Kazu Kibuishi & Google for the unintended aid in getting me noticed by the right people and lastly to all of the amazing artists who contributed to the Oddly Gallery in the back of this book.

Thanks also to the readers. I hope those of you who read the series or the trade paperback have enjoyed it and have found something in the tale that resonates. And for those of you who are wondering . . . yes, there is more "Oddly Normal" to come.

And last, but certainly not least, many MANY thanks to Jim Resnowski and Jessie Garza for discovering and publishing "Oddly Normal". You've made my dream of being a published storyteller come true, and I will always be grateful.

Otis Frampton
Newport News, Va
April 3rd, 2006

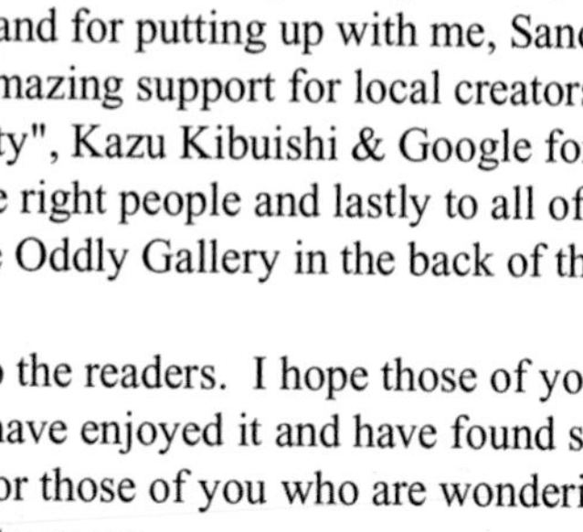

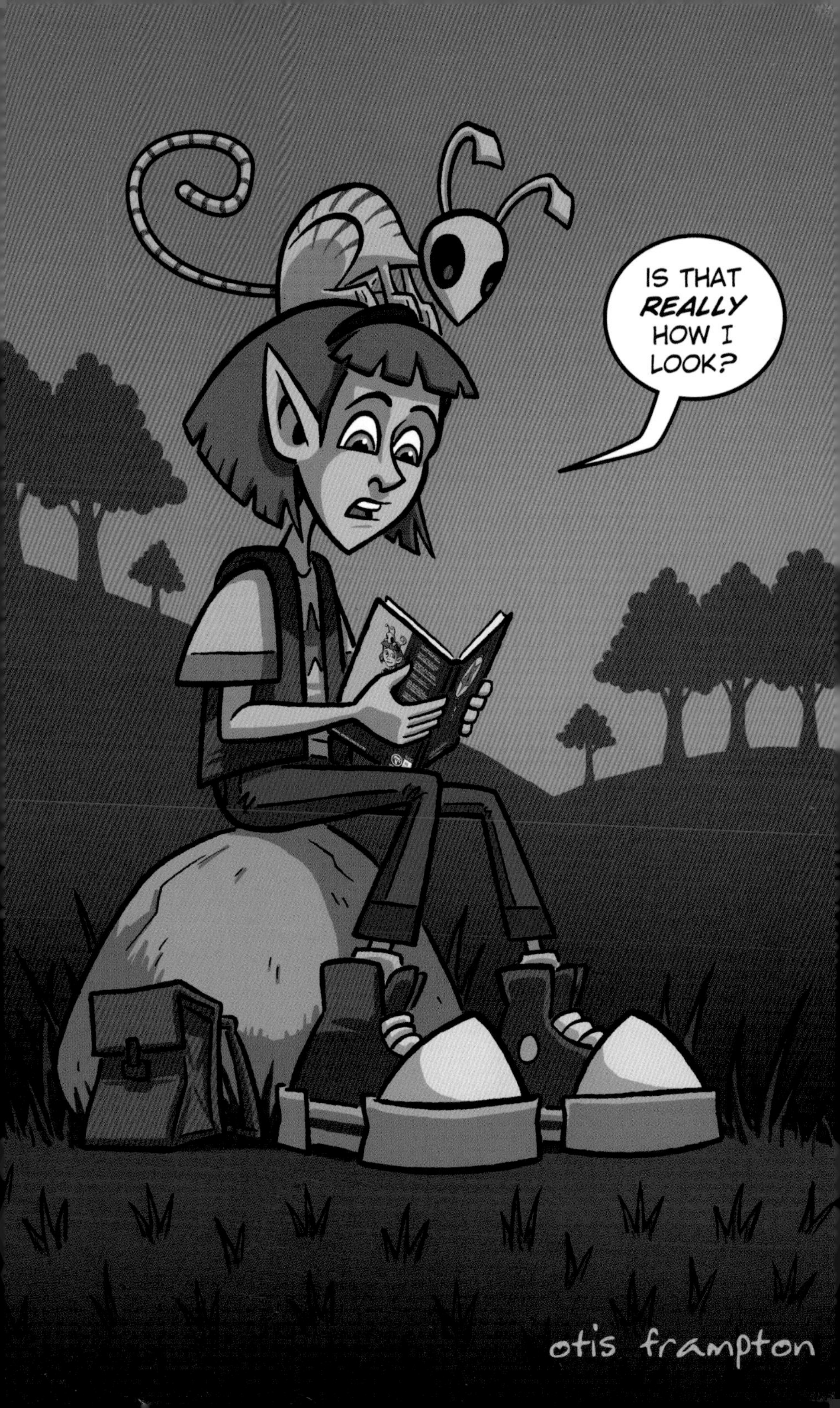
IS THAT *REALLY* HOW I LOOK?
otis frampton

Oddly Gallery

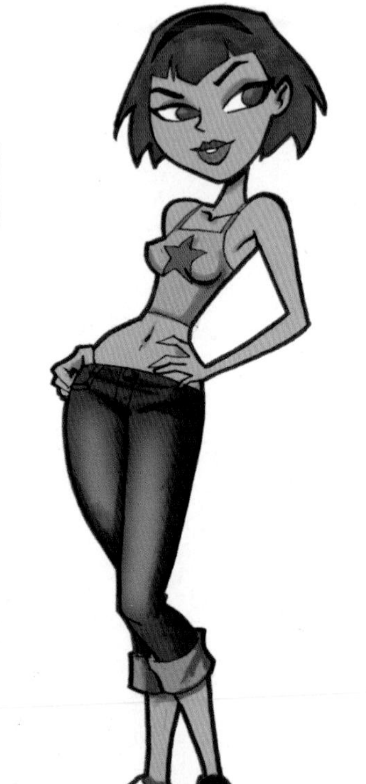

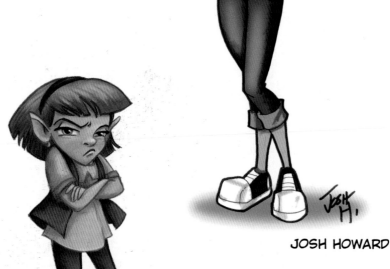

JOSH HOWARD

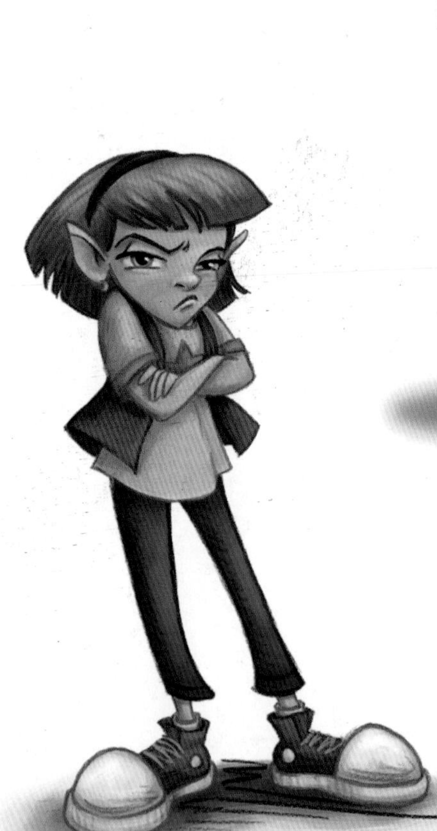

MARYN ROOS

DERRICK FISH

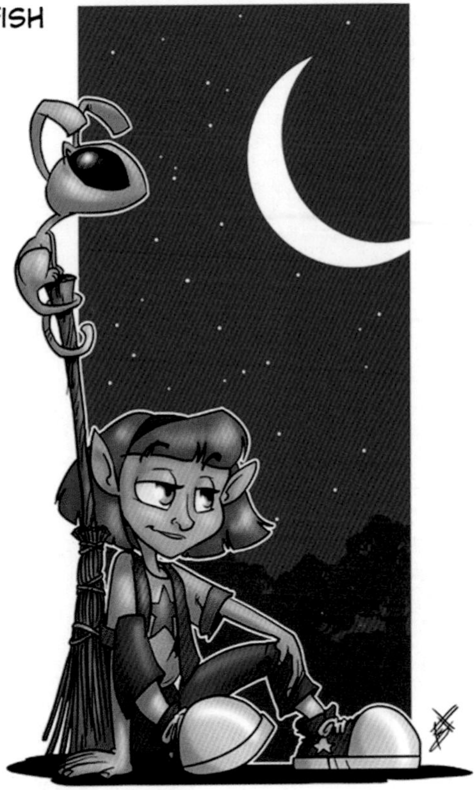

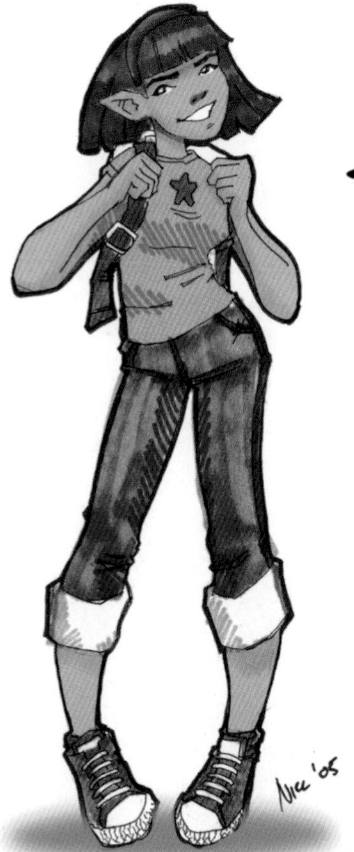
Nicc '05

NICC BALCE

TOM KURZANSKI

GRANT GOULD

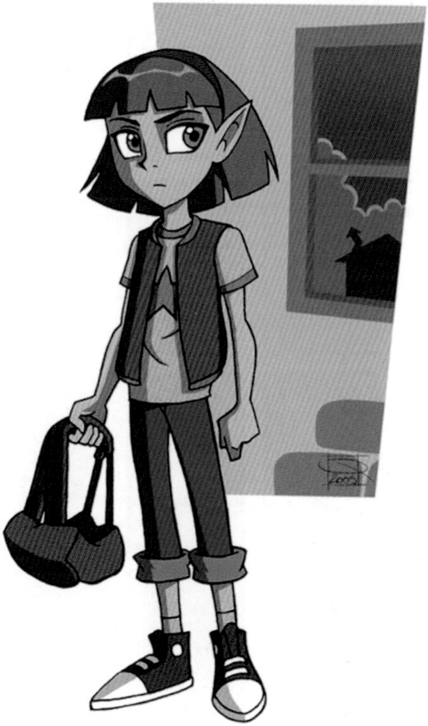

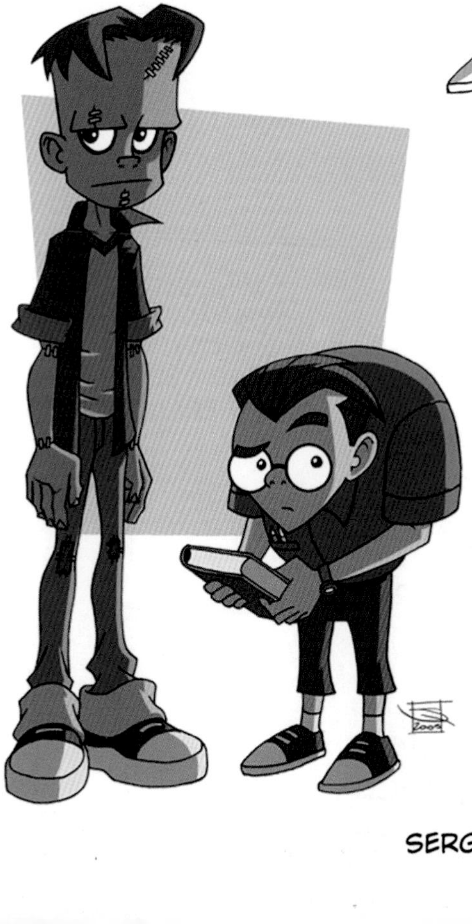

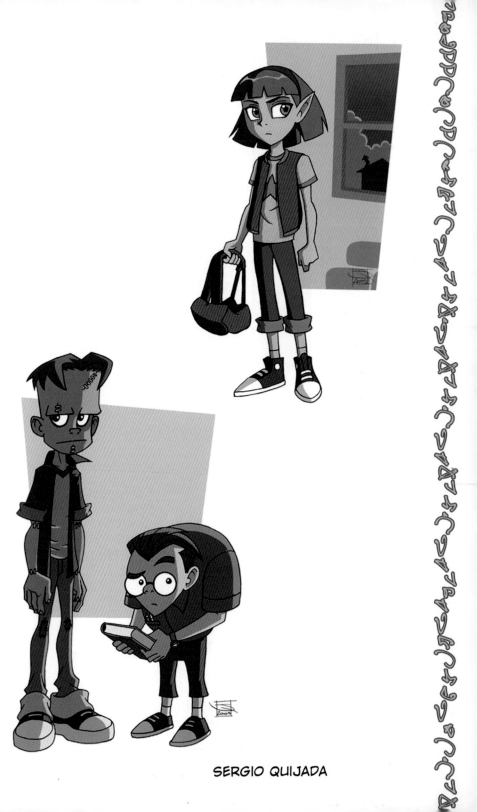

SERGIO QUIJADA

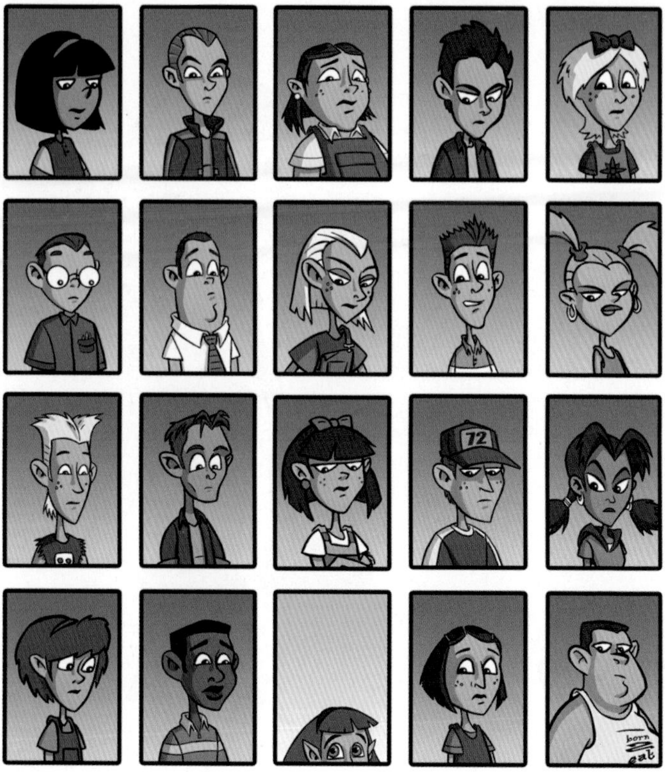
72

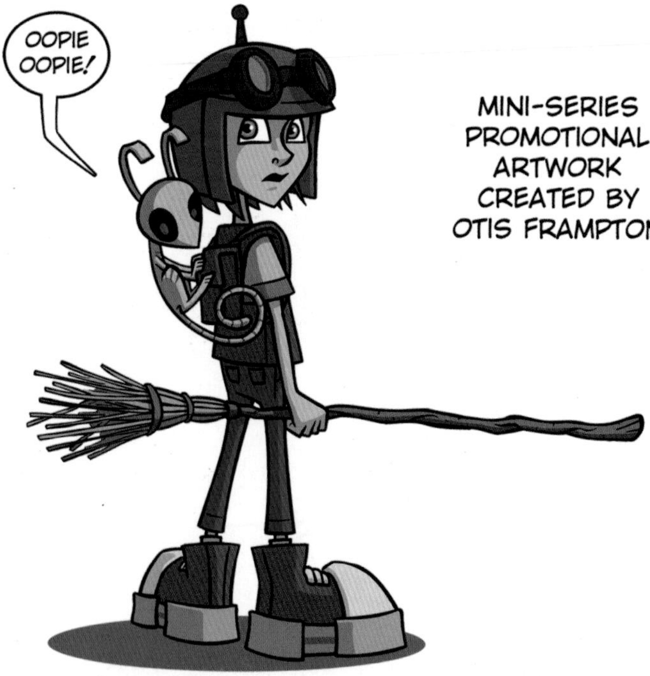
OOPIE OOPIE!

MINI-SERIES
PROMOTIONAL
ARTWORK
CREATED BY
OTIS FRAMPTON

ODDLY NORMAL HISTORY

"Oddly Normal" began life as a webcomic which premiered at Girlamatic.com on May 15th, 2003. How Oddly went from Girlamatic to being published by Viper Comics is quite a story, and it all started with a rejection. Joey Manley (head honcho and big cheese of the Modern Tales family) had put the call out: "I need a new series for Modern Tales!" And submissions poured in.

At the time, I was thinking about starting a webcomic series about a little girl with a smidge of weirdness about her. I had some sketches and ideas, but little else. It was an uncooked concept at best, but I thought it was worth putting on the stove. I had an inkling that it might be just the series that Joey was looking for.

But what to do? I had no series, just a concept, and the deadline for submissions loomed large. So I kicked it into high gear, finalizing character concepts, hammering out a storyline to kick off the series, and working on 3 or 4 pages of the comic itself to "wow" JM and his council of webcomickers.

And did the proposal "wow" the folks at Modern Tales? Well, yes and no. I received a couple of very supportive e-mails from two of my favorite creators, and thought I had a good chance of being selected. But alas, it was not to be for Oddly and MT. Joey let me down gently, telling me that he would still like to work with me in some capacity or another, maybe providing art for a different project. But I still believed in Oddly, and its potential to be something really good (maybe even great).

So I shamelessly suggested that if there was ever an opening at Girlamatic.com, Oddly might be a good fit. I expected a response along the lines of, "Right. I'll get back to you on that one (never)." Instead, Joey said that he thought I might be right, and told me that he would pass the idea along to the splendiferous Lea Hernandez (the editor of Girlamatic).

I figured this was a polite brush-off, and expected never to hear a word from anyone at from the Modern Tales world ever again. To my amazement, I received an e-mail from Lea just a few hours later saying that she'd love to add "Oddly Normal" to the Girlamatic line-up.

I was truly shocked. Joey Manley earned my instant respect for being a man of his word, and Lea earned the title of "splendiferous". Now, to the more jaded folks out there, the previous sentence will probably sound like the big kiss-up. But I assure you, it's not. I value intergrity, and Joey could have just as well brushed me off. But he didn't, he followed through on his word, which means the world to me.

"Oddly Normal", the webcomic, premiered at Girlamatic.com on May 15th, 2003 and it received quite a good response from readers during its run. But when my initial contract was up, I decided to end my association with Girlamatic.com. I absolutely loved being at Girlamatic, and this departure came with no regrets or displeasure about having been a part of the Modern Tales family. But I felt that it was time to take my comic solo.

Once Oddly was on its own, the archives sitting on my personal website, it drew the attention of Jim Resnowski, who just happened to be the art director at Viper Comics and the man in charge of finding new books for Jessie Garza to throw money behind. Jim was Googling Kazu Kibuishi's "Daisy Kutter", to see what the word on the web was for the new comic they had recently added to their publicaion schedule. His search led him to a piece of Daisy fan art I had recently done, and Jim eventually found his way to my site and "Oddly Normal".

The rest, as they say, is history . . .